D1081279

Gender, Crime and Justice

Gender, Crime and Justice

EDITED BY

Pat Carlen and Anne Worrall

Open University
Milton Keynes · Philadelphia

Open University Press
Open University Educational Enterprises Limited
12 Cofferidge Close
Stony Stratford
Milton Keynes MK11 1BY, England

and

242 Cherry Street
Philadelphia, PA 19106, USA

First Published 1987

British Library Cataloguing in Publication Data
Gender, crime and justice.
  1. Female offenders
  I. Carlen, Pat   II. Worrall, Anne
  364.3'74   HV6046

ISBN 0-335-15505-7
ISBN 0-335-15504-9 Pbk

Library of Congress Cataloging in Publication Data
Main entry under title:
Gender, crime and justice
  Bibliography: p.
  Includes index.
  1. Female offenders—Great Britain.   2. Women
prisoners—Great Britain.   3. Sex discrimination in
criminal justice administration—Great Britain.
4. Criminal justice, Administration of—Great Britain.
I. Carlen, Pat.   II. Worrall, Anne.
HV6046.G46   1987   364.3'74'0941   87-1510

ISBN 0-335-15505-7
ISBN 0-335-15504-9 (pbk.)

Text design by Clarke Williams

Typeset by GCS, Leighton Buzzard, in 10/12 point Bembo
Printed in Great Britain by St. Edmundsbury Press,
Bury St. Edmunds, Suffolk.

Contents

About the Editors and Contributors

The Editors

Pat Carlen, BA, PhD. Reader in Criminology at Keele University and Director of The Keele Centre for Criminology. Publications include *Magistrates' Justice* (Oxford, Martin Robertson, 1976); *Women's Imprisonment* (London, Routledge & Kegan Paul, 1983); *Official Discourse* (co-authored with Frank Burton, London, Routledge & Kegan Paul, 1979); *The Sociology of Law* (ed. Keele, University of Keele, 1976); *Radical Issues in Criminology* (ed., with Mike Collison, Oxford, Martin Robertson, 1980) and *Criminal Women* (ed., Polity Press, 1985). On the editorial boards of *Law in Context, Contemporary Crises, Howard Journal of Criminal Justice* and *Journal of Law and Society*. Most recent book, *Women, Crime and Poverty*, to be published by Open University Press, 1988.

Anne Worrall, BA, MA, CQSW. Lecturer in Social Work at Manchester University. Formerly a probation officer. Part-time PhD student at Keele University (Centre for Criminology). Published in *Probation, Howard Journal of Criminal Justice* and *British Journal of Criminology*.

The Contributors

Hilary Allen, BSC, RMN, PhD. Psychiatric nurse and erstwhile researcher in Sociology and Law. Doctoral research concerned the excessive psychiatrisation of female offenders. Lectured and published on various aspects of feminism, law and psychiatry – most recently a discussion of psychiatry and gender in P. Miller and N. Rose (eds) *The Power of Psychiatry* (Cambridge, Polity Press, 1986).

Gerry Chambers, MA, MSC. Research Fellow at the Policy Studies Institute. Previously worked in the Criminological Research Branch, Scottish Office. Publications include *Investigating Sexual Assault* (with Ann Millar, Edinburgh, HMSO, 1983), *Prosecuting Sexual Assault* (with Ann Millar, Edinburgh, HMSO, 1985); and *The Scottish Crime Survey* (with J. Tombs, Edinburgh, HMSO, 1983).

Dee Cook, BA, MA. Lecturer in Sociology at Telford College of Arts and Technology. Part-time tutor, Open University. Formerly Inland Revenue Tax officer and Department of Health and Social Security. Part-time PhD student Keele University (Centre for Criminology). Published in Civil and Public Services Associations *Red Tape* and Inland Revenue's Staff Federation's Journal *Taxes*.

Mary Eaton, BEd, PhD. Head of the Department of Sociology at St Mary's College, Middlesex. Publications include *Justice for Women? Family, Court and Social Control* (Milton Keynes, Open University Press, 1986). On the editorial board of *Sociology*.

Susan S.M. Edwards, BA, MA, PhD. Presently writing a book entitled *Women, Policing and the State*. Publications include *Female Sexuality and the Law* (Oxford, Martin Robertson, 1981); *Women on Trial* (Manchester, Manchester University Press, 1984); *Gender, Sex and the Law* (ed., Beckenham, Croom Helm, 1985). On the editorial boards of *Victimology* and *Reviewing Sociology*.

Elaine Genders, BSoc. Sci, MPhil. Research Fellow, Centre for Criminological Research, University of Oxford. Co-author of *Sentencing in the Crown Court* (Occasional Paper No. 10, Centre for Criminological Research, 1984) and 'Women's Imprisonment: the Effects of Youth Custody' (with E. Player, *British Journal of Criminology*, October 1986).

Frances Heidensohn, BA. Senior Lecturer in the Department of Social Science and Administration, Goldsmiths' College, University of London. Author of *Women and Crime* (London, Macmillan, 1985). Associate Editor of *British Journal of Criminology*.

Ann Millar, MA, MSc. Senior Research Officer, Criminological Research Branch, Scottish Office. In addition to recently published work on civil debts and fines, she has also co-authored *Investigating Sexual Assault* (with Gerry Chambers, Edinburgh, HMSO, 1983) and *Prosecuting Sexual Assault* (with Gerry Chambers, Edinburgh, HMSO, 1985).

Josie O'Dwyer. Previously full-time Development Worker for Women in Prison. Member of the Clean Break Theatre Company. Co-author of *Criminal Women* (with P. Carlen *et al.* Cambridge, Polity Press, 1985).

Elaine Player, BSc. Research Fellow at the Centre for Criminological Research, University of Oxford. Registered for PhD on Women and Crime at London School of Economics. Co-authored *Sentencing in the Crown Court* (with Elaine Genders, Occasional Paper No. 10, Centre for Criminological Research, 1984); 'Women's Imprisonment: the Effects of Youth Custody' (with Elaine Genders, *British Journal of Criminology*, October 1986); and *Women in the Penal System* (with N. Seear, London Howard League for Penal Reform, 1986).

Judi Wilson, BA. Previously full-time co-ordinator for Women in Prison and member of the Board of Management of the Women Prisoners' Resource Centre.

Acknowledgements

We would like to thank Anne Kerr at Manchester University and Doreen Thompson, Freda Mainwaring and June Poppleton at Keele University for their secretarial help at the editorial stage of this book.

Introduction:

Gender, Crime and Justice

Pat Carlen and Anne Worrall

When I was studying sociology and I got up to the crime bit, I thought it was absolute shit. People steal for different reasons but *not* because something causes it. They don't *have* to steal, but they look around and they think of ways to get what other people take for granted and they decide that the only way to get it is to steal.

(Kim, aged 28)

Courts feel it's more normal for men to commit crime. But they don't realise how hard it is out there for women. I don't depend on nobody, but they look on that as wrong. That's why they come down harsh on women in court.

(Cindy, aged 22)

Kim and Cindy are not philosophers. They are practising criminals. Yet because they have been perennially called to account for their actions in numerous courts of law, psychiatrists' clinics and probation offices, they frequently ruminate upon two related questions. To what extent is an individual free to shape her own actions, identity and consciousness independently of the economic, ideological and political circumstances in which she finds herself? What is the relationship between criminal justice and social justice in general? These two questions, the first relating to issues traditionally debated under the legend of free-will versus determinism, the second relating to questions of class exploitation, racism, gender, culpability and the power to punish, are also fundamental to any analyses of women's lawbreaking and/or criminalisation. For women who break the law have, like all other Western women, been born into material and ideological conditions structure by two major sets of relationships: the class relationships of a capitalist mode of production and the gender relationships of a patriarchal system of social reproduction. Additionally, black women (and black men) in Britain will have had both their life-chances and their experiences of the criminal justice and

1

penal systems, shaped by racism (Home Office 1986; Southgate and Ekblom 1986).

This book focuses primarily upon *women's* lawbreaking and criminalisation. The emphasis throughout is upon analysing the relationships between the position of women in society and their representation and treatment as gendered subjects of the criminal justice and penal systems. At the same time, the analyses raise two further questions: about the relative importance of both class exploitation and racism in engendering women's lawbreaking behaviour; and about both class and racist biases in the administration of criminal justice for women. Thus, although the articles are actually organised into three sections on women in crime, courts and custody, three theoretical concerns dominate and crosscut the volume as a whole:

1. Women's ideological representation in, and experience of, the criminal justice and penal systems (Chs 1 and 4–10).
2. The relationships between class exploitation and/or racism and discourses of femininity in the social control of women in general *and* in their representation as criminals in particular (Chs 2, 3 and 8).
3. Questions about the actual, proper and possible relationships between formal criminal justice and the substantive inequities stemming variously from racism, class exploitation and patriarchal domination (Chs 1, 3, 5 and 7).

All chapters of the book contribute to the feminist project of deconstructing the dominant ideological discourses present constitutive of media, judicial and popular conceptions of the criminal justice system's gendered female subjects. Central to such conceptions of women lawbreakers are the typifications of femininity that distinguish between 'normal' and 'abnormal' women.

Femininity and the Construction of the Normal Woman

Femininity is routinely constituted within a number of discourses which circumscribe not only a woman's behaviour but also the images which she has of herself and her relationships with other people.

Women's experiences of 'being female' are mediated by their bodies, their minds and their social interaction. The discourses within which these experiences are structured are constituted by sets of relationships which cluster around notions of domesticity, sexuality and pathology. These discourses themselves interrelate and are not mutually exclusive. As with the images of a kaleidoscope, each discourse organises its components uniquely but not arbitrarily. A discourse may contain paradoxes and discontinuities, but in its realisation these are transformed into unity, coherence and hierarchy. As Mark Cousins (1978) has observed, the categories of maleness and femaleness

> are not simply categories which oppose each other on a neutral ground. They are set
> up in a 'violent hierarchy', for they are already organised by the privileged term in

relation to which the other term is both necessitated and subordinated

(Cousins 1978)

Women, then are always-ready *not men*. Femininity is constructed on the site vacated by masculinity, and this absence of maleness is manifested in two opposing sets of expectations, revolving around the socially ambiguous status of dependence (Eichenbaum and Orbach 1983). On the one hand, femininity is characterised by self-control and independence. Being a normal woman means coping, caring, nurturing and sacrificing self-interest to the needs of others. It also means being intuitively sensitive to those needs without them being actively spelt out. It means being *more than man*, in order to embrace and support Man. On the other hand, femininity is characterised by lack of control and dependence. Being a normal woman means needing protection (Hutter and Williams 1981). It means being childlike, incapable, fragile and capricious. It is being *less than man* in order to serve and defer to Man.

Domesticity

Motherhood is regarded ambivalently in our society. The young mother is a valued category (Ardener 1978) and it is assumed that the normal young woman is either a mother or a mother-in-the-making. Adolescent girls are regarded as potential mothers, and their behaviour as daughters is viewed as indicative of their capacity for future home-making and child-caring (Hudson 1983). Ideally, mothers produce and socialise the next generation of workers and mothers, and are also the guardians of morality. Motherhood is therefore promoted as a vocation, as a worthy career in itself (Calvert 1985). Becoming a mother is one of the ways in which an ideal woman demonstrates that she is 'more than Man' and that, in both a literal and metaphorical sense, she encompasses Man. At the same time the woman's ability to reproduce is a characteristic that inspires in men fear as well as celebration. The realisation that the internal processes of the female body are crucial to, yet beyond the control of, men can provoke anxiety and a desire to contain, limit and punish. Beyond the point of insemination men cannot control the physiological processes of reproduction. They can, however, structure the material and ideological conditions under which women become, and remain, mothers.

Approbated motherhood is (1) dependent motherhood within the structure of the nuclear family and (2) responsible, co-operative motherhood within the structure of the welfare state. The normal mother is both economically and emotionally dependent on the father of her child, and it is considered essential to that child's welfare to have two parents *in situ* in the family home (Barrett and McIntosh 1982). 'A mother without a male for support is seen as a social problem' (Calvert 1985; Cook, Ch. 2 below).

But the buttressing of the nuclear family does not render it autonomous or impervious to the influence of the state. Rather, the family is seen as an agency of 'supervised reproduction', supported by means of 'contract and tutelage'

(Donzelot 1979). The means for achieving this objective varies with the class of family, but the key site of intervention is always the woman as mother. The offer to the middle-class family is that of a contract, an alliance between the family welfare professionals (doctors, psychiatrists and social-workers) and the mother. By promoting the mother as educator and medical auxiliary, the state secures its influence over the family, and the mother increases her power within the domestic sphere. But for 'unstructured', 'rejecting' or 'deficient' families the objective must be achieved by a different means. It is then the mother herself who requires education and supervision – not directly, but through the medium of social work and child psychiatry, with their emphases on the needs of her children. In this way 'the prophylactic cravings of psychiatrists and the disciplinary requirements of the social apparatuses' converge (Donzelot 1979: 131).

Yet the ideal woman is not only a mother. She is also a wife. The ideology of wifeliness involves additional, conflicting expectations of coping yet not coping. Being a good wife means maintaining a clean, tidy, welcoming home, yet giving the impression of doing so with a minimum of effort, which leaves sufficient energy and motivation to be attractive, attentive and seductive. The home may be one of the few places offering a genuine outlet for women's creativity, but that creativity is 'submitted to a visual ideal whose main statement is the absence of the work they do, and absence of conflict about that work' (Coward 1984). Evidence of labour, conflict or mess is interpreted as evidence of failure rather than as a true reflection of the reality of women's domestic lives.

The discourse of domesticity is legitimised by privileged (predominantly male) professionals who are empowered to circumscribe the behaviour of women through alliance or tutelage. Their power is frequently delegated to (predominantly female) semi-professionals (e.g. nurses and social-workers), who mediate between them and the women who enter the roles of patient or client. These are the 'wise women' (Heidensohn 1985) who, in addition to translating 'expert knowledge' into 'common sense' for the consumption of the always-already failing woman, also purvey an authoritative role model of normal womanhood (Hutter and Williams 1981). But the widest dissemination of the 'Ideal Homes' ideology (Coward 1984) is through the influence of women on each other as peers.

Sexuality

Post-Freudian attempts to explain the development of gender consciousness – or sexuality – have struggled with contradictory interpretations of his writings. The discovery of the unconscious and its influence on the construction and organisation of sexuality has been used both to prescribe and proscribe the socialisation of women as wives and mothers. The power of the professional to invoke a reading of Freud that supports politically conservative theories of healthy gender-role adjustment, has been challenged by a feminist reading which argues that what Freud really did was to identify the *myth* that facilitates the ideology of masculinity and femininity.

The underlying thesis of psychoanalysis is that the discourse of sexuality is a discourse of conflict, and that, while the discovery of conflict is the entrance to power for the little boy, it is the portent of powerlessness for the little girl (Miller 1976). In order to become normal women, little girls have to be *transformed*: they have to recognise and come to terms with 'castration'–with that of which they have been deprived. They must recognise that they are lacking, that they are 'other', that they are 'different from normal people (who are men)' (Orbach 1978). Following this recognition, a woman can choose from three possible reactions (Mitchell 1974). She can fear her own sexuality and become inhibited and neurotic; she can refuse to abandon her sexuality (as represented by the clitoris) and remain in a pre-Oedipal 'masculine' phase; she can exploit the passive aims of her sexual drive (as represented by the vagina and uterus), transferring her affection from mother to father and desiring the phallus, thus 'successfully' resolving the Oedipal complex and becoming a 'normal' woman. Through this latter course, the woman embarks on an exchange relationship with the phallus, reproducing within the personal the economic relations of production that underpin capitalist society. Thus the personal is political.

Central to this process is the resolution of the conflict between the reality and the representation of loss–what Adams (1983) calls the 'lack-in-being'. The obligation on the mother is simultaneously to provide objects that satisfy her child and to disillusion the child about the guaranteed predictability of such provision. Coming to terms with the unpredictability and uncontrollability of drive satisfaction is the essence of the Oedipal stage of development; though while the little boy can compensate for the loss of the mother by gaining identification with the father (the phallus, the definer), the little girl is left to identify with the failed provider, the forever lacking mother, the defined.

The consequence of this necessary transformation of consciousness is that women come to believe that their own desires and needs are not their own but someone else's and that they can only be satisfied through serving the needs of others. In this way women allow men to off-load unresolved conflicts about their own sexuality (Miller 1976; Eichenbaum and Orbach 1983).

Yet women also 'know' that sexuality is not *only* about service and fulfilling the needs of others. Men may depend on the service of women but they do not usually love them for that reason (or for that reason alone). Service may be essential, but it is unattractive, so women must serve while giving the impression of not serving. Intrinsic to the role of normal womanhood is the concept of 'appearance'. 'Appearance' is an ambiguous word, for it means both 'what is seen' and 'what is not real'. It implies both visibility and pretence. Women are constantly exhorted to attend to their appearance – both physically and emotionally. 'Looking good' is of paramount importance (Coward 1984). But the hidden messages in this exhortation are that the normal woman looks good even if she doesn't feel good (pretence for the benefit of others) *and* that she will feel good if she looks good (pretence for the benefit of self). The preoccupation of so many women with their body shape and size reflects precisely this conflict between the felt reality of a woman's existence and her desire to present herself in an acceptable, conforming and attractive way to the world (Orbach 1978).

The construction of femininity through the discourse of sexuality is dependent, then, on a gender consciousness that develops from early childhood through the unconscious mental struggles of the little girl to make sense of the conflicts and contradictions of the reality of her physical and emotional world. Such struggles are reinforced by privileged intermediaries such as teachers, social-workers and doctors; *and* by those trapped within the same ideologies – mothers, fathers, family relations and friends.

Pathological 'Otherness'

It has been argued here that the ability of women to give birth to live beings arouses a fundamental fear of the female body in men together with a need to limit and control the environment of personal relationships within which a woman is allowed to become a mother. It has also been argued that the ideology of femininity is internalised by women from an early age and that the development of gender consciousness is a struggle which a woman has with herself as much as with other people. In this relationship with herself, the normal woman becomes aware of the conflicting expectations of the in-control/out-of-control dichotomy.

This dichotomy is further manifested in a discourse that constructs female biology as a *disease*. The description of the normal woman as 'sick' derives from two sources. First, the normal woman's body is perceived as intrinsically 'abnormal' in that though capable of more than a man's body, it is less reliable. Menstruation, pregnancy, childbirth and the menopause all result in 'hormonal imbalance' – a phrase which connotes that the woman may herself be 'imbalanced' during those times. Second, women are statistically over-represented amongst those who use medical facilities; in particular, they appear to suffer disproportionately from ostensibly gender-neutral mental illnesses.

The ideology of 'normal abnormalities' that surrounds reproductive processes has become so powerful since the development of 'scientia gynaecologia' (Edwards 1981) in the nineteenth century that it is rarely explicitly restated. The normal woman accepts and accommodates the 'naturalness' and inevitability of the power of her bodily functions to dictate her self-image and restrict her behaviour. The corollary of this ideology is that women who suffer gynaecological dysfunctions, or who reject the controlling influence of the reproductive cycle (e.g. by taking the Pill), become problematic and potentially 'out of control'. The alternative means of controlling such women involve the making of moral judgements about either their sexual proclivities (the 'promiscuous' woman) or their genuineness (the 'malingering' woman). In practice this poses a dilemma relating to the *eligibility* of women for inclusion in the medical category 'normal woman'. The dilemma is exemplified in the ambivalent attitudes of medical and judicial professions towards the potentially excusing condition of Pre-menstrual Syndrome (Dalton 1964, 1978).

The political implications of accepting a theory which maintains that many (most?) women are physiologically, emotionally and behaviourally abnormal for between a quarter and a half of their reproductive lives, have clouded the recognition of what could be seen as an otherwise valuable clinical exploration of a neglected area of medicine. The conservative (male dominated) medical and legal establishment fears that women will exploit such theories to develop a 'trained incapacity' to evade the moral and/or legal consequences of their behaviour; feminists fear that such theories reinforce assumptions about the inherent inferiority of women (Edwards 1984). Our own position would be that while we would totally agree with analyses that reject any notions that women are forever tied to their biology, we would also argue that sociological reductionism is as unhelpful in understanding women's crimes as is biological reductionism. Now that some of the more extreme forms of biological positivism and essentialism have been discarded, maybe we should be looking forward to analyses that, rather than denying female biology and difference, try to represent more fully the complex relationships between biological, physiological and social causes of women's behaviours and experiences and the heterogeneity of the interpretations given them. (cf. Birke 1986).

The ideology of female biology as disease, like the ideology of the family, has its roots in the Victorian era, when its parameters were defined by the male-dominated medical profession that, in collusion with wealthy, white, middle-class husbands, was vigilant to distinguish the 'silly, self-indulgent and superstitious' malingerer from the genuinely weak and sickly woman, who needed constant rest and (expensive) medical care (Ehrenreich and English 1973). Interestingly, such distinctions were always less relevant for poor and working-class women, who were conveniently deemed inherently stronger and less in need of lengthy medical treatment anyway. Yet the legacy of such distinctions remains, and the assessment of women's eligibility for medical help constitutes a 'practice of exclusion' both from 'normal' femininity and 'normal' medicine. Allen (1986) has observed that disturbances arising from women's reproductive cycle – along with those deviations of gender role that have come to be defined as 'personality disorders' (sexual deviance, violence, rejection of family relationships) – have been increasingly marginalised by the medical profession. Since they do not display a 'proper' psychiatric symptomatology, women so categorised are excluded from 'proper' psychiatric treatment and are increasingly defined as requiring social-work intervention. Thus certain women are doubly restricted by being constructed within a discourse of sickness which nevertheless denies them access to the means of health.

The effectivity of the discourse of 'pathological otherness', unlike that of the discourses of domesticity and sexuality, emanates from the elasticity of its parameters. The boundary between normality and abnormality is constantly blurred. Three factors contribute to this elasticity. First, health is implicitly defined in relation to maleness, in the sense that the 'normal' female body is regularly and predictably abnormal or 'unhealthy'. Second, the emphasis in the ideologies of both femininity and current psychiatric practice on 'coping' (Allen 1986) predisposes women to define themselves as 'sick' when they feel they are not coping. Third, the centrality to the construction of femininity of the dilemma of having to be both 'in control' and 'out of control' poses a routine problem for women. While they may perceive themselves to be crossing the boundary between normality and abnormality many times a day, that journey is itself a feature of normal femininity. The point at which women become 'genuinely' sick is therefore never clear. Such confusion is functional to the controlling of women's behaviour and may explain the preventive use of medication by many women who learn to dread the debilitating self-hatred that results from not knowing whether they are – or should be – in control of their bodies, their minds and their relationships with other people.

Femininity, then, is constructed within the ideological discourses of domesticity, sexuality and pathology. The essentially *normal* woman does not exist. Nor are all women equally oppressed. Gender expectations have effects variously on women whose consciousness and social experiences are differentially structured within the inequities of a society based on class exploitation and crosscut by racism. Even so, the study of women, crime and justice is now sufficiently advanced for it to be confidently asserted that the majority of criminalised and imprisoned females are victims of gender typifications that discriminate primarily against working-class and black women. The articles in this volume specifically discuss the experiences and ideological representations of women in crime, courts and custody. In so doing they also raise questions about the relationships between gender and justice.

Gender, Crime and Justice

Part One's title 'Women in Crime' is a reference both to women's representation in criminology, courts and penal policy, and to their actual experiences of lawbreaking and criminalisation. In Chapter 1 Frances Heidensohn gives an elegant exposition of the advances made in the study of women in crime, courts and custody, together with a stimulating exposition of some of their implications for criminology. Then in Chapters 2 and 3 respectively, Dee Cook and Susan Edwards in turn analyse the ideologies and social conditions conducive to the lawbreaking and discriminatory regulation of, first, female supplementary benefit claimants and, second, women engaged in soliciting and other sex-related offences. By the end of Part One, therefore, the political, ideological and economic context conditioning women's experiences of crime, courts and custody has been well outlined, the recent deterioration in their economic position firmly established. The empirical studies of Parts Two and Three subsequently detail how the patriarchal domination both constituted by, and constitutive of, the ideological and economic oppression of women discussed in Part One, also inseminates the courtroom and the prison to such an extent that women's experiences of courts and custody are very different from men's. But the following essays do not *only* demonstrate that the administration of criminal justice realises and amplifies all those substantive gender (and other) inequalities that the formal notion of social justice denies. As Frances Heidensohn suggests in Chapter

1, they also raise questions about the significance of gender studies for criminological theory and judicial and penal policy.

What significance do gender-studies have for criminological theory?

Gender studies have significance for criminological theory in three main respects:

1. They call into question previous theories of lawbreaking and/or criminalisation.
2. They suggest new lines of investigation for empirical research programmes.
3. They either provoke new uses for old concepts or displace old theories by new ones.

This book of course owes its very existence to the fact that so many previously held theories have already been called into question by Heidensohn's (1968) and Smart's (1977) pioneering work on women and crime, so we will limit this discussion to the other theoretical issues and research possibilities raised by studies of crime and gender. They all centre around questions concerning the relative importance of gender in relation to other variables such as class, racism and age in the routine production of:

1. Socially identifiable groups of both the powerless and the powerful as known lawbreakers.
2. A selection of those (mainly powerless) lawbreakers as convicted criminals.
3. A further selection of those convicted criminals with even more social characteristics in common — other than the seriousness of the offence or the persistence of the nuisance — as recidivist prisoners.
4. Specific groups of crime victims.

Though only three of the following chapters (i.e. Cook's, Edwards's and Carlen's) analyse some specific social contexts conditioning women's lawbreaking, (and only one of them even begins to touch on the relationships between racism and criminalisation), we would argue that, taken together, the eight empirical studies reported here indicate that there is still a need for investigative research in the interactionist tradition.

First, only empirical studies can begin to chart the complex interplay between historically specific social contexts and gendered consciousness in producing the decision to engage in one or more types of lawbreaking. Thus, for instance, the chapters on supplementary benefit claimants, prostitution, young women in care and bail decisions (Eaton, Ch. 6) do not only indicate that some women choose to break the law under ideological conditions that, incorporated into both statute and judicial decisions, reinforce women's dependency upon, and regulation by, men. They suggest, too, that certain combinations of gender and class factors are also strategic in determining the extent to which some women will 'see through' the controlling occlusions of the 'gender deal' and consequently decide to go it alone – even if it means that in order to 'have what everybody else takes for granted' they have to break the law.

Second, once we compare women's experiences of lawbreaking with those of their criminalisation and imprisonment, it becomes plain that the distinct processes conditioning women's lawbreaking, criminalisation and imprisonment need separate analysis; that, though each may later be incorporated into a model that indexes the points at which judicial and penal intervention produce or exacerbate the conditions conducive to lawbreaking, these separate analyses should neither be conflated nor be assumed to have symmetrical effects. For example, though the articles of Mary Eaton and Hilary Allen separately demonstrate that women (like men, but for different reasons) are not held in custody according to the seriousness of their crimes, a comparison of Allen's chapter with Carlen's indicates that the same patriarchal assumptions that result in the earlier and more repressive regulation of young women's deviance than young men's, can also result in women who commit certain serious crimes of violence receiving much lighter sentences than those imposed on men who have committed similar crimes. This reminder, that the effects of ideologies can vary, lends further support to the argument that it is only through empirical investigation that new forms of ideological domination and economic exploitation can be socially (though not necessarily theoretically) located.

Third, and conversely, empirical research into the relationships between gender and other variables in the production of women's lawbreaking, criminalisation and penal incarceration highlights the urgent need to develop conceptualisations that in explaining why contemporary women's lawbreaking and judicial and penal regulation take the forms that they do take, also deny to women's experiences of crimes, courts and custody a necessary and unitary existence. Furthermore, it is because there is no such unitary object as 'women's lawbreaking' that it cannot be in a symmetrical relationship with a unitary 'women's conformity'. In other words, the inversion of a control theory explaining why the majority of women appear to be law-abiding will only partly explain why *some* other women break the law in the first place. It will be even less useful in explaining why a few of all women lawbreakers go on to become recidivist criminals and prisoners. Instead, therefore, of only analysing the processes that condition the conformity of women who are law-abiding, it might also be useful to conceive of the diverse processes that converge in the production and representation of those who are *not*, as being epiphenomena of women's *powerlessness*. It is a powerlessness that is most dramatically visible when women (1) resist it by engaging in minor property crime or self-destructive acts of violence or drug abuse, (2) are victims of male violence and (3) appear in the courts as either offenders *or* complainants (see Chambers and Millar, Ch. 4 below). The various forms that these manifestations of women's powerlessness (and resistance to it) take will depend, as we have already suggested, upon the interplay of a variety of social factors, dominant amongst them being gender, class, racism and age. Through empirical investigation and theoretical analysis of their combinatory effects on lawbreakers, courts and prisons, it might be possible to suggest at what stages (if any) racism, social class or age become more important than gender in the lawbreaking, prosecution and imprisonment of women.

What significance do gender studies have for judicial and penal policy?

People with a philosophical and practical interest in questions of crime and punishment should find the following essays both thought-provoking and frustrating. And the frustration will most probably be greatest amongst those who accept the two major conclusions of the analyses: that some women's lawbreaking is in part provoked by legislation and forms of economic regulation that discriminate against women by reinforcing their dependency upon men; and that women are dealt with by courts and prisons according to typifications of femininity that disadvantage all except some of those very few women accused of the most serious crimes.[1] For where do such analyses get us? Even if they are suggestive of the effective relationship between certain ideologies, economic conditions and crime, they do not provide the answers to a whole range of jurisprudential questions concerning culpability, penal regulation and the power to punish. To indicate the conditions that socially overdetermine the lawbreaking and/or criminalisation of some women, is a task for social theory; argument about the degree of their culpability, or the most judicious method for calculating it, are tasks for political jurisprudence. Sociological analyses (like the ones in this book) only suggest that under certain relatively rare *combinations* of otherwise general economic and ideological conditions some women are more likely than not to choose to break the law, and are more likely than not to be criminalised and/or imprisoned. Such analyses do *not* assume or imply that the women involved have no choice. Nor do they entail arguments that lawbreaking women should be treated either according to a principle of positive discrimination or as if they were men! Instead, therefore, of claiming that any 'feminist', 'socialist' or other policy implications can be 'read off' from these essays, we just hope that they will stimulate new discussions about possible and appropriate ways to reduce the inequities presently suffered by women in the courts and prisons. The arguments and analyses of the rest of the book have moved us to conclude this introductory chapter by making some observations on the possible implications of gender studies for judicial and penal policy.

WOMEN'S LAW
There is a case for establishing Women's Law as a special area of study.[2] In Chapter 1 (and in Heidensohn 1986) Frances Heidensohn, in confronting some of the problems of relating gender, crime and justice studies to policy, asks, 'What would a woman-centred justice system be like?' It is a question that is also implicit in much of the work of the Institute of Women's Law at the University of Oslo, where Women's Law has been established as a special area of study within the Faculty of Law and interwoven into its degree scheme, not just as an optional subject but as a component too of all the first year compulsory subjects (see Stang-Dahl, 1987). Similar programmes in Britain, in addition to examining further the

issues discussed by Heidensohn, might also place the following interrelated questions on a Women's Law agenda.

1. *Is it inevitable that the assumptions, language and practices of the courts and prisons reflect and reinforce the prevailing picture of women's 'proper' and relatively powerless place in the social order?* This question, explicitly posed by Mary Eaton on page 100 below, and implicit in all the other chapters, concerns the extent to which criminal courts and prisons should (or indeed could) develop policies that might contribute to a diminution (rather than an amplification) of the gender injustices that women have already suffered well before they enter the criminal justice arena (see Carlen 1983b, and 1984).

2. *To what extent is it either desirable or possible for magistrates and judges to take into account either biological difference or differential gender experience in their decision-making?* One might be tempted to argue that, given the malign effects gender stereotyping has already had on the treatment of women in courts and prisons, we should work towards making the legal and penal systems gender-neutral. But they cannot be gender-neutral. For as Tove Stang-Dahl has recently observed, while we live in societies where women and men have very different life chances and experiences, 'legal rules will necessarily affect men and women differently' (Stang-Dahl 1986: 1). Accordingly, and rather than attempting to make judicial and prison personnel gender-blind, we should try first to persuade them that all their thinking about women in the judicial and penal systems is (like other people's) infused with gender typifications, and then get them to examine the implications and effects of those stereotypes. But what then? Magistrates might well be alerted to the inappropriateness of sentencing on the basis of out-of-date or sexist gender expectations, but could even the most gender-alert magistrate make allowance for the multiple and different inequities of sexism, racism and an exploitative class system when deciding upon the guilt of the accused or the punishment of the guilty? Which leads to question three.

3. *Is it either desirable or possible for courts to calculate individual responsibility and culpability in terms of biological difference and the differentials of gender-experience and power?* This difficult question is implicit in Cook's chapter on supplementary benefit fraud, Edwards's on prostitution and, in acute form, Carlen's on young women in Care; and it is explicit in Allen's chapter on women's crimes of violence. As it is a question that provokes people into flinging out accusations about biological determinism, sociological determinism, positivism and a host of other sociological sins, let us make our own position clear.

As we have already claimed, to say that under certain combinatory conditions women choose to break the law is not also to argue that such women have no responsibility for their actions. Certainly they are responsible. Moreover, under present conditions of class exploitation, sexism and racism, questions of individual culpability will in any case ultimately be decided in the courts after a calculation of the political feasibility (or not) of appearing to imply that specific clusters of social disadvantage license crime (cf. Carlen 1979). And we ourselves, well appraised of the dire discriminatory effects that individualised sentencing based on either biological or sociological determinism has already had on women (and working-class children) would certainly not recommend that the sentence be tailored to fit the woman rather than the crime. Yet, while we are not suggesting that more women on trial should be pathologised and have their intentionality denied in the way that Hilary Allen so carefully describes in Chapter 5, we do think that these essays call for a radical rethinking of the concept of culpability in terms of what a *reasonable woman* might be justified in doing under certain circumstances. For there is increasing evidence that the concept of the reasonable *man* biases the logic of courtroom proceedings against women. And nowhere is this more apparent than in Chambers and Millar's article, where it is clearly demonstrated that the questioning of rape victims is frequently based on moralistic assumptions about, for example, what *moral* women *should* do when threatened with rape, that are quite opposed to what *reasonable* women (often with prior experience of male violence) actually do. In fact, Chambers and Millar's article makes explicit the logic that is implicit in most judicial and penal approaches to women – that if they had been reasonable (i.e. moral) women, they would not have stepped out of their proper place and found themselves in the courts and prisons at all (cf. Worrall 1981). It is because of that sexist logic and because legal rules *do* affect women and men differently that we argue for a rethinking of the concept of culpability in terms of at least a recognition that, because of their relative powerlessness, '*reasonable* women' often choose to act in ways that are opposed to the logic of the 'reasonable man' whose thinking dominates the courts. (Even when the magistrate is female! See Anne Worrall, Ch. 7 below.)

4. *Does biological difference and differential gender experience justify the provision of different facilities for women in courts and prisons?* On the evidence of Eaton (Ch. 6) Genders and Player (Ch. 9) and O'Dwyer, Wilson and Carlen (Ch. 10) we argue that the crucial test is whether any specific provision for women will either empower them to gain greater control over their courtroom or prison experiences or, conversely, worsen their position by reinforcing debilitating gender roles or stereotypes. Thus, for instance, greater recognition that the formalities of courts especially disadvantage women (whose domestic isolation will have given them fewer chances for public performance than men) could lead to much-needed changes in courtroom spacing, placing and practice that would certainly benefit women (and many men too). Similarly, greater recognition by the prison authorities of women's special health needs during menstruation, pregnancy and the menopause should result in the enforcement of minimum standards of sanitation and a more sophisticated, woman-oriented system of health provision in the women's prisons. Such changes would also give women more control over their prison experience.

5. *To what extent do men also suffer gender injustices in the courts and prisons?* This question (implicit in Allen's chapter) is important for women because answers to it might usefully result in entirely different penal regimes for men. For it seems to us that contemporary demands for harsher sentences for rape and other crimes of violence against women could be counterproductive, while men's gaols continue to be run in such a way that violent men are brutalised still further.

MONITORING SEXISM

There is a case for monitoring sexism within the criminal justice system and for providing 'gender-stereotyping awareness' training for social-workers, probation officers, prison officers, magistrates and judges, in the same way that some police forces have been investigated for racism. Additionally, magistrates, probation officers and other court personnel should be sensitised both to the gender-stereotyping that precludes consideration of contemporary women's actual gender problems and powerlessness, and to the courtroom practices that especially inhibit women. Likewise, it is to be hoped that the Prison Department will be sufficiently inspired by the excellent analysis of Genders and Players (Ch. 10) to introduce similar training for prison officers. For as Anne Worrall shows in Chapter 7, common sense is not enough. Women on trial (whether as criminals *or* victims) are still seen primarily as abnormal females rather than rational persons. Constant vigilance, analysis and campaigning are required to expose and oppose the institutionalised sexism routinely celebrated in British courts and prisons.

Notes

The views in this chapter are those of the editors and are not necessarily subscribed to by every contributor. Anne Worrall wrote the section on 'femininity' (pp. 2–8). Pat Carlen wrote the rest.

1. Though women convicted of certain very serious crimes are likely to receive a worse press than their male counterparts— as the media persecution of Myra Hindley has shown.
2. This concept of 'Women's law' is taken from Tove Stang-Dahl (1986) and the whole of this section was inspired by her account of the work of the Institute of Women's Law in Oslo.

Part One

Women in Crime

1

Women and Crime: Questions for Criminology

Frances Heidensohn

Criminology seems to be in one of its crises again. There is the predictable loss of confidence, and as Downes and Rock put it,

> the analysis of rule-breaking and rule-enforcement has failed to be cumulative. That analysis is composed of an extended train of partially examined and partially exhausted ideas.
>
> (Downes and Rock 1982: 251)

Cohen suggests that students of deviance are caught and immobilised between the two contradictory and self-cancelling poles of 'analytical despair' and 'adversarial nihilism' (1985: 240). Young (1986), in the most thorough of recent accounts, analyses the failure of what he calls 'social democratic positivism'. His recipe for future success involves what he calls 'left realist criminology'.

During the past ten or twenty years, when paradigms have faded as rapidly as pop stars, there have been significant developments in the study of women and crime. Indeed, the fact that women and crime has been studied seriously at all is a significant development in itself. There can be no doubting the extensive range and volume of work published on women and crime in recent times. Yet how significant and how effective has been the impact of that literature on its various audiences of criminologists and penologists, politicians and policy-makers, and women themselves? Almost two decades after 'The Deviance of Women' (Heidensohn 1968) was published and a decade after *Women, Crime and Criminology* (Smart 1976) seems an appropriate point to review what has been achieved and what remains to be done at this critical point for criminology.

I have suggested elsewhere (Heidensohn 1985: 145–50) that contemporary studies of women and crime derive from two key sources. First, the modern feminist movement provided a critique and set of concepts, especially in the social services of mainstream academic discourse. Second, in criminology itself, there was growing dissatisfaction of scholars with the omission of gender from theories of crime, and the marginal and distorting treatment given to women in such discussions. Much of the work of the past two decades which can be indexed under the heading 'Women and Crime' deals with the last two points, that is with making women visible in the study of crime and with ensuring that the image of them so rendered was not a mere gargoyle-like stereotype. In both these areas real advances have been made, even though important questions remain. I want to outline what seem to me the key insights and the remaining questions, and then to look at the more difficult issue of gender and criminality in the same way.

Characterising Female Offenders

A whole litany of writers (Heidensohn 1968; Klein 1976; Smart 1976; Shacklady Smith 1978; Leonard 1982; Millman 1982) have shown the fundamental flaws in traditional criminological writing on women, focusing particularly on the way in which folk myths about the inherent 'nature' of women were taken over by criminologists and used as the basis of pseudo-scientific psycho-biological theories (Lombroso and Ferrero 1895; Thomas 1923; Pollak 1950). What is striking about these theories is not merely their sexism, or even their misogyny, but their resilience and persistence. A second generation of writers (Cowie, Cowie and Slater 1968; Richardson 1969; Gibbens 1971) continued to put forward such views about female offenders until quite recently. As the Dobashes show (Dobash, Dobash and Gutteridge 1986) these notions were crucial in forming the basis for the treatment of women offenders in the 'new' Holloway and at the Scottish women's prison at Cornton Vale.

Clearly, then, a reasoned critique of traditional theories was vital both intellectually and because the stereotyped assumptions on which they were based has profound policy implications. Recent work on women and crime has not only challenged past assumptions, it also offers alternative views: we can now say much more confidently what women offenders are like and how they make sense of their own experiences. On women in prison, in the UK for example, there have been three major studies published in the 1980s (Carlen 1983a, Dobash, Dobash and Gutteridge 1986; Mandaraka-Sheppard 1986) as well as several autobiographical accounts (Carlen *et al.* 1985; Peckham 1985) of imprisonment. While the methods and approaches of all these authors differ in significant ways, their findings broadly confirm the main hypotheses of the feminist critics of traditional criminology.

Four major characteristics of many of the female offenders studied stand out and are worth highlighting. These are:

1. Economic rationality.
2. Heterogeneity of their offences.
3. Fear and impact of deviant stigma.
4. The experience of double deviance and double jeopardy.

Economic Rationality

Female criminals have been consistently portrayed down the ages as peculiarly evil and depraved, and as unstable and irrational. Often their irrationality is linked to their biological and their psychological nature. Paradoxically, they have been depicted as unfeminine and hence unnatural (Lombroso and Ferrero 1895) or all-too-feminine (Pollak 1950). More modern sociologists of deviance were also guilty of making similar assumptions by claiming that female deviance was mainly sexual in nature (Cohen 1955). Yet the overwhelming evidence from the studies under review is that women offenders, whose offences are, for the most part property crimes, are largely economically motivated. Thus Mandaraka-Sheppard concluded from her study of women in six English women's prisons that

> 40 per cent of the women were in extreme financial difficulties before and during the crime... the meaning of their crime for them, by and large, was mainly an act of supporting their children... the women made a conscious decision to offend as a solution to their problem for survival and support to their children.
>
> (Mandaraka-Sheppard 1986: 10–11)

Dobash, Dobash and Gutteridge also point to the 'dismal' employment histories of the inmates of Cornton Vale and to the poverty and deprivation of their lives (1986: 171–2). Carlen's more sophisticated analysis of women's imprisonment in Scotland shows how the interaction of family life, male dominance and Celtic culture make working-class women dependent and vulnerable, and yet responsible for family and finance, and lead some of them into a downward spiral 'of crime, prostitution and drinking' (Carlen 1983a: 44–6). McLeod too has voiced the views of many prostitute women who roundly contradict the thoughts of those who for generations have seen them as sex offenders; theirs is, they insist an economic activity: 'I do it purely for money' (McLeod 1982: 26 [see also Ch. 3 below]). Chris Tchaikovsky, after describing her criminal career in detail and its considerabale financial benefits sums it up thus:

> I had enjoyed both the dangers and the rewards, and my criminality was the result of a rational choice – nobody had coerced or cajoled me into it.
>
> (Tchaikovsky, in Carlen *et al.* 1985: 56).

Now, it would not of course be true to say that all women offenders are solely motivated by need (or greed) when committing crimes. Peckham, for instance, insists that she was mentally ill for some considerable time before her offence (1985: 16) and that so were many of those remanded with her (p. 240). But it is vital to redress the balance of the conventional account of female crime. Women offenders have been seen as less rational than male, as mere puppets jerked on the strings of sexual motives or pulled by darker tides of the reproductive cycle and its moon-based phases.

Variety of Deviance

Recent studies confirm that what distinguishes the pattern of female from male criminality is its frequency, scope and seriousness, not essential qualitative differences (Heidensohn 1985: 5–10). Women commit fewer crimes than men, are less likely to be recidivists or professional criminals and contribute very little to the tariff of serious violent crime. However, these differences are rooted in differential opportunities, different forms of socialisation and social control, not in innate characteristics. Women do in fact commit almost every kind of offence, however modestly: in the last two decades women have been notably involved in violent terrorist activities in several countries (Becker 1977; Iles 1985) and several studies have shown that girls and young women do join delinquent gangs and do get involved in fighting (Shacklady Smith 1978; Campbell 1984). The growth of historical studies of crime trends also suggest alternative patterns of deviance in the past. Women for instance were heavily involved in 'popular protests associated with bread production and distribution' (Dobash, Dobash and Gutteridge 1986: 27) and often led community action which involved threats and violence (Thompson 1971). Beattie argues from an analysis of crime trends in the eighteenth century that female criminality changed during this period both in its form and incidence because women's experience of life in the growing cities and industrial areas was quite different from men's (Beattie 1975).

Stigma

Goffman's classic work *Stigma* is subtitled 'the Management of Spoiled Identity' (1968), and this phrase succinctly summarises a notable problem for women criminals: most women perceive themselves and are perceived as being damaged or spoiled by criminalisation. This also happens, of course, to male criminals, but women offenders, because they are rarer, because their crimes may be more sensationally treated in the media [see Ch. 2 below] and because of the impact on their family lives feel their stigmatisation very deeply (Carlen 1983a; Heidensohn 1985; Iles 1986):

> Prison takes everything away from us, our identity, our children and whatever was valuable for us in life.
>
> (Mandaraka-Sheppard 1986: 206)

> I felt set apart, branded. . . . My good character is blemished.
>
> (Peckham 1985: 228–36)

Describing the impact on her of the 'Kerry Babies' Tribunal, which was not a criminal trial but an investigation of events, Joanne Hayes says,

> Nothing will ever repair the damage done . . . newspaper headlines have created an image of me in the public mind, as if I was some kind of scarlet woman rather than the perhaps rather naive and inexperienced person I am.
>
> (Hayes 1985: 169)

Double Deviance and Double Jeopardy

It is perhaps not surprising that, since women offenders come before the courts so comparatively rarely, they should be regarded as odd, unusual or even bizarre. However, in addition there is increasing evidence to show that women offenders often face a vicious double circle. They are seen as twice, or doubly deviant – as rare, abnormal female offenders for breaking social rules and as 'unfeminine and unnatural' women who have broken out of their conventional roles. Edwards reports from her study of female defendants before the Manchester City Magistrates' Court that women were much more likely to be subject to an oppressive and paternalistic form of individualised justice:

> Female defendants are processed within the criminal justice system in accordance with the crimes which they committed *and the extent to which the commission of the act and its nature deviate from appropriate female behaviour.*
>
> (Edwards 1984: 213, emphasis added)

Eaton also found in a magistrates' court in Greater London that it was women's adherence to conventional familial roles that was crucial in determining their court experience. This also happened to men, but Eaton notes certain important points of difference. Women were much more firmly and narrowly seen in a conventional domestic context: 'the probation officers place women within the domestic sphere' (Eaton 1985: 134 [see also Ch. 6 below]). Paradoxically, women were seen both as properly located as *dependants* in a traditional family setting (Eaton 1985: 136) and also responsible both for their own 'proper' behaviour and for those around them in the home. Farrington and Morris suggest a similar possible conclusion from their Cambridge study (1983a: 245), and Carlen found Scottish sheriffs especially punitive to women offenders whom they perceived as bad mothers (Carlen 1983a: 66). A collection of essays on the American criminal justice system also has as its central theme that there are considerable differences in the system's response to males and females with sexual stereotyping in terms of gender image being especially crucial for females (Hahn Rafter and Stanko 1982).

Double deviance, in short, can lead to paternalism, protectiveness and excessive punishment for women offenders. One group for whom this is especially clear are young offenders where a combination of 'welfare' ideology and double standards has produced a pattern of excessive interference in girls' lives for trivial offences (Chesney-Lind 1973; Parker, Casburn and Turnbull 1981; Casburn 1979; Webb 1984 [see also Ch. 8 below]). Women and girl offenders may therefore be entitled to feel that they are placed in 'double jeopardy'; that is, they risk punishment, or are actually punished, twice. They face the usual sanctions of the criminal justice system, but in addition they may be more harshly treated because they are deviant women who are *deviant as women* (Heidensohn 1985). One of the least surprising features to emerge therefore as characteristic of women offenders' experience is their widespread reaction to criminal justice as particularly unjust to them (Carlen 1983a; Carlen *et al.* 1985; Edwards 1984; Heidensohn 1986).

I have tried here briefly to give an account of important recent findings which develop and, for the most part, confirm the insights already offered by the modern critique of mainstream criminology's myopic view of women. It is clear that an immense amount has been achieved in quite a short time. Yet a whole series of questions still remain. Some are obviously suggested by the discussion so far, others go beyond its range.

The key points I have already listed indicate many areas for further exploration. Some accounts by women themselves of their experiences of crime have been published and further research will be published shortly (Carlen 1988), but there is still very little available. Links between the 'feminisation' of poverty and female crime also clearly need further exploration. Women's perceptions of themselves as 'deviant', the damage done by criminalising them, all need much closer more careful study so that we can appreciate the processes involved. Comparative aspects of such questions are important, if hard to achieve. It can be all too easily assumed that only women are subject to sexual stereotyping. Men are of course, too, although as subtle analyses like Eaton's shows, there are critical differences in how this operates. Unconventional counter-intuitive crimes by women as well as divergent historical trends are largely unknown terrain. One forthcoming study suggests that 'sexual' murders of the predatory 'Ripper' or 'monster' kind, are never committed by women, only by men, although their victims may sometimes be men as well as women and children (Fraser and Cameron 1986). Can this really be so and will it always continue? Participation by women (or the lack of it) in recent civil disturbances in Britain has been almost completely ignored, although as the research quoted above suggests, there is a longstanding tradition of popular protest led by women as well as their participation in peace camps at Greenham Common and elsewhere.

This is merely a short agenda of interesting possible questions suggested by existing work. Wider queries remain to be tackled. The largest group of these undoubtedly concern aetiology: what causes the patterns of women's crime, why does it differ significantly from men's and how far and in what ways are these gender divisions linked to other crucial divisions of age, class and race? In an earlier work I argued that these questions should be recast to emphasise the production of conformity rather than deviance in women, and that social institutions, values and culture operating in mutually reinforcing ways to create this. But the debate obviously needs to be taken much further.

It is one thing to describe, to applaud even, the substantial achievement of analysis and explanation of female crime. What is both much more difficult and also probably more crucial is to assess the wider impact of this achievement. Has anyone, save for a small, select audience been listening? Have they taken it seriously? Have they changed their minds, their research studies or their institutional practices? It is to these issues that I want to turn next. These matters pivot around the central point of gender, perhaps the most critical issue for criminology today. If studies of women and crime have not carried that message home, then they have not achieved a great deal at all.

Gender and Crime

Gender appears to be the single most crucial variable associated with criminality.
Put more bluntly, most crime is committed by men; relatively little crime is
committed by women. As Gregory puts it,

> the crime statistics of all countries, despite considerable legal and cultural variations
> tell the same story: that women have a lower crime rate than men.
>
> (Gregory 1986: 54)

The differences are very striking: in England and Wales more than 80 per cent of
serious crimes are carried out by males (Heidensohn 1985). Although women
outnumber men in the population as a whole, in the prison population men are in a
ratio to women of about 24:1. As an explanatory variable, as the possible
beginning of a theory of criminality, gender might therefore seem promising. Yet,
on the contrary, most criminologists have resisted this obvious insight with an
energy comparable to that of medieval churchmen denying Galileo or Victorian
bishops attacking Darwin. Classical and neoclassical theorists certainly looked at
sex differences, and some tried to account for them, though their explanations
always overpredicted the incidence of female crime. For instance, if females'
biology is causally linked to their crime, then all or most women share common
crimogenic experiences. The disappearance of gender from the more modern
sociological studies of crime and deviance is much more blatant. Leonard has
carefully and convincingly shown how all the major theories of crime are
fundamentally flawed by their failure to build gender into their explanations (as
with Merton's anomie theory, critical criminology, labelling theory, etc.) or
because of their marginal or wholly inadequate treatment (as in, for example,
Sutherland's differential association and Cohen's subcultural theories).

Some concern with explaining gender differences in recorded criminality was
manifested. Indeed, the criminological cottage industry of self-report, victim and
crime surveys owes its origin in part at least to a concern with establishing the
'true' sex–crime ratio, that is with finding a cache of hidden female criminality.
Far from doing so, such studies have largely confirmed the message of official
figures. Women and girls are involved in hidden, unreported crime, but so are men
and boys, and the size of the hidden 'iceberg' does not appear to alter the relative
shares (Box and Hale 1983; Heidensohn 1985).

Gender, then, is critical. That is the message of both mainstream criminology
and of the tributaries which have flowed in increasing numbers in recent years.
How has this message been received? What has its impact been? It ought to have
worked in at least two ways: first, by reinforcing the primacy of gender in all
theories of crime, and hence to undermine those which omit it; second, in asserting
the primacy of gender, any theory has to include both men and women.

It is possible to conduct an exercise in which one searches recent criminological
literature for gender awareness. (Just as, indeed not so long ago, it was standard
practice to note the omission of women from all such work). As Leonard puts it,
Critical Criminology [Taylor, Walton and Young 1975] does not contain one word

about women' (1982: 176). In my (admittedly non-random and idiosyncratic) survey, I have found three categories of response rather like delinquents' reaction to conviction: continued denial, shamefaced awareness and born-again acceptance.

Cohen's *Visions of Social Control* (1985) seems to me to be fundamentally flawed at its heart by its failure to take any account at all of the gender dimensions of social control. Downes and Rock (1982) in their more conventional textbook on deviance, perceptively weigh and find wanting the major schools of deviancy theory on many counts, but lack of a gender dimension is not one of them.

Into the category of 'shamefaced awareness' we have to sweep a whole genre of youth culture studies whose attitude to gender is neatly summed up in Brake's brief and apologetic chapter 'The Invisible Girl' (Brake 1980: 137). What this approach exemplifies is what I can only characterise as the 'lean-to' or 'added extension' approach to gender and deviance. Gender is no longer ignored in this approach, but it is consigned to an outhouse, beyond the main structure of the work and is almost invariably conflated with *women*; males are not seen as having gender; or if their masculinity does become an issue, it is taken-for-granted and not treated as problematic. Thus Brake throughout his study keeps asserting that

> youth cultures and subcultures tend to be some form of exploration of masculinity. These are *therefore* masculinist, and I have tried to consider *their effect on girls*.
> (Brake 1980: vii, emphasis added)

What, one cannot help wondering, of their effect on boys? Willis (1977) has been praised for at least acknowledging the power of gender in male working-class youth culture (Gregory 1986: 63) and for evincing a token shudder at the rampant sexism, racism and philistinism of 'the Lads'. But he, too, fails to analyse 'masculinity' fully, and by focusing on 'the Lads' and ignoring the wimpish 'earholes', only gives us one side of the picture and, in the process, reinforces a particularly charmless image of 'masculinity'.

Those writers who have, apparently, been reconstructed and enlightened (as distinct from those who always acknowledged the importance of gender) are relatively few, but their 'conversion' accounts provide instructive case studies. Wood, for instance, thoughtfully analyses his own responses to a series of gender-power confrontations in a unit for 'disruptive' school-children. Observing his own reactions he notes,

> Partly because of the tradition within which I was working, I went time and time again for the male and the spectacular in my ethnography. Perhaps I imagined it to actually equal youth culture (I take McRobbie's point ... here about male accounts of youth culture often being displaced autobiography and/or wish fulfilment).
> (Wood 1984: 68)

Wood goes on to give a thoughtful analysis of masculinity, its contradictions and weaknesses, above all recognising that it is necessary to explain masculinity – that it is not a category merely to be taken for granted nor, in either of the obvious ways, just to be asserted.

In an article on heroin use by young working-class males in the 1980s Auld and his colleagues suggest that sexual divisions play an important part in use of the drug (Auld, Dorn and South 1986). They stress masculinity as a key issue, but do not really explore the considerable contradictions they raise. Thus for them masculinity is constructed not only in terms of male economic and social *power* (p. 177) but also in a kind of vulnerability and dependence on girlfriends and mothers, which is, they suggest, seductive (p. 179). Only masculinity is explored in this account, and the massive contradictions in their concepts of gender are not accounted for; nevertheless, this is an interesting attempt to give gender a central place in the understanding of male deviance.

I am not as convinced by some of the other papers in the same collection or from the same stable, despite their eager stress on the centrality of gender (Young 1986; Lea and Young 1984). Essentially, what that means in practice is acknowledging the gender of the victims of crime and the validity of gender-related fears of crime (Young 1986: 22). Indeed, the recognition that much 'real' crime has a gender dimension is the single most telling impact which the study of women and crime has had. As Young puts it,

> the pioneering work of feminist criminologists both in the field of women as victims and as offenders has been of prime importance in forcing radicals to re-examine their positions on punishment and the causes of crime

(Young 1986: 27)

It is in the area of victimisation too, of course, that media and policy reactions have been most marked. There have been some attempts to handle rape victims more sensitively (Blair 1985 [but see Chambers and Millar, Ch. 4 below]) and even to overcome police-culture sexism over domestic violence. The law has been changed on kerb crawling, and there is growing recognition of the problems of the sexual abuse of children in families (Stanko 1984).

The deeper understanding which studying women and crime brings to criminology ought to result in a paradigm shift. Gender, and hence the explanations of gender-related patterns, should become central. That has clearly not happened. Instead, there is now a vast store of material on women offenders, women and crime and women and penology which is, no doubt, taken seriously and widely used for its impact *on women*. But the importance of gender for criminality is only perceived in terms of victimology. Important though these are, crimes with victims are only a small proportion of all crimes, even though violence does for most people constitute the crimes they fear. A central question therefore remains about gender: how can it be built into criminology to play the central part in explanation and analysis which it clearly must?

Social Control and Crime

I have already suggested that one of the most fruitful and fascinating areas of research which has developed from the study of women and crime has been work on social control and the processes by which conformity is achieved. Lees, for example, has developed her earlier work to show how schoolgirls are constrained and controlled by the reputations given to them (and taken away) by boys, and how this is related to their socialisation into adult sex-roles and acceptance of marriage in a realistic and unromantic way (Lees 1986). What we also need are the answers to a whole series of comparable questions about boys: how does their adolescent experience differ from girls, and how is it that power and control are already gender-related even among teenagers? Does this merely reflect adult society and its relationships? How important are class and race in these structures and processes? 'Family life' is often represented, for instance, in studies of delinquency as though it were a homogeneous, universally understood category. Yet any first-year sociology student knows that it is a highly problematic concept.

In the current moral panic about crime, which is centred especially on violence in the inner city, almost all the proffered remedies involve amazingly traditional solutions designed to reinforce conventional male behaviour, they range from quasi-militaristic short, sharp shocks to adventure training. The gender dimensions to the majority of attacks is all but ignored.

There are many areas of social control we know little about: the experiences of adult women have been studied remarkably little. This is as true of their roles *in* control as well as of their responses *to* control. The British police now seem to share their squad cars with sociologists almost as often as the Navaho Indians used allegedly to share their homes with American anthropologists. Of the values, ideologies, culture, strategies, and so on, of the (mainly male) police force we know a great deal. Yet of the vast 'soft control' forces who operate in social-work, nursing and teaching (and are predominantly female) we know far less.

Another aspect of informal social control and support which is related to a wider understanding of women and crime, has been the growth of supportive sisterhoods. A range of these have developed, several formed by groups of prostitute women campaigning for law reform, changes in police practice and destigmatisation. Others have brought together former prisoners and have used the media to try and demolish stereotypes and change specific penal practices, such as in the psychiatric wing at Holloway Prison [see Ch. 10 below]. These groups raise fascinating questions for criminology. Are they unique to women? Are they a response to stigma and damage?

Asking Questions

It is a popular truism that any social research study will end by asking more questions than it answers and follow this by requesting a research grant to fund the enquiries. With the recent study of women and crime certain exceptions can however be made. It is possible to answer far more queries now than we could ten or twenty years ago. Anyone who cares to look beyond stereotypes (and no one has any longer a real excuse not to) can learn a great deal. Women who do offend are much more like male offenders than is ordinarily supposed. But far more women than men are successfully held back by social controls and fears of social reaction.

There are three important levels on which these insights should be having some impact: in academic criminology; in the various formal agencies such as the police, prisons, and so on; and in the media. I have already suggested that academic criminology has given some house room to the study of women and crime in recent years, but it tends too often to be the lumber room or the attic rather than the visible and visited public rooms. What is still lacking is the integration of all this work into the mainstream. Partly this reflects the wider crises in the subject, but it is also related to institutional and political factors which conditions today do nothing to help. Ironically, though, control theorists and administrative criminologists have missed their most fruitful source of insight. If they are serious about wanting to contain and control crime, they could examine why it is that girls and women accept stricter social control and discipline than boys and men, and how far the processes are transferable. The answer to football hooligans might not then be identity cards, barbed wire enclosures or life sentences, but rather the feminisation of socialisation. Some agencies of formal control have had to adapt to new experiences and perceptions of women and crime. I have already noted the responses to feminist-led campaigns against violence to women. But these have generally been isolated outcrops in a sea of conventional and heavily stereotyped assumptions. All the recent findings on women's prisons suggest that they are still run on the assumption that women are housewives and mothers, to whom real, non-domestic work, education and training are unimportant (Dobash, Dobash and Gutteridge 1986). Discipline based on a high degree of (much resented) control is still the norm in most women's prisons, and they are *therefore* as Mandaraka-Sheppard (1986) shows, peculiarly hard to run. But so have they been for 150 years, and it seems incredible that insights about women's perceptions and experience of socialisation and control have not been applied. Some of those working with female offenders have become very concerned about possibly sexist practices, notably those engaged in intermediate treatment with young girls (Bottoms 1986; Stone 1985), and there have been serious efforts to reform and evaluate practice. The main problems and questions here seem to lie not so much in the willingness to change as in the real confusion as to what good, gender-conscious policies are and how to achieve them. This again is an area in which criminology ought to have much to offer, both in exploring the meanings of 'gender justice' for girls and boys and women and men, and in examining the alternative treatment strategies which might be achieved. Should women and men be treated exactly equally in the criminal justice system, for example? What would a woman-centred justice system be like? (See Heidensohn 1986 for some ideas on this.)

The role of the mass media in influencing public perceptions of crime is critical. 'Moral panics' about teddy boys, seaside gang fights and drug abuse have all been largely created and fed by the media. As far as women and issues of gender are concerned there are several points to note. Clearly, the media play a very important part in helping to form people's fears about crime, and it is notable that the media still help to perpetuate the 'evil stranger' on the street myth rather than recognising the threat within the home. The media have recognised the seriousness of rape and of child abuse, although perhaps not surprisingly various manifestations of patriarchal power are not linked in any extensive analysis. Instead, they are separated and individualised.

Media stereotypes have been far less flexible when female criminals are concerned. The narrow range of witch, whore or bewildered mother are still paraded. In a remarkable case in 1985, a dead woman was initially presented as an evil and depraved international drugs dealer who had killed her parents and children and then herself in a drug-induced orgy. Only when local community pressure resisted this stereotypical presentation did the media stories change and the police pursue other enquiries. Of course, some academics have fed the media a new modern stereotype, the 'liberated female criminal' who allegedly slays and steals all before her in the name of equal opportunities.

Can any of these institutions be changed? Can their practices be modified? These remain amongst the most crucial questions for all social scientists, not just criminologists today. The answers must surely lie in a range of approaches. There is undoubtedly a different climate for work on women and crime, as this book and others testify, and it is now far more receptive. The 'core' audience of women offenders themselves, the professionals and committed researchers is greater than ever. In some countries, such as Australia and the Netherlands, and perhaps also in the UK, some very interesting advances have been made. With a home 'base' and an overseas 'market' it is possible to air and debate new ideas and for them eventually to gain wider currency.

No crisis in criminology can be solved by using the insights and knowledge gained from the study of women and crime. Nevertheless, criminology is poorer in all its forms because those messages are not yet fully accepted and integrated. There is much to be gained for mainstream criminology, and for more radical kinds, by pursuing the questions I have raised here. For students of female criminality, too, there is the possible benefit of their work contributing to changes in some of the most stubborn paradigms and stereotypes in the whole of the social sciences.

2

Women on Welfare: In Crime or Injustice?

Dee Cook

Fiddling supplementary benefit is a type of lawbreaking open to increasing numbers of women. They see it as a rational response to living in poverty. As economic conditions have steadily worsened in the 1980s, women, more likely than men to be already living on the breadline, have been particularly hard-hit (Townsend 1979; Donnison 1982).

A large proportion of females claiming supplementary benefit are lone mothers. Their activities are likely to be policed both formally by the Department of Health and Social Security (DHSS) staff and informally by neighbours and community. They are thus doubly regulated: by DHSS rules that define their claims to benefit as being either legitimate or fraudulent; and by tacit ideological demands that they fulfil the traditional role of housewife-mother within the framework of the idealised nuclear family (Oakley 1974; Sharpe 1984). The status of female supplementary benefit claimants is thus problematic in both law and ideology. They are mothers but not wives; instead of being dependent upon a traditional breadwinner-husband, they are dependent upon the state.

In terms of current Conservative political-economic philosophy, women on welfare are not heading 'proper' families at all:

> The family is formed by the institution of marriage which is a union for life and is the vital link which binds together the family.
> (Conservative Political Centre, quoted in Loney, Boswell and Clarke 1983: 48)

So, women on welfare are regarded as deviant (if not criminal) by virtue of their lack of economic and emotional dependence upon a male. Furthermore, any formal rule-breaking, by fiddling social security payments for instance, is likely to provoke a negative reaction to their deviant *personal* status as well as to the criminal act they have committed.

This chapter argues that female supplementary benefit claims are regulated in terms of formal DHSS departmental rules and informal social mores; the nature of both sets of constraints are constructed economically and politically. The arguments are based upon current research into the treatment of supplementary benefit fraud cases[1] and past work experience within the DHSS. The chapter is structured so as to locate the problems of female benefit claimants within the wider context of debates concerning the politics of the family and the nature and role of the welfare state in Britain in the 1980s. The analysis focuses upon:

1. The structural position of women within the welfare state as it has been variously constituted from the time of Beveridge to the present.
2. Media representation of female 'scroungers'.
3. The precise conditions under which women commit fraud, the justifications they offer for fiddling, and the techniques they employ.
4. DHSS techniques used to police female claimants. (These will be analysed in order to locate DHSS practices within a framework both of anti-fraud policy and the broader political-economic philosophy that has resulted in the deteriorating position of poorer women in Britain in the 1980s).

Women, Poverty and the Welfare State

The Beveridge Report published in 1942 provided a blueprint for the postwar welfare state. While recognising the importance of women's arduous and unpaid labour in the home, it none the less rested upon prewar assumptions concerning the family (Wilson 1980). Distinctions were drawn between married and unmarried women:

> The attitude of the housewife to gainful employment outside the home is not and should not be the same as that of the single woman.
>
> (Beveridge 1942: 49)

In putting a 'premium on marriage' Beveridge saw married women's role as 'ensuring the continuance of the British race and of British ideals in the world' (Beveridge 1942: 52). Insurance classes reflected distinctions between married and single, men and women. In terms of the benefits paid out, single men and women were treated equally, but benefits for married persons were gender-specific (Allatt 1981). The postwar welfare consensus based upon Beveridge therefore rested upon belief in the contribution principle. This, in turn, assumed not only female dependency but male life-long employment. Sickness and unemployment were assumed to be transient, merely short breaks in the breadwinner's insurance contributions. By the late 1970s, economic stagnation and mass unemployment had seriously weakened such principles (Mishra 1984; Esam, Good and Middleton 1985).

Demographic changes and alternative family structures nowadays provide a challenge to the original Beveridge conception. With an ageing population, lifetime breadwinner contributions do not prove sufficient to finance retirement pensions for an increasing number of elderly over a longer period of time. Additionally, the dramatic upturn in divorce during the early 1970s created a new phenomenon, the single-parent family, whose numbers doubled between 1961 and 1983.

There are now over one million single-parent families in Britain, the vast majority being headed by females, over half of whom rely on supplementary benefit (Central Statistics Office 1986). As Beveridge assumed the universality of the nuclear family (with wife at home, husband at work), his plans did not include provision for single parents (Esam, Good and Middleton, 1985).

There are two important conclusions to be drawn: first that the welfare state itself and informal social norms support the existence of an ideal-type nuclear family that does not represent the way in which an increasing number of women live; second, that supplementary benefit, widely held to be the 'safety net' within the social security system, is designed to ensure that 'nobody need fall below a minimum level of income which is intended to cover basic needs' (Lynes 1985: 19). Official definitions of poverty frequently use supplementary benefit level as indicating the 'poverty line' (Holman 1978). Increasing numbers of women therefore are living in poverty because of their inability to fulfil their role in the economic marriage of breadwinner–dependant, assumed to be the family norm since Beveridge (Smart and Smart 1978; Wilson 1977).

The breakdown of the welfare state consensus led to a reassertion of individualistic free-market values that have had a profound effect upon women, particularly those in poverty. In what is termed New Right political philosophy,[2] the welfare state is seen as both bureaucratic and interfering. In order to accomplish the political shift from interventionist to minimalist state, the role of the family is reconstructed. In order progressively to withdraw from catering for individual needs, the state sheds its welfare functions in favour of the family (Fitzgerald 1983; Esam, Good and Middleton 1985). New Right ideology centres upon the traditional two-parent family, earning, consuming, prudent and well disciplined. Within this family women are central, and they should be at home! For as Patrick Jenkin told the 1977 Conservative Party Conference,

> If the good Lord had intended us to have equal rights to go out to work, he wouldn't have created men and women. These are biological facts.

Similarly, Ferdinand Mount, an important adviser on family policy to Mrs Thatcher, referred to a 'nesting instinct' or 'biological ethic'; an instinct and ethic, presumably, that render married women suitable candidates to take over the duties of caring for all those sick, disabled, handicapped and mentally ill currently being denied support by the minimalist state.

At the same time, in the eyes of New Right policy-makers, women claiming social security are invariably deviating from the family ideal. They are likely to be single parents, they are not self-supporting through earnings, and they are unable to consume the fruits of capitalism. Additionally, the media presents them as being both imprudent (bad managers) and breeders of undisciplined problem' children.

Yet as former Supplementary Benefits Commission chairman David Donnison argues, 'their problems are unlikely to be solved by lectures on domestic science' (Donnison 1982: 3). None the less, ideologies that stress individualism invariably construe poverty as culpable, the product of failed individuals.

Echoes of the nineteenth-century advocates of the New Poor Law are present in explanations of poverty as the product of idleness, fecklessness and vice (Fraser 1984). Former minister for social security Rhodes Boyson coupled such explanations with an attack upon the cosseting welfare state:

> The moral fibre of our people has been weakened. The state which does for its citizens what they can do for themselves is an evil state.... No one cares, no one bothers – why should they when the state spends all its energies taking money from the energetic, successful and thrifty to give to the idle, the failures and the feckless?
>
> (Boyson 1971: 81)

The sapping of moral strength and hazards of moral turpitude are themes that are never far apart within anti-working-class rhetoric. Where working-class young *women* are concerned, Sir Keith Joseph, speaking over a decade ago, has no doubts as to the threat they pose to our 'human stock':

> They are producing problem children, the future unmarried mothers, delinquents, denizens of our borstals, sub-normal educational establishments, prisons, hostels for drifters.
>
> (Joseph 1974 [but see Ch. 9 below for an alternative explanation])

A familiar tautological argument is in use here: problem families produce problem behaviour that is attributed to the problematic nature of the family (Eaton 1985). And despite their dubious logic, individual pathological explanations for poverty and deviance remain powerful at an ideological level. They link poverty, criminality and non-nuclear family forms with a belief in individual culpability. In blaming the family (most often, the mother) the responsibility of the state for social problems and social inequality itself is absolved. At the same time the reactionary familism of the New Right justifies doubly harsh regulation of women who are poor.

Women with children claiming supplementary benefits suffer a series of double-binds within a social security system based on the nuclear family as the key 'assessment unit'. Hilary Land (1985) has argued that the conditions under which men receive maintenance from the state reflect the goal of maintaining work incentives, whereas the conditions under which (married) women acquire maintenance from the state are determined by the need to keep them performing unwaged 'caring' work for their families.

There are additional disincentives operating upon lone mothers. These act both as a means of deterring their claim to supplementary benefit and also as an encouragement to work part-time in order to augment inadequate benefit levels. For example, the 'obstacle course' presented to lone mothers claiming for the first time is daunting, stigmatising and degrading (see pp. 35–36 below). Also, for the first year of their claim (before the higher long-term rates of benefit become payable), single mothers are as effectively subject to the same incentive to work, through low levels of benefit, as are the unemployed. But one advantage that single parents have over the unemployed is a higher level of disregarded earnings. For instance, a single parent may keep up to £12 of net earnings of £20 whereas an unemployed person keeps only £4, the remainder being deducted from his/her benefit. However, this regulation could be seen as merely confirming the inadequacy of benefits paid to single parents and the necessity to supplement them through part-time work. Crucially, for women, inducements to work part-time serve to maintain the inferior and disposable status of females in a dual labour market.

Lone mothers who seek part-time employment to augment supplementary benefit payments can therefore be seen as doubly oppressed – first, in relation to their weak position in the workforce and, second, in relation to their contradictory position as claimants. Their very existence is seen to contradict the norms of family life underpinning the nature and form of the welfare state from Beveridge to New Right. Equally, they contradict public perceptions of the 'good family'. For the 'good family' is not dependent upon the state, is neither poor nor idle and is certainly not female-headed. The financial independence lone mothers gain as claimants in their own right is contradicted by ideologies concerning a 'natural' order in which women should be forever emotionally and financially dependent upon men (Allatt 1981, Wilson 1980). It is therefore hardly surprising that single-parent status is socially regarded as a transient phase for women because 'sooner or later it is likely, and even hoped, that a mother will solve her problems by marrying again' (Atkins and Hoggett 1984: 98). This assumption clearly underlies the policing of women on welfare. The unequal or harsh treatment of lone mothers is justified as an indirect spur to them to 'solve their problems' by marrying. Women who do not choose to escape poverty through either marriage or economic dependency on a man have few alternatives open to them. Social security fraud may present itself to some as being the *only* route to financial security. [But see Ch. 3 for another route.]

The Media Tale

Media coverage of supplementary benefit fraud bears all the hallmarks of a classic amplification spiral (Cohen 1972). Mass media, government departments and judiciary reinforce and amplify stereotypes adopted from each other. The sum total of their reaction far outstrips the reality of the social threat that 'scroungers' pose.

In recent years academic attention has been focused upon 'scrounger-mania' (Golding and Middleton 1982; Deacon 1980). The emphasis has been on the role of the national daily press in creating negative attitudes towards the unemployed. Scroungers are seen as the 'whipping boys of the recession' by providing ready stereotypes for idleness, shamelessness, lack of motivation and the undeserving poor (Golding and Middleton 1982). Those on the edge of the welfare state are most susceptible to stereotyping as scroungers. Their susceptibility is increased during economic recession (Furnham 1985; Golding and Middleton 1982).

What remains invisible in such critiques is an analysis of the specific imagery concerning female scroungers. Agreed, it is essential to look at the *modus operandi* of both the journalists creating such stories and the politicians feeding them, but societal reaction is not just directed against the unemployed. Media images of female scroungers are sexualised. They involve a distinct type of stereotyping in addition to those so well described by Golding and Middleton.

Deviant women are represented by the media within a fairly limited range of characterisations. For instance, portrayal of the Greenham Common women frequently stresses their lack of orthodox femininity. Under a headline 'The ugly face of the sisters of peace', *The Sun* (14 December 1982) referred to 'militant feminists and burly lesbians ... the storm troops in the front line'. Their activities are linked with those of 'punks', 'skinheads', ' IRA sympathisers' and 'weirdos'. The juxtaposition of these images with those of (respectable) 'police girls', 'shocked middle-aged women' and 'sincere housewives' serves to reinforce the essential deviance of the ugly, political non-housewives. The threat such non-women pose for traditional gender roles is translated into ideological form under the guise of maintaining political and social order. Prime examples are also frequently found in the local press, a much neglected source of public imagery.[3] One typical letter to the editor headed 'THEIR PLACE' reads as follows:

> Allow me to put forward my cure for unemployment. Replace all the working married women with ... males. This will return the woman to her rightful place in the home as housewife to look after her (probably adolescent children) and will help to reduce the crime figures. It will also establish the man as being the breadwinner – as he should be. As women usually only work to earn 'extra money' on top of their husband's, no unemployment benefit should be paid.
>
> (Ex-soldier, Royal Engineers, *Shropshire Star*, 4 December 1985)

Deconstruction of this one letter reveals a cluster of assumptions concerning breadwinner-dependent, the housewife/mother role, and maternal deprivation as a prime cause of delinquency. When *any* women deviate from their proper place media reaction can be venomous. It can be especially so in the case of female benefit fraudsters.

In February 1985 a Wolverhampton couple and two accomplices were jailed for a £50,000 supplementary benefit fraud involving the setting up of a series of claims using false names and addresses in the West Midlands. Coverage in the local press was headed 'Life on the Scrounge'. Significantly, the report relied more upon neighbours' comments than the actual court proceedings:

> Neighbours spoke today of the spend, spend, spend life-style of a Wolverhampton couple who fiddled £50,000 in social security handouts. Kathleen Smyth and her husband Tom were always rolling in money.
> Kathleen Smyth known as the 'tattooed lady' admitted 12 charges. ... While they were enjoying the good life Smyth, a 19 stone mother of six, drank much of the cash away in pubs and her husband bet heavily on horses.
>
> (*Express and Star*, 15 February 1985)

In this case a woman's official deviance (benefit fraud) merges with unofficial deviance such as heavy build, tattoos and drinking – '15 pints a night'. The result is a grossly exaggerated stereotype demonstrating not only all the necessary ingredients of a scrounger story – massive amounts of cash, 'sponging' life-style, heavy drinking, gambling – but also a dash of circus-like titillation in the portrayal of the woman involved. Her crime was not only in defrauding the DHSS, she also failed to conform to gender expectations concerning self-presentation, family propriety and, above all, femininity. Nowhere in the story is her love for her six children doubted, yet the hidden agenda behind the story implies that 'good mothers' neither get drunk, nor engage in economic crime. The moralising is insidious; the woman is judged both as an offender and as a woman.

Women are an important part of scrounger mythology, and in many instances they are represented as being anathema to the 'madonna' version of femininity. This is evident in Ros Franey's analysis of the criminal claimant as portrayed in the media immediately following Operation Major in Oxford on 2 September 1982. (This involved the mass arrest of 283 'homeless' claimants at a bogus benefit office in Oxford.) Follow-up stories were rife following an anti-fraud swoop which was alternatively dubbed 'The Oxfraud Incident' (BBC *Grapevine*) or 'The Sting' (*Daily Star*, *The Sun*). Racism underpinned a good deal of the scapegoating. For instance, a *Sun* cartoon following Operation Major depicted a courtroom conveyor belt holding twelve 'scroungers', four of whom were black (*The Sun*, 4 September 1982). On the same day the *Daily Mail* told of seven itinerant 'Irish' scroungers. And another less familiar scapegoat emerged in the form of the

> trickster from Nottingham who 'swindled £13,000 by claiming she was an unmarried mum' when all the time she was driving an £8,000 sports car'.
>
> (*The Standard*, quoted in Franey 1983: 49)

The Sun, meanwhile had already introduced the sex angle in the story about the Leeds man who drew £3,000 in benefit 'while his wife, a top class stripper, earned over £14,000' (Franey 1983: 49), while in the *Daily Mail's* catalogue of fiddles women featured prominently – husbands hiding in wardrobes while their wives claimed alone (fictitious desertion): single mothers claiming while being 'kept' by boyfriends (cohabitation); married women claiming under their former names (known as 'Maidens' money'); and, of course, women working while drawing benefit (*Daily Mail*, 4 September 1982).

Female scroungers are depicted towards the less favourable end of the madonna–whore continuum. The 'unmarried mum' media-stories usually suggest, too, that 'the temptress' imagery is at work. Single mothers who do not adhere to society's norms concerning marriage and dependence are perceived as threatening when they strive for economic independence by either working or claiming welfare benefits in their own right. The general moral panic concerning female criminality and the assertive, aggressive nature of so-called 'liberated women' is reinforced by the panic concern about female scroungers. Women on welfare are therefore as much prone to deviant labelling by virtue of their life-style and sexual relationships as they are by their official 'crimes'.

So far this discussion has centred upon women who have been found guilty of falsely claiming supplementary benefit. Because such offences are repeatedly made much of by the media, many legitimate claimants fear that they will be scapegoated and stereotyped. In 1982, for instance, a single mother of a handicapped child wrote, 'I am now more worried than ever, as I will probably be considered as one of the scroungers by investigators employed by Social Security' (Child Poverty Action Group 1982). These fears are unlikely to be allayed. In a confidential document the DHSS admitted that the impact of their specialist investigation squads was 'greater on women than on men' and that 'impact was less on registered unemployed claimants than on single parent families'.

The reality of investigation policy rests upon two assumptions: that lone women are easily intimated; that lone women are highly likely to be fiddling. In the course of translating the results of anti-fraud efforts into the public idiom the distinction between the vulnerable, poor woman and the deceitful temptress is lost. If reference *is* made to the difficulty of eking out a living and raising children on supplementary benefit alone, media coverage treats such information as spurious excuse rather than genuine cause for mitigation.

The sexualisation of both the crimes and personal conduct of female 'scroungers' obscures the political questions that should be raised in relation to women's position within the welfare state. Despite legislation promoting sexual equality in many other spheres of British social life, the welfare state stubbornly lags behind, clinging to sexist principles for the unprincipled reason that they are too costly to abandon. These discriminatory 'principles' are informally bolstered through the ideological representations of the mass media.

The Woman's Position

During the 1970s, legislation on equal pay, sex discrimination and domestic violence seemed to signal great advances against women's oppression (Smart 1984; Ungerson 1985). At the same time, rising divorce rates coupled with the beginnings of economic recession fuelled debates in which woman's proper place was once more said to be in the home.

In relation to divorce, it was held that 'economic equality for women and the high divorce rate are not independent events' (Allen 1982: 16, quoted in Smart 1984: 134). Fears for the very survival of the institution of marriage were expressed. Fears for the well-being of children were articulated. In the late 1970s both the Home Office's consultative document 'Marriage Matters' (1979) and the Church of England's expressed concern were symptomatic of a growing fear of family instability caused implicitly by the changing demands and experiences of women (Smart 1985). Additionally, economic recession and growing unemployment provided the conditions under which it would be functional for the minimalist state to reassert woman's place in the home, leaving space (ideologically as well as practically), for male breadwinners in a contracting employment market. As Carol Smart (1985) has argued, Thatcherism not only embodied the familiar ideology which valorised the role of 'mother' within the family, but it created the material conditions under which increasingly large numbers of women had no option but to conform to this ideal. Cuts in educational, health and social services, coupled with the vulnerability of women within a dual labour market, meant that many women were forced out of jobs. Simultaneously, the rhetoric and reality of 'community care' proved regressive for women; effectively, 'community care' means family care, 'family care equals care by women' (Finch and Groves 1985: 230). It is within this material context that the position of women living on supplementary benefit must be understood.

The progress and regress of the 1970s and 1980s has had a profound impact upon the lives of women who are poor. Not only are there far more of them but also they are more likely to be experiencing gross contradictions in their lives. For instance, women's awareness and aspirations, much heightened during the 1970s by progressive legislation and the mythology of the 'liberated women', are confounded by their conditions of existence under which their economic dependence (upon men or the welfare state) remains little changed (Smart 1985; Ungerson 1985). Such contradictions are rendered apparent when women claim supplementary benefit.

The process of claiming supplementary benefit and the attitudes of non-claimants almost invariably lead to loss of self-esteem and stigma in the individual who is 'asking for help'. The most common epithet used to describe the claiming process is 'degrading' (Foster 1983). Because of the nature of the questions asked by DHSS officials, lone mothers suffer acutely. One woman (Carol) vividly recalled the official response to her initial claim to benefit in 1975 when she said, 'They wanted all the mucky details, not to help me. They asked who I'd had sex with, where, when and how many times. It was disgusting.' Follow-up visits centred on boyfriends:

> They wanted to know who he was, did he visit often, did he live with his parents? But when I asked about the cohabitation rule much later they wouldn't tell me, just said that if I was thinking about it to send my book in.
>
> (Carol)

It can be argued that many aspects of the claiming process – delay, lengthy questioning, feelings of humiliation, loss of personal worth – apply to *all* supplementary benefit claimants male and female, young and old. However, the extent to which Carol's treatment was gender-specific is revealed in an example quoted by David Donnison (last chairman of the Supplementary Benefits Commission, abolished in 1980).

A postgraduate student at Oxford was visited by a DHSS official who found the claimant's room scattered with cosmetics belonging to the girl (working as a secretary) who was sharing it 'for this term':

> The DHSS did not cut off his benefit, deciding that this was not what most people meant by a husband and wife relationship. Not in Oxford, anyway. 'And besides',

said the visiting officer, 'how do you argue with a man who's studying to be a Doctor of Philosophy?'

(Donnison 1982: 108)

Not only was the claimant male, he was also confident, articulate and middle class.

It may well be the case that women on welfare suffer doubly as a result of their gender and their working–class situation. Paradoxically, it is often argued that some lone mothers are 'better off' when leaving male partners who are either low paid or fail to hand over sufficient of their wage to their wives for 'housekeeping' (Beltram 1984; Harrison 1983). Yet rather than providing evidence of the adequacy of benefit levels, this argument in fact provides evidence that 'For some families sickness, unemployment or marital break-up means, in material terms, a tightening of the screw of chronic shortage of money' (Beltram 1984: 89). In this respect some women suffer doubly from the problem of dependency; initially upon poorer men, thereafter upon the state. Also, the operation of 'liable relative' cases in practice forces separated women to claim maintenance from the fathers of their children to save the DHSS money. Mothers are thus pushed back into financial dependence upon men from whom they are separated.

The position of women on supplementary benefits has been well summarised by Esam, Good and Middleton:

> The harsh earnings rule, low pay and 'liable relative' and cohabitation tests place obstructions in the way of women single parents who wish to work or enter into any kind of friendship. They must either make a dramatic change – go to work full-time or set up joint home with a man – or stay as they are. Most women single parents and their children face the choice between poverty and dependence.
>
> (Esam, Good and Middleton 1985: 65–6)

There is a third option: to engage in crime. [See Ch. 3 below for a discussion of the relationship between poverty and prostitution.] As one lone mother of three, Susan, told me, 'It's simply lack of money. You don't have enough to live on so you fiddle for the necessities'. Hardship, not greed, is the major cause of benefit fraud, and in addition the vagaries of the benefit system itself are often cited. For instance, official income from earnings (or from spouse or relatives) is sometimes not declared by claimants who fear that already erratic benefit payments may become even more irregular. They do not perceive such behaviour as being fraudulent but instead, as part of the 'swings and roundabouts' of the benefits system. To some extent fiddling is seen as compensation for both low levels of benefit and the delay and complexity in the administration of benefit payments.

'Fiddling' may take a variety of forms. They range from failure to declare earnings, altering girocheques, falsely claiming to have 'lost' a purse on benefit payday, and so on, to fraud connected with what was termed 'the cohabitation rule'. According to the DHSS, of all cases considered for prosecution in 1984/5, 49 per cent involved the claimant failing to declare earnings, 12 per cent involved failure to declare the earnings of a dependent (usually a wife) and 7.4 per cent were connected with cohabitation and fictitious desertion (DHSS, in personal communication, 1986). In a league table of offences considered for prosecution

these were ranked first, second and third, respectively, and although no
breakdown along gender lines is available, the third category would be almost
exclusively female. Undoubtedly women also engage in the most prevalent form
of supplementary benefit fraud (working and claiming), but of the 25,513
claimants considered for prosecution for this offence in 1984/5 it is impossible to
guess how many were female. In addition, it is impossible to assess the extent of
undetected fraud despite wild guesstimates (DHSS 1986). None the less the 3,680
claimants considered for prosecution for cohabiting or fictitious desertion are by
definition almost always female, although this 'official statistic' may bear no
relation to the true extent of this form of fraud.

Working and claiming, fiddling giros and concealing income are all crimes of
omission, the motivation clearly an economic one. Yet although a couple's motives
for *cohabiting* are *not* necessarily economic, the DHSS presumes an economic
relationship between couples whom they adjudge to be 'living together as
husband and wife'. Within the welfare state, as elsewhere, the relationship is still
assumed to be that of breadwinner–dependant (Smart and Smart 1978; Wilson
1977). The error of such assumptions is evidenced by one lone mother who lived
(undetected by the DHSS) with her (divorced and working) boyfriend: 'It wasn't
wrong. He didn't give me any money so my commitments still stood and I needed
my benefit. It was really me keeping him!' Nevertheless, had the DHSS been
aware of her situation, a husband and wife relationship (based upon subjective
assessments of shared expenses, stability of relationship, 'public appearance' and
sexual relations) would have been assumed and her order book, together with her
financial independence, confiscated.

In the eyes of many feminists, the living together rule is tantamount to assuming
payment for sexual and domestic services, a form of prostitution (Wilson 1983;
Fairbairns 1985). Official sanctions serve to reinforce women's position in terms of
their emotional and economic dependence on men. At the same time, the state
enters and polices the private arena of personal relationships where female
claimants are concerned, and one may indeed well ask, 'How on earth did the state
get into all this?' (Donnison 1982: 109). The answer lies in the household means-
test for the poor in which the traditional nuclear family pattern is first assumed and
then, if not in evidence, actively promoted (through stigma, deterrence and
investigation methods) in the policing of female claimants.

DHSS Practice

> Supplementary benefit staff, although better informed than most of their fellow
> citizens, are exposed to the same ideological climate and do not not, on the whole,
> seem inclined to take an excessively liberal view of claimants' needs.
>
> (Beltram 1984: 115)

Although at first sight this might appear to be an understatement on the part of
Beltram (a former high-ranking civil servant), it does indicate the need to locate
DHSS practice, and the behaviour and attitudes of its officers, within a broader

ideological framework. Social policy in general, and departmental anti-fraud policies in particular, are implemented by individual officers and determined by political objectives. Recent policy shifts affecting the lives of women on welfare are broadly twofold. First, changes have taken place in response to EEC directives addressing the need for equal treatment for women within the social security system (Ungerson 1985). Second, changes in the priority given to, and means of investigating, fraud and other abuse have resulted in a more proactive role being adopted in the policing of supplementary benefits. Paradoxically, formal moves towards equality in the operation of the welfare state have resulted in discriminatory treatment of many women on social security who are now informally regarded as potential fraudsters by virtue of their (lack of) marital status.

In relation to the first set of changes it can be argued that moves towards formal equality between men and women in matters of social security have been very limited. For example, recent changes enabling women (in theory) to become the claiming partner for supplementary benefit purposes have had negligible effects in practice:

> The rules for selecting who should be the claimant favour the partner who has recently been in work or signing on as available for work – and men are more likely to meet these conditions.

> (Esam, Good and Middleton 1985: 60)

Inequalities in the labour market thus render formal rules impotent, and unequal treatment persists.

Another instance of the limitation of recent formal changes is evident in the renaming of the infamous 'cohabitation rule' – now known by the more vernacular phrase 'living-together cases' – though little else appears to have changed! Admittedly couples are now assessed by more senior officers on criteria involving the stability of the relationship, its public appearance, degree of sharing of household expenses and duties, and the existence of a sexual relationship. But, although more refined, these rules echo the shorthand assumptions underlying the old cohabitation rule – common purse, common bed and common table.

In theory the intrusion into the private lives of female claimants and the humiliation they suffer should be lessened, but it is difficult to see qualitative differences in the treatment of lone mothers. Lip-service may well be paid to EEC directives and the consequent demands for equal treatment for women within the welfare state, but as Esam, Good and Middleton argue, 'Despite moves towards formal equality, little seems to change in practice; women still get a significantly worse deal from social security.' (1985: 59).

A second set of changes in the area of anti-fraud policy negated many of the official efforts to counter sex discrimination in the social security system. In 1980 the then minister for social security, Reg Prentice, set up Special Claims Control Units (SCCUs) to spearhead his new anti-fraud drive (Hansard, 1980, Vol. 978: 118). These new 'swoop' squads marked a radical departure from earlier anti-fraud policy in three respects. First, their *proactive* nature contrasted with the previous investigative work, which had been *reactive*, often anonymous letters and tip-offs. 'S.C.C. is a means of taking the initiative against fraud and abuse' (DHSS circular FIG 1983). Second, they targeted the groups of claimants who were assumed to be the most likely fraudsters. They did so

> by selecting for investigation cases whose characteristics correspond to those where experience has shown that there is a high incidence of fraud. Such cases are commonly to be found within the E (registered unemployed) and MC (lone mother with dependent children) load.
>
> (DHSS circular Fraud Investigators' Guide (FIG) 1983)

Random selection of such cases for further investigation clearly involved an anti-fraud blitz on the most vulnerable of supplementary benefit claimants. But equally important was the *aim* of such investigations – to avoid prosecution where appropriate. So, third, the emphasis on 'non-prosecution interviews' marked an important shift because it signalled cost-effectiveness as being investigations' primary goal. Guidelines issued to fraud officers reminded them that there was 'no additional direct cash return for a prosecution' and that, therefore, the cessation of a claim in appropriate cases was the most 'cost-effective way of dealing with the matter' (Moore 1981: 375).

The watchwords 'financial return' and 'cost-effective' are in keeping with a political philosophy concerned with results in cash terms. But, according to worried DHSS trades unions, this could lead to an emphasis on benefit savings at the expense of claimants' rights (Civil and Public Services Association (CPSA) 1984; Society of Civil and Public Servants (SCPS) 1984). Descriptions of the treatment of women by SCC investigators suggest that there *is* cause for concern.

> Women [are] interviewed in locked rooms by – sometimes – two SCC team members. Late in the afternoon is a favourite time with mothers pre-occupied about their children at school, home or SCC waiting rooms. Evening home visits by two SCC team members. . . . Threats to women that their children will be taken into care by Social Services because they are unfit mothers. False stories of having watched and followed claimants for days and having obtained evidence of working or cohabitation. . . . .Threats to prosecute if order books are not handed over.
>
> (DHSS official 1981)

This official argued that in the first year of SCC operation over half their time was devoted to accepting order books from women who were persuaded they were living with men as members of a single household. Another officer confirmed,

> It seems that single women are particularly vulnerable. . . . This situation is compounded by the predominance of male SCC investigators . . . this also applies to general Special Investigation work.
>
> (DHSS office 1982)

A special conference organised by DHSS staffs' trades unions in October 1983 maintained that SCC was 'part of a rigid authoritarian, anti-woman, anti-minority elite within the welfare system' (CPSA 1984).

In recent years increased pressure has been put upon the DHSS by a variety of interest groups seeking the abolition of SCCUs (NCCL 1983). Tighter guidelines were issued to investigators and, according to a DHSS official, the department was forced to reduce grossly exaggerated statistics for 'benefit savings' which stood at £103 million for 1984, although operational costs were still estimated at £38.9 million. (It can only be assumed that cost-effectiveness does not necessarily apply to the expenses incurred by SCC investigators.) Nevertheless, SCCUs were no longer 'sex snoopers' of the old school. Welfare workers believed that 'they don't care if you are sleeping together. They're pursuing a different tack – they are less concerned with what *is* the economic connection than what *ought* to be' (quoted in B. Campbell 1984: 30).

In line with current pragmatic, neo-liberal political thought, the DHSS now asks fewer questions regarding sex and more concerning household duties. Higher-grade officers conduct interviews for cases that are no longer labelled 'cohabitation' but 'living together'. Whether this marks a genuine improvement for women on welfare who are attempting to be economically independent is debatable.

In May 1986 it was announced that the seven regional SCCUs were to be abolished, and that they were to be replaced by thirty-one national fraud squads focusing upon providing extra help for local benefit fraud staff in chasing individuals rather than looking for whole categories of suspected claimants' (*Guardian* 16 May 1986). Whether this will have any positive impact on the treatment of lone mothers on supplementary benefit remains to be seen. It seems likely that old prejudices and assumptions concerning likely cases for investigation will die hard. In an ideological climate within which the poor and the problem family (centred upon an inadequate mother) are perceived as both deviant and culpable, any positive shift in DHSS practice appears unlikely. Furthermore, the abolition of SCC may yet prove to be not a victory for feminists and interest groups advocating social equality, but rather a pragmatic victory for cost-effectiveness. It was in this latter respect that SCC conspicuously failed.

It could be argued that the *worst* of the discriminatory practices in the treatment of women by DHSS investigators have been eliminated. Certainly lip-service has been paid to legal directives prohibiting the grosser investigative methods (Atkins and Hoggett 1984). But the basic principles underlying the policing of female claimants remain the same. They embody the deeply held assumptions concerning the desirability of women's economic dependency that have been rooted in the welfare state since its inception. Thus, while the struggle for change in the treatment of female claimants (whether defrauding or not) goes on, social policy trails behind. As Campbell writes, the state 'fails to provide the infrastructure for mothers' independence – shelter, child care and jobs. And what affronts the system most of all is the idea that the state could help to *support* women's independence' (1984: 30).

Until it is acknowledged that women who are forced to rely upon the welfare state should be truly independent of men and not merely 'in-between' men, it seems probable that the dual regulation of women on welfare will continue, first in the administration of DHSS rules and second in familial ideology. This ideology is enforced by neighbours as well as by politicians. According to a report in *The Times* in 1985, the most profitable referrals for SCCUs emanated from disgruntled neighbours. As David Donnison noted, most letters complaining about too many handouts, layabouts and scroungers 'rarely came on headed notepaper from leafy suburbs. Most of them are written by ordinary voters and taxpayers' (Donnison 1982: 48). Yet the clusters of beliefs that constitute reactionary ideologies are forged within a political context. Undoubtedly the politics of the New Right have led to a worsening in the condition of women on welfare and to their closer surveillance by the regulatory agencies.

I have argued that the position of women living on supplementary benefit is one of privation, degradation and imparity. Those who refuse to remain in poverty have only two legitimate courses open to them: they can either work (an option not open to many in times of recession) or they can be pushed back into a relationship where they are once more financially dependent upon a male. A third option is social security fraud or other crime. Despite what the media would have us believe, the women's motivation is not greed nor are their characteristics mendacity and immorality. Rather, they engage in economic crime primarily because levels of supplementary benefit are simply too low to allow them a decent standard of living. Formally, of course, they *are* engaged in crime; arguably, also, they are resisting class and gender injustices.

Notes

1. The research upon which this article is based forms part of an ongoing PhD study entitled 'Rich Law, Poor Law: The Differential Treatment of Tax and Supplementary Benefit Fraud' (Keele University Centre for Criminology). To date, informal interviews have been conducted with claimants, DHSS officials, magistrates and welfare rights officers. The first year of the research was funded by an ESRC studentship.

2. The term 'New Right' describes a 'neo-conservative counter-revolution in social thought', principally in the United States and Great Britain, in the late 1970s. Implicit in the ideology of the New Right are criticisms of both government bureaucracy and 'overload', and of government (particularly welfare state) policy failures (Mishra 1984: 27–32).

3. The combined national evening newspaper sales of over five million comprise but half of the combined national daily circulation. However, the local press achieves a far higher penetration in many areas coupled with more readers per copy than do the national dailies (British Rate and Data, Marketing Research, 1986).

3

Prostitutes: Victims of Law, Social Policy and Organised Crime

Susan S.M. Edwards

Since the coming to power of the Thatcher Government in 1979 there has been a dramatic increase in the number of prosecutions for offences relating to prostitution. In 1979 prosecutions totalled 3,167. In 1980 they rose to 3,482, in 1981 to 4,324, in 1982 to 6,062 and in 1983 they reached a peak of 10,674. They levelled off at 8,836 in 1984 (Fig.3 1). These increases have been due, in part, to changes in legislation and policing. The figures for 1983, in particular, reflect the adoption by the Metropolitan Police of a 'get tough' policy towards the increasing numbers of prostitutes on the streets following the abolition of imprisonment for soliciting offences by the Criminal Justice Act 1982. Yet, even without these peripheral factors, the official figures for soliciting had been rising; they reflected a 'real' increase in the numbers of prostitutes working the streets. The increase in the number of women engaging in prostitution has been a response to the deterioration of women's economic position (see Chapter 2). The erosion of women's employment opportunities and the gradual demise of state welfare have placed increasing numbers of women within the poverty trap. Any analysis of present trends in prostitution, therefore, must look beyond the operational response of the police and courts. It must examine the factors contributing to women's poverty as being the primary preconditions for prostitution.

This chapter develops earlier analyses of prostitutes as victims of sexually repressive legislation and male exploitation and control, (see James 1978a, 1978b; Barry 1979; Mukherjee and Scutt 1981; Russell Frey and Reichert 1981; McLeod 1982; Bracey 1983; Barry, Bunch and Castley 1984; Edwards 1984; Ohse 1984; Russell and Owen 1984; Edwards 1986a, 1986b). It also extends this contextual analysis to examine three interrelated factors: (1) the rise in prosecutions for

43

Table 3.1 Prosecutions for loitering for the purpose of prostitution 1979–84

Year	1979	1980			1981			1982			1983			1984		
		Tot.	17–21	21+	Tot.	17–21	21+	Tot.	17–21	21+	Tot.	17–21	21+	Tot.	17–21	21+
Total prosecutions	3167	3482	1324	2125	4324	1582	2706	6062	2151	3886	10674	3450	7210	8836	2379	6425
Withdrawn/Dismissed	142	140	44	93	182	55	124	247	54	192	215	53	161	211	61	149
Otherwise dealt with	14	8	2	6	7	1	5	11	6	5	5	1	4	–	1	5
Total found guilty	3014	3336	1278	2030	4127	1523	2571	5804	1192	3688	10442	3390	7059	8605	2312	6263
Absolute discharge	14	25	9	15	39	17	22	30	9	21	62	13	48	114	26	88
Conditional discharge	578	513	185	320	686	267	409	746	257	480	800	270	528	706	97	501
Probation	279	324	144	180	379	155	224	448	176	272	251	109	142	184	74	110
Fine	1609	1880	758	1108	2389	889	1490	3983	1488	2482	9294	2989	6298	7588	2014	5558
Community Service Order	42	116	39	77	115	32	83	96	19	77	5	–	5	–	–	1
Suspended Sentence	245	254	75	179	288	90	198	298	87	211	13	4	9	–	–	–
Up to 1 month	78	108	{205}		144	{204}		131	{187}		4	1		1	1	
1 mth up to 2 mths	19	32			26			12			1	1		–		
2 mths up to 3 mths	85	64			31			43			1			–		
Over 3 mths	2	1			3			1			–			–		
Other disposals	38	19			7			11			5					

{ } = Imprisonment (combined)

Criminal Justice Act 1982 abolished imprisonment for prostitution.
Source: Home Office, Criminal Statistics England and Wales, 1979–84; Supplementary tables from 1980, Vol. 1, s.1 1(a).

soliciting; (2) women's poverty and (3) the increase in state repression and control of female prostitutes.

First, I shall argue that while legislation and its enforcement unfairly penalise the streetwalker, the behaviour of the client is exonerated. Second, I shall argue that official figures reflect the fact that more women are taking to prostitution as a direct consequence of their worsening economic position. Third, I shall discuss the insidious and unchallenged growth in the organisation and control of prostitutes by male ponces and managers. I shall argue that inadequate legislation, under–enforcement and difficulties in obtaining evidence have resulted in a situation where prosecutions are few and women are left vulnerable and unprotected.

Law and Policing

Women Prosecuted

In law, only women are defined as prostitutes and prosecuted for the offences of loitering and soliciting in pursuance of that activity. No male or trans–sexual male is liable to prosecution for loitering or soliciting, though those who offer a sexual service to other males are liable to arrest for 'importuning' in the pursuit of an 'immoral' activity. Despite the many forms that prostitution can take, legislation has been primarily concerned with the tightening-up of controls as they affect the street prostitute. Nowhere is this more evident than in the Street Offences Act 1959, where section 1(1), makes it an offence for a woman to loiter or solicit for the purpose of prostitution. The aftermath of this Act was characterised by the almost triumphant proclamation that the diminished visibility of street activity and the decline in prosecutions for soliciting were evidence of its overnight success. As Edwards writes,

> 'whilst the numbers of prosecutions and convictions for offences relating to prostitu-
> tion declined drastically from 19,663 before the introduction of the Act, to 2,726 in
> 1960, this by no means reflected a real diminution in police activity or in prostitution'.
>
> (Edwards 1984: 30)

What was reflected was simply a change in police *prosecution* procedures, brought about by the introduction of a system that provided for the cautioning of women on two occasions prior to arrest and charge.

The apparently more lenient approach after 1959 was countervailed by the restoration of other police powers to their former nineteenth–century glory. These permitted a constable to 'arrest without warrant anyone he finds in a street or public place and suspects, with reasonable cause, to be committing an offence under this section' (section 1 (3)). If some women were deterred from using the streets, they merely used other means of contacting clients, thereby avoiding police detection and ultimate imprisonment.

Ironically, it was in the *other* arenas of prostitution that women were to experience the grossest victimisation, control and male violence. Increasing numbers of women prostituted themselves in clubs, saunas and massage parlours. They lost their autonomy and were rapidly subjugated under the control of male manages, ponces and pimps. Police claims that evidence of lawbreaking was difficult to establish means that these enterprises were outside police control. Women's vulnerability to male violence had thus been increased.

By December 1982 the Criminal Law Revision Committee, assisted by the Policy Advisory Committee, published the working paper on 'Offences Relating to Prostitution and Allied Offences'. It was the fourth such review in the last fifty years, its predecessors being the Street Offences Report of 1928, the Wolfenden Report of 1957, and the working papers on 'Vagrancy and Street Offences' of 1974 and 1976. From 31 January 1983 and in accordance with Home Office Circular 2/1983, following section 71 of the Criminal Justice Act 1982, imprisonment for loitering and soliciting was abolished. Though many claimed that this was a humanitarian move, it was more likely to have been a politically expedient measure, calculated to deal with the problem of prison overcrowding. With the abolition of imprisonment, magistrates could no longer make the community service orders, or the suspended and partially suspended sentences that had hitherto been alternatives to custody. Legal practice dictated that the probation order and the fine were the only remaining viable options.

The result has been that, while the use of probation orders has declined, the use of fines has increased, as has their amount, representing a 'get tough' policy on prostitution. In Sheffield, for example, in November 1983, a 24–year–old woman was fined £650 after admitting only four offences! Previously, an average fine for four offences would have been about £50. Lord Justice Stephen Brown has backed this policy:

> The magistrates in Sheffield deserve to be congratulated upon a careful and realistic approach to what undoubtedly appears to have been a major problem in their area.
>
> (*Sheffield Star,* 8 March 1985)

Despite the abolition of immediate imprisonment, the use of more and heavier fines has led to a steep rise in the number of women being sent to prison for fine default (Home Office 1982, 1983, 1984a). In 1981 a total of 2,087 women were received into prison; 825 were fine defaulters, of whom forty–four were prostitutes (constituting 2.1 per cent of the total population). In 1982, 2,185 women were imprisoned, with an increase to 1,030 of fine defaulters, fifty–seven of whom were prostitutes (2.6 per cent of the total population). By 1983 receptions of women into prison had fallen to 2,178, partly as a result of the guidelines on police cautioning for certain offences, implemented in 1982. There were 1,041 women imprisoned for fine default, 128 of whom were prostitutes, constituting 5.9 per cent of the total population. By 1984 this figure had risen to 193 – over 8 per cent of the total prison population. A recent report by the Howard League (Seear and Player 1986: 16) proposes that 'no woman should be sent to prison for the non-payment of fines'.

Table 3.2 Prosecutions for prostitution offences since the Street Offences Act 1959, England and Wales 1959–1984

Offences		1959	1960	1961	1962	1963	1964	1965	1966	1967	1968	1969	1970	1971
Procuration	(M)	32	15	13	18	18	5	12	20	11	58	59	38	42
24	(F)	3	11	11	8	7	5	5	7	3	9	5	4	6
Brothel-keeping	(M)	68	42	72	41	41	41	51	35	69	63	62	32	29
107	(F)	130	108	121	122	145	103	126	130	161	152	120	132	120
Male living on prostitutes earnings	(M)	283	235	277	325	275	304	300	321	267	355	358	371	276
187	(F)	8	8	11	18	22	1	22	4	1	0	2	0	0
Female living on prostitutes earnings	(M)	121	29	0	0	0	0	0	1	1	0	0	0	0
187	(F)	578	28	0	0	0	12	14	10	2	4	5	5	6

Offences		1972	1973	1974	1975	1976	1977	1978	1979	1980	1981	1982	1983	1984
Procuration	(M)	39	40	36	45	44	66	70	225	362	322	375	337	360
24	(F)	6	6	10	9	10	4	8	25	17	19	18	23	21
Brothel-keeping	(M)	29	23	16	22	31	25	38	33	30	47	33	50	28
107	(F)	157	116	85	95	141	83	118	115	95	113	67	109	68
Male living on prostitutes earnings	(M)	344	239	226	231	233	202	223	–	–	–	–	–	–
187	(F)	0	1	0	1	0	0	1	–	–	–	–	–	–
Female living on prostitutes earnings	(M)	1	2	0	0	0	0	0	–	–	–	–	–	–
187	(F)	1	6	22	10	9	7	7	–	–	–	–	–	–

*These ambiguous cases are due to the opposite sex aiding and abetting the principal offence, latterly errors in recording or more possibly trans-sexualism.

†After 1978, categories 187 were included in category 24 (Procuration), following Part III of the Criminal Law Act 1977 which redefined mode of trial. 187 became triable-either-way and were reclassified and included with indictable offences.

Source: Home Office Criminal Statistics England and Wales 1959-83; Supplementary tables, from 1980, Vol. I, s.1 1(a).

Male Punters Exonerated

Legislation and policing have reflected a preoccupation with the streetwalker, while the activities of male punters have been outside the law, and pimps and ponces find themselves rarely prosecuted (Fig.3 2). Legislators have been content with the illogicality of penalising women for being prostitutes rather than penalising men for seeking or accepting prostitution. Women, prostitutes and non–prostitutes alike, have remained unprotected from the unwelcome advances of punters, yet they are blamed and prosecuted if they accept such advances. 'Improper' suggestions are only illegal if made to young girls under 16 years and the law has historically required women who find advances from men offensive to protect themselves – by staying at home! Women who choose not to do this have been regarded as being responsible for their own fate, being at the least negligent and at the most downright provocative. While such attitudes persist, women remain vulnerable on the streets to punters who, as McLeod (1982) discovered, are not always 'ordinary' men.

Two stereotypes characterise popular understanding of punters or clients. On the one hand, they are 'ordinary' men, husbands, fathers, brothers and lovers. On the other, they are perverted and dangerous, potential sex offenders, child molesters and rapists.

The Manchester study (Edwards 1984) confirmed McLeod's earlier finding in Birmingham that some punters are indeed 'ordinary' men. 'Most are very nice men...some are well educated...and most are married men who don't want to get seriously involved'. This characterisation persists, too, in the minds of police patrol officers and court personnel. Consider, for example, the following extract from a trial dialogue at City Magistrates' Court, Manchester, 1981, between the defence solicitor and the arresting police officer in a trial for soliciting:

Q. Did you take the number of the Escort?
A. It is not our policy.
Q. Wouldn't it have been at the time – December in Moss Side – because of the Ripper?
A. No, we had stopped doing that a few nights before.
Q. But it was only a few weeks before then that the Ripper was caught in the same kind of situation?
A. I know.
Q. Don't you ever take names and numbers?
A. As far as I'm concerned it was an ordinary punter.
Q. But that was the sort of person that the Ripper turned out to be, the man you were trying to catch.
A. Yes.

(Quoted in Edwards 1984: 73)

On the other hand, many punters are perverted. Prostitutes who spoke to McLeod (1982) and Edwards (1984) had also experienced serious physical violence from their clients. 'One punter cut my face with a razor blade', said one. Another woman remarked, 'I won't do foreigners, they just frighten me. Once I nearly got strangled'. Few cases of this kind ever come to court. As McLeod (1982: 54) indicates, violence is regarded as 'one of the hazards of the job'.

On 11 September 1985 the Sexual Offences Act provided, for the first time, for the prosecution of the kerb–crawler or punter. The introduction of this legislation appears to owe more to the patriarchal campaign of bourgeois lawyers for the protection of wives and daughters and the defence of the respectability of their neighbourhoods than it does to the efforts of legislators, policy–makers or the feminist movement. The Sexual Offences Bill that preceded it offered protection from male harassment to all women, but this clause was later dropped. The final drafting of the Act provided only for the criminalisation of the 'persistent soliciting' of prostitutes by punters.

Not all women's organisations have supported this legislation, some regarding it as a further move in the direction of the criminalisation of prostitution and further repression of the streetwalker. The English Collective of Prostitutes, for example, contend that the prohibition of kerb-crawling will adversely affect their trade and drive potential clients away.

What has happened since the implementation of the 1985 Act parallels the response of streetwalking women to the 1959 Act. Prostitutes are finding other ways of contacting clients through advertising and through working in hotels, clubs and massage parlours – indeed, anywhere that provides an unpoliced venue. Women who continue to work the streets find that, in order to avoid police arrest, a contract must be quickly agreed upon. Certainly, Jackie Murray, who was murdered in November 1985, might not have met with this fate had she had time to check out the man who approached her.

Equal Protection?

Women who prostitute have every justification for feeling themselves the victims of repressive legislation that does nothing at all to protect them. They feel particularly vulnerable to assault. One woman complained: 'If a prostitute gets raped or battered, the police won't do anything about it unless they have got a car number. They just haven't got time to make note of it . . .ridiculous!' (Quoted in Edwards 1984: 132). Prostitutes therefore rarely report violent assault perpetrated against them, not only for fear of further reprisals (Wilson 1983: 80–97) but also because the police are reluctant to do anything about it.

The handling of the Yorkshire Ripper inquiry is a further salutary reminder of the inequality in police protection afforded prostitute women:

> The distinction between prostitutes and 'totally respectable' women victims clearly testified to a value that the lives of prostitutes were worthless and that Sutcliffe's mission in wiping them out was somehow justifiable.
>
> (Hollway 1981: 31)

West Yorkshire's Acting Assistant Chief Constable, Jim Hobson, in a statement, could not make the position clearer. He said of the Ripper:

> He has made it clear that he hates prostitutes. Many people do. We, as a police force, will continue to arrest prostitutes. But the Ripper is now killing innocent girls.

Sir Michael Havers, the Attorney General, reinforced this distinction when he said of Sutcliffe's victims, 'Some were prostitutes, but perhaps the saddest part of this case is that some were not'.

Chambers and Millar (1983) in their study of the police investigation of rape, found that women who had particular backgrounds encountered great difficulty in establishing credibility. Of the complainant sample, 19 per cent were critical of the CID, who they said had attributed blame to them, alleging either that they were drunk or were prostitutes (p. 79).

The application of criminal law further discriminates against and victimises known prostitutes. The author recalls an attempted–rape trial at Manchester Crown Court in 1976, where the woman was asked in cross–examination whether she had a conviction for soliciting some fifteen years previous (Edwards 1981: 185). Since the 1976 Sexual Offences (Amendment) Act, rape trials in particular have been monitored for the degree to which they are conducted in accordance with section 2 (1) of the Act. If at a trial any person is for the time being charged with a rape offence to which he pleads not guilty, then except with the leave of the judge, no cross–examination shall be adduced or asked at the trial, by or on behalf of any defendant at the trial about any sexual experience of the complainant with a person other than the defendant. Yet, if the complainant is a prostitute, past moral character is still admissible, in accordance with this section. Adler's research (1982, 1985) has revealed that the applications by counsel were more readily allowed if the moral character of the complainant was in doubt and particularly if the complainant was a prostitute. The conundrum is that such evidence is admissible and considered relevant to the issue of consent (Adler 1985). The decision to admit such evidence remains capriciously at the judge's discretion (or 'judgment'). The cases of *Lawrence* (1977 Crim. LR at 493) and *Mills* (1978 68 CR. App. R 154) hold that evidence of prostitution would always be relevant.

In the event of injury following criminal assault, claims for compensation made by prostitutes may be considerably reduced or indeed rejected altogether, simply because of their 'life–style'. Consider, for instance, the application made by Marcella Claxton to the Criminal Injuries Compensation Board, following injuries received in May 1976 by Peter Sutcliffe, the Yorkshire Ripper. Her original claim for compensation in 1978 was refused on the grounds of her supposed way of life, and that she had 'clearly misled the police and provoked the attack' (*Yorkshire Post,* 22 December 1982). After five years the Board acknowledged that there was no question of provocation (and remember we are talking about the Ripper!) following evidence from the police officer who had interviewed Sutcliffe when he pleaded guilty and admitted that he had attempted to murder her. Ms Claxton was finally awarded £17,500. The Criminal Injuries Compensation Board considers the moral character of the victim and her way of life (para. 6 (c) new scheme as per 1979) to be relevant to the success of an application.

Social Policy

Women prostitute against a background of (1) low–paid part–time and seasonal work, (2) dependency on state benefit and (3) their own centrality within the family, with its increasing demands of responsibility for the care of children and relatives. Prostitution is thus an institutionalised occupational choice related to the non–viability of other work opportunities (Reiman 1979; Jaget 1980; Bujra 1982).

Women, Wage Labour and Unemployment

Peggy Kahn (1985: 79) has shown that changes in employment law since the return of a Conservative government in 1979, have further weakened already inadequate regulation of women's work. Because of the woman's role within the family, part–time work is especially attractive. But part–time workers receive low pay and they are excluded from statutory rights. Yet, as Kate Marshall (1985) points out, the main change in women's working patterns has been the growth in part–time work. From 1972 to 1984 the number of part–time workers increased by 1. 3 million, most of them being women. However, many if not most prostitutes arrested and prosecuted are unemployed, either without benefit of any kind or else in the process of claiming state benefit. Women's recorded unemployment has risen dramatically in the last ten yers. Department of Employment figures reveal that in 1974, 0.9 per cent of women were registered unemployed, in 1975 the numbers rose to 1.8 per cent, by 1980 to 4.8 per cent, in 1981 to 6.9 per cent, in 1982 to 8.0 per cent, in 1983 to 8.9 per cent and in 1984 to 9.4 per cent. As Kahn (1985: 80) has indicatd, these figures do not fully express the magnitude of women's unemployment for since 1982 figures were derived only from those claiming unemployment benefit. Since many women are not entitled to benefit, they were removed from the statistics.

State Benefit

Women who are married, cohabiting or presumed to be cohabiting are also discriminated against. As we saw in Chapter 2, for most state benefits, women are regarded primarily as economic dependents and as home–makers. As economic dependants they cannot claim benefit in their own right. The most glaring example of this inequality is the cohabitation ruling where benefit may be stopped if the DHSS suspects a single female to be cohabiting (the standard test being that a man stays for more than three consecutive nights). Women who are known prostitutes or suspected of prostitution are certainly the first to be harassed in this manner.

As 'homemakers' women are excluded from a series of benefits over which the Sex Discrimination Act (1975) apparently has no jurisdiction. Married women continue to be regarded as homemakers although in reality many are breadwinners. Until November 1983 married women could not claim Family Income Supplement unless they were separated. As in the case of supplementary benefit, a woman living with a man was precluded.

The centrality of a woman's role as carer in the family serves to discriminate against her even further. Discrimination is made in the benefit system between married, cohabiting and single women. For instance, men and single women looking after persons in receipt of an attendance allowance have qualified for Invalid Care Allowance since 1975. Though designed to assist those who have sacrificed work opportunities to care for a dependent relative, this allowance is not available for married and cohabiting women.[1] The Non-Contributory

Invalidity Pension (NCIP) is based on the same assumption, that the primary role of the married/cohabiting woman is that of housewife and carer. Invalided housewives were excluded from the scheme until 1977, when the Housewives' NCIP was introduced, but benefit was extended to them only if they could show that, in addition to being incapable of paid work, they were also incapable of performing normal household duties. On 29 November 1984 the Severe Disablement Allowance was introduced. It replaced the NCIP and the HNCIP but the retention of the household duties test still excludes many women from receiving this benefit.

In the summer of 1985 the Green and White Papers on the Reform of Social Security (DHSS 1985a, 1985b) were published, followed by the Social Security Bill in January 1986. The Bill contains proposals for a dramatic reorganisation and cutback of social security provision which will affect single people in particular; including the abolition of single and urgent needs payments. These are to be replaced by a social fund which is cash limited, and from which payments will be made by way of a grant of repayable loan.

Economic Imperatives: Reasons, Excuses and Negotiations in Self Reportage

It has been argued that women's engagement in prostitution is related to economic powerlessness. Motivations for entrance into prostitution have been studied, using a variety of research methods, by James (1978a, 1978b) McLeod (1982) and Edwards (1984). Edwards employed three research methods. The first examined the accounts given by women to the writers of their social inquiry reports. The second involved court observation of a sample of cases (N = 50), examining what solicitors said on behalf of their prostitute clients in mitigation. The third involved discussions with individual women arrested and charged at police stations for offences related to prostitution (N = 22). What follows is an analysis of women's justifications for prostitution.

Prostitutes overwhelmingly accepted full responsibility for their behaviour, but within this acceptance of responsibility a variety of styles of accounting became apparent. Glover's statement (in Smart 1976) that women become prostitutes because of sexual problems and greed found no place in these self-perceptions. Instead, financial imperatives dictated prostitution within this sample. Of the 108 women whose primary motive was financial, only five were employed, either as cleaners or in similar part-time employment. The remainder of the total sample also found themselves in dire financial straits but identified other reasons for their prostitution, including threats from men and the need to sustain a drink habit. Most of the women were single parents whose marriages or cohabitation had broken down and who felt isolated and often desperate at having to rear several children unassisted. The ages of the women ranged from 17 to 46, proportionately as follows:

Age	No.	%
17—21	60	40
22—26	39	26
32—37	20	13
27—31	23	16
37—46	8	5
	150	100

During childhood, a significant proportion had been in Care [cf. Ch. 8] and a similarly significant proportion had experienced violent and sexual assault at the hands of parents or guardians.

Many women were unemployed and some were in receipt of neither unemployment nor supplementary benefit. One woman stated that she felt unable to 'sign on' because she thought that the DHSS would make enquiries as to why she had been able to survive without claiming benefit. Some women claiming benefit talked of the need to supplement it with prostitution. Others described the long wait for DHSS benefit, and, in the interim, of being without money for food, clothing, heating or lighting. Threats from men, although only on occasions cited as a primary motive, were more significant in the case of profiles:

> She has become involved with various boyfriends, but all of these relationships proved to be unsatisfactory and shortlived. On occasions she has become pregnant but has suffered miscarriages. On at least two occasions she was assaulted and ran into problems.

The women themselves often experienced situations where men were taking money off them.

That prostitution is the consequence of economic disadvantage is abundantly clear. Eileen Fairweather came to a similar conclusion regarding the impoverishment and social vulnerability of the prostitutes she studied. They were 'single parents who wanted off the game just as soon as they had saved enough money decently to support their children' (Fairweather:1982:138)

Organised Crime

Finally, I wish to argue that legislative manoeuvres have done more to expose women prostitutes to the victimisation and control of male managers than to provide equality of treatment or relaxation of legislative measures.

Since the 1959 Street Offences Act women have become victims of prostitution as organised crime, controlled largely by male ponces and male managers (Russell, Frey and Reichert 1981; Barry, Bunch and Castley 1984; Ohse 1984), though the actual extent of this control is hidden. There are few complainants to instigate reactive policing, and, if the totality of prosecutions for procuration, brothel-keeping and allied offences is any indication, there is little proactive policing or enforcement of existing legislation. (Fig. 3.2 indicates the very few prosecutions for these allied offences.) A report by Camden Council's Women's Committee in the London area came to similar conclusions. Police figures for 1981 in the Metropolitan area revealed a total of five prosecutions for living off immoral earnings, ten prosecutions for soliciting (Deighton 1983).

The Wolfenden Committee remarked in 1957 (para. 286) that

> It must be accepted that for so long as prostitution exists, the prostitute will seek customers and the potential customer will seek prostitutes. If the prostitute is not allowed to find her customers in the streets, then presumably she and her customers will find other means of meeting each other.

Over the years disproportionately little attention has been paid to enforcing the law with regard to these allied offences when compared with the over-enforcement of legislation affecting the streetwalker. In this respect, the Criminal Law Revision Committee's 17th Report (1986) is to be welcomed. 'Prostitution: Off Street Activities', is primarily concerned with the exploitation of female prostitutes through organised prostitution. This worry is made evident in the opening remarks that 'all too often those who practice prostitution are likely to become the victims of exploitation or to contract venereal disease'. The real mischief is the large-scale facilitation of prostitution (para. 2.17) and other insidious means of its control (para. 2.14). The report has suggested some changes within the law, but nearly six months after the publication of the report it appears to have made little impact on informed discussion, policing or proposed legislation.

Poncing

The legislation relating to ponces is ambiguous and confusing. Most of the regulatory measures are contained within the Sexual Offences Act 1956 where some offences are 'sex specific', for example a *man* living off prostitution (s. 30) and a *woman* directing or controlling prostitutes (s. 31). These measures not only penalise the coercive ponce but also male members of a prostitute's household who may have been unaware of her prostitution. The Criminal Law Revision Committee's 17th Report has suggested that this section be repealed, since the focus of attention should be on those who organise, control and assist prostitution for gain. Alongside this specific legislation is the *Criminal Attempts Act 1981,* which has a far wider application and makes it an offence to attempt procuration. The question of 'poncing' was considered by the Criminal Law Revision Committee in their working paper on 'Offences Relating to Prostitutes and Allied Offences 1982' (p. 15). They heard evidence of the extent of intimidation and violence 'used to enforce the ponce's will on his women or simply to keep her subjugated'. McLeod (1982: 45–6, 49) makes a distinction between 'heavy' poncing involving violence and taking virtually all a woman's money, and poncing where the man simply lives off her earnings. Additionally, there are the 'small time' ponces who may have two or three women working for them and who may be involved in other minor illegalities. McLeod's work (1982: 49) reveals the extent of violence used by ponces to direct control. It is these aspects of coercion the law wishes to guard women against.

Contrary to the popular belief that few women have ponces, McLeod estimated that 75 per cent of prostitutes have ponces. Since prosecutions for soliciting totalled 10,674 in 1983, and since prosecutions for procuration (including poncing) were 337, it appears that many ponces are outside the law. There may be good reasons for their non-prosecution. If the ponce is a husband or cohabitee, there are problems in securing a conviction. Proof of controlling or living on the earnings of a prostitute is said by the police and courts to be difficult to establish, since the uncorroborated evidence of the prostitute is insufficient in practice. To obtain evidence, observation over a period of something like four or more days should be kept by experienced plain-clothed officers. The CLRC here pointed to the problem of getting satisfactory evidence and enforcing section 30 (2.13). The Criminal Law Revision Committee (1982) concluded that sections 30 and 31 of the Sexual Offences Act 1956 (man living on the earnings of prostitutes and women exercising control of a prostitute) should be released and replace by much more detailed provisions: 'It should be an offence for a person to gain or exercise control or direction over a prostitute or to organise prostitution'. (Para 2.7 p.48)

The Committee also invited comment on the necessity to penalise poncing where the ponce plays no part in prostitution. Unless, however, the law is more prepared to protect women in general from domestic violence, to give to prostitutes the same rights extended to men prostitutes, changes along the lines suggested by the Committee would be unlikely to be enforced.

Procuration and 'Fronts' for Prostitution

It is an offence to procure a woman to become a prostitute (Sexual Offences Act 1956, s. 22) (Criminal Attempts Act 1981, s. 1(1)). The appellant Brown in *R v Brown* (CA 1 WLP: 1211) raised the defence that he had not procured her...because he believed she was already a prostitute. The judge ruled that 'his belief' (a concept which has vexed rape cases) was, in this offence, irrelevant. He changed his plea and was convicted. The appeal court overruled this, declaring 'his belief' relevant. It held that if a man genuinely believed on reasonable grounds that a woman was a prostitute, he could not be said to be trying to procure her.

The Sexual Offences Act 1956, sections 33 to 36, makes specific reference to brothels such as it is an offence for a person to keep a brothel, or to manage, or act or assist in its management (s. 33). It is an offence for a landlord or his agent to let a premises knowing it to be so used (s. 34). The Criminal Law Revision Committee have suggested that the notion of 'a brothel' is now no longer relevant as widely differing kinds of establishments may qualify. Since the 1959 Act a wide variety of premises have proliferated as 'fronts' for prostitution. The committee proposes that the law should allow two prostitutes to share a house without it coming within the definition of a brothel. In the case of Farrugia (1979, 69 *Cr. App. R.* 108) the manager and employees of an escort agency who received payment from prostitutes' clients were convicted under section 30. In Broadfoot (1976 *3 ALL ER* 753), the manager of a massage parlour was convicted under section 22 of the Sexual Offences Act for procuration. He had invited job applicants to earn extra money by masturbating clients. In cases where prostitutes are employed as night-club hostesses and negotiate independently, managers commit no offence. Again, several days' police observation is required to secure evidence. Evidence sufficient to convict a streetwalker is comparatively easy to obtain, being merely the word of two police officers. In terms of detection and conviction rates, therefore, emphasis on the streetwalker is a more attractive proposition. Meanwhile, women prostitutes are controlled, exploited, intimidated and assaulted beyond the reach of the law.

Conclusion

Prostitution, as Engels has argued, symbolises the ultimate objectification and appropriation of women as sexual objects, as commodities. I do not take the view that women prostitutes have a freedom – that the ultimate control of the transaction is in their hands. In a society where women are oppressed and exploited, prostitution can be nothing more than an extension of the general oppression. Since 1979 decreasing job opportunities and the erosion of welfare benefits have together resulted in more and more girls and young mothers drifting into prostitution. At the same time, enforcement patterns have ensured that while women who work the streets are subjected to incessant police harassment, those operating elsewhere are controlled, exploited and intimidated beyond the reach of the law. The deterioration in women's economic position has thus been accompanied by a crisis in sexual exploitation. Law, social policy and organised crime presently combine to ensure that while women engaged in prostitution face high risks of either prosecution or exploitation, pimps, ponces and others benefiting from the prostitution business remain relatively free to exploit prostitute women's increasingly vulnerable position in both law and economy.

Notes

I would like to acknowledge the Greater Manchester Probation Service, and the West Midlands Probation Service for permitting access to data used in this article, and the co-operation of the Greater Manchester Police. The Economic and Social Research Council provided financial support. Grant number HR/7588/1.

1. Editors' note: on 23 June 1986 Mr Norman Fowler, the social services secretary, announced an extension of the Invalid Care Allowance; the benefit will now be paid to an extra 70,000 married women, who did not qualify previously, at an estimated cost of £55 million a year (*Guardian*, 24 June 1986).

Part Two

Women in Courts

4

Proving Sexual Assault: Prosecuting the Offender or Persecuting the Victim?

Gerry Chambers and Ann Millar

In recent years considerable attention has been focused on the conduct of rape trials, and although a new framework within which evidence could be led in England and Wales was established by the Sexual Offences (Amendment) Act of 1976, there has been considerable disquiet at the way the new rules are being interpreted (Adler 1982). In addition, individual instances of lenient sentencing in rape trials have continued to attract adverse comment.[1] As part of our research on sexual assault within the context of the Scottish criminal justice system, we have been able to obtain detailed information about what happens at sexual-assault trials and in particular on how the complainer's evidence is presented by the prosecution and challenged by the defence (see Chambers and Millar 1983, 1986).

Apart from recent research by Adler which examined the exercise of judicial discretion in allowing in otherwise 'prohibited' evidence of the woman's previous sexual history, there has been no thorough examination of how rape and other sexual-assault trials are conducted. In both England and Wales and Scotland the most important sections of these trials, during which the complainer gives evidence and is cross-examined, are closed to the public, and so people have been dependent on the graphic and often chilling accounts given in newspapers and journals by individual women who have been courageous enough to narrate their own experiences after the event. Rather ironically the anonymity now guaranteed for complainers in rape trials by legislation in England and Wales and by 'gentleman's agreement' in Scotland has in itself inhibited any systematic assessment of how rape trials operate since the public are excluded from knowing fully what goes on there and court observation by researchers is problematic.[2] Our research suggests that while such anonymity is clearly in the interests of women and is welcomed by most of them, the requirement to clear the court of the public also operates to provide a cover for loose and irrelevant questioning during the trial. Such rules of evidence as existed during the course of our research study were frequently flouted in ways which we describe later.

Clearly, not all incidents of sexual assault[3] reported by women to the police result in a trial, and it is worth setting in context the data on trials that we present in this chapter. During a fifteen-month period (in 1980 and 1981) we collected information on all incidents of serious sexual assault that occurred in the two cities of Glasgow and Edinburgh. The 196 incidents recorded by the police during this period became the basis of our sample. Our research showed that there is considerable case attrition at identifiable points since only forty of these incidents resulted in trials. Figure 4.1 summarises the key attrition points for cases in our study.

However, because of the way the study was designed, two facets of case attrition could not be examined in an empirical way, and we begin by considering these. First, and perhaps to state the obvious, not all rapes and sexual assaults are reported to the police. Estimates of the ratio of unreported to reported rapes have varied from 1.5 : 1 to 20 : 1 to 100 : 1 (Katz and Mazur 1979: 32). British data on this question is available from at least two sources: crime victimisation surveys and the records of rape crisis centres.

Crime surveys are a fairly new phenomenon in Britain. The first British crime survey, conducted in 1982, found that in Scotland only 7 per cent of sexual assaults (including the usually less serious crime of indecent assault) were reported to the police (Chambers and Tombs 1984: 15). In England and Wales the same survey found the number reported to be 28 per cent (Hough and Mayhew 1983: 11), while the repeat of that survey in 1984 found that only 10 per cent had been reported to the police in England and Wales (Hough and Mayhew 1985: 21). A major problem with the crime-survey method is that crimes of sexual violence are possibly just as unlikely, and some would say are less likely, to be made known to survey interviewers as to police officers. Hall (1985) attempted to overcome some of the difficulties of formal crime surveys in the Woman's Safety Survey conducted by women against rape. Two thousand questionnaires were distributed at a variety of distribution points throughout London: 17 per cent of respondents reported a rape and 31 per cent a sexual assault. Despite the unreliability of crime-survey data for incidents of sexual assault, the indications are that fewer incidents get reported to the police than comparably serious acts of non-sexual violence.

Records from rape crisis centres are another source of information about non-report to the police. A report from Edinburgh Rape Crisis Centre (ERCC) states that for 1981, 56 per cent of a sample of women who contacted the rape crisis centre also reported the crime to the police (ERCC 1981: 9), and in its report for 1982 London Rape Crisis Centre (LRCC) states that only 25 per cent of women who contacted the centre reported to the police (LRCC 1982:37). But data from rape crisis centres also has limitations since it is unknown to what extent women who contact the centres are representative of all women who experience sexual violence, and the crime definitions used by centres may not match the legal criteria

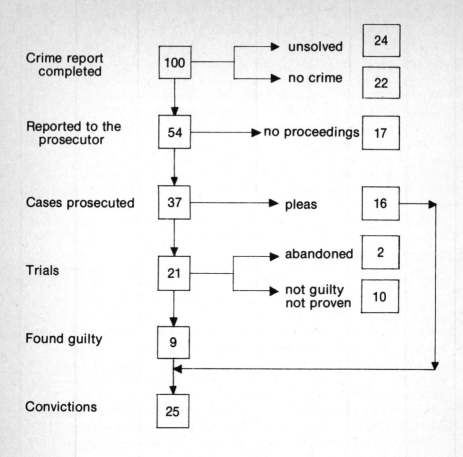

Figure 4.1 *Case attrition in sexual-assault cases. Figures are percentages based on the number of incidents (196) in the sample; 16 per cent of incidents involved more than one offender and therefore the number of offenders exceeded the number of incidents. In multiple-offender incidents only the outcome for the **main** offender has been considered above. A more detailed analysis of case progress which is **offender**-based is presented in Chambers and Millar (1986).*

used by criminal justice agents, making direct comparisons with official statistics problematic.

A second point to make is that official records of the incidence of sexual assault, as is the case with all crimes, may be incomplete for reasons other than non-report. There is reason to doubt that all 'criminal' incidents reported to the police by victims, bystanders, witnesses or other people, get recorded as crimes. There are of course some fairly obvious reasons why this should be so. A person may report a theft of an item which has in fact only been misplaced by the reporter. Anonymous calls to the police of incidents of vandalism or rowdiness or street brawls have to be verified before their occurrence can be logged. It is not difficult to imagine scenarios which result in no official crime report being filed for a sexual-assault incident. Police officers have claimed to know women who, they said, regularly turn up to police stations as a matter of habit to say they have been sexually assaulted. Other officers have said they might be approached on the beat with 'exaggerated' claims which, they said, turned out to be unfounded and that the situation was defused after talking it over.

Although there may be scope especially outwith the police station for deflecting claims of victimisation, this is unlikely to reflect any systematic or officially sanctioned practice, but rather the informal exercise of discretion by the officer to whom the incident is reported. Opportunities certainly exist for police officers to avoid recording incidents which can be defused, deflected or talked out, and, if the complainer fails to pursue the matter further, there may be no official record. Our own information about the extent of such 'renegotiations' in sexual-assault cases is, however, mainly anecdotal.

Our research began with incidents which were officially recorded by the police on a crime report form and which as a consequence, became the subject of investigation by a detective. One major reason for case attrition in this sample of cases was the practice of filing cases as 'no crimes' after initial enquiries have been conducted. Figure 4.1 showed that 22 per cent of all cases initially recorded by the police as a crime of rape, attempted rape or assault with intent to rape were filed as 'no crime'. We have described elsewhere how investigators approached sexual-assault complaints with a high degree of scepticism arising, in part, from their general approach to detective work and, in part, from the widely held belief, common also outside police circles, that women were likely to fabricate complaints (Chambers and Millar 1983:81–87). Reasons given to us by police officers for complaint fabrication included the following: to explain a pregnancy; as an excuse for getting home late; out of spite; because of a hyperactive imagination or remorse. Such scepticism appeared to be learned in training and was part of the general police culture. Because of this assumption about the high likelihood of false complaints, police officers felt that women had to be scrupulously cross-questioned. The research found that not only were detectives acting as collectors of evidence but that they were also acting as interpreters of the legal significance of evidence (a role normally thought to belong to the prosecutor), and they could thus decide not to pass cases on to the prosecutor if evidence seemed to be lacking.

There were two ways in which cases could be marked as 'no crimes'. First, cases could be filed as 'complaint withdrawn', although this did not necessarily mean that the woman had herself initiated or suggested the withdrawal. In fact it was a very rare occurrence for a woman who had reported an offence to the police to completely retract or withdraw a statement. The suggestion that a woman should not pursue her complaint, on occasions, came from police officers themselves. In addition, some cases were filed as 'complaint withdrawn' although the woman might have no recollection of having withdrawn. A second group of 'no crime' cases were those which were filed as unfounded, unsubstantiated or groundless, such cases being regarded by the police as straightforward fabrications or exaggerations.

A further source of attrition arises from the fact that a proportion of cases remain unsolved by the police. Crimes of serious violence however have a high clear-up rate due to the fact that victims of violence (unlike, say, burglary victims) are often able to provide substantial information about their offenders, sometimes including even a name and address. In this sample about one-quarter of cases were unsolved (see Fig. 4.1), and they were mainly attacks by strangers where recognition by the woman was not a factor in the detecting process. The next major attrition point occurs when a decision is made as to whether or not to embark on a prosecution. Prosecutors decided not to initiate proceedings in a further 17 per cent of the cases in this sample, that is in about one-third of all those cases actually reported by the police to the prosecutor with a view to prosecution. Thus, in only 37 per cent of all cases which started off in our sample were steps taken to initiate prosecution proceedings against an offender.

In cases of serious crime, prosecution decisions are made in Scotland on two separate occasions. On receipt of a written report of a crime from the police the procurator fiscal marks the case, either by continuing it for case preparation or, alternatively, by deciding there should be no further proceedings. Once a case has been prepared and all the evidence available to the prosecution has been gathered and documented, the case papers are then examined by Crown counsel, the collective name for the group of Crown advocates-depute, one of whose number will be prosecuting the case if it goes to the high court. Crown counsel either agrees that the accused should be indicted or decides not to proceed with the case. We have considered in greater detail elsewhere the reasons which enter into the decision to prosecute, in sexual-assault cases (Chambers and Millar 1986: Ch. 3). To a large extent these relate to judgments about evidential sufficiency and the likelihood of a successful outcome for the prosecution. However, such judgments are not grounded exclusively in legalistic considerations and the prosecutor's expectations of the issues likely to be considered important by a jury in determining guilt or innocence are crucial in narrowing the options available to the prosecutor. We take up this point later on in the chapter.

Trial before a jury is undoubtedly seen by many people as the cornerstone of our system of justice and it is its most visible and public feature. However, not all cases which are prosecuted result in contested trials and, of course, in Scotland only the most serious of these, are tried by a jury. An accused person will want to take the advice of his solicitor on how strong is the evidence against him, that is on the risks surrounding going to trial. Many accused may feel that they will want to get things over quickly by pleading guilty because they know that their chances of getting off at a trial are very slim. On the other hand, it is the accused's right to plead not guilty and, when facing serious charges, to have the evidence against him heard by a jury; many will therefore want to avail themselves of that option, which allows the possibility of full acquittal.

There are of course considerable bureaucratic pressures within the criminal justice system itself to resolve cases without going to trial. An early indication by the accused's agent that an offender will plead guilty relieves administrative work on case preparation for the prosecutor. In addition, guilty-plea cases are much less costly on the public purse than trials and, the more accused persons who plead guilty, the more quickly cases can move through the system, thus expediting the administration of justice for witnesses, victims and offenders alike.

In this sample, 43 per cent of prosecutions were resolved by the accused submitting a plea of guilty. Not all of these, however, were guilty pleas to the charges on which the accused had been indicted. Over half of the guilty pleas were to lesser charges resulting from plea bargaining between the accused's agent and the prosecutor. Thus seven men charged with rape, twelve charged with assault with intent to rape and two charged with attempted rape pleaded guilty to lesser charges and avoided going to trial.

The normal course of events at a trial in Scotland is for a jury of fifteen members – after listening to the evidence from the prosecution and defence, and after instruction by the judge on the law and on the legal significance of the evidence – to be invited by the judge to retire and return a verdict. A jury will be told that three verdicts – guilty, not guilty and not proven – are possible and that a decision can be arrived at on the basis of a simple majority. They will also be told in rape cases that if they do not believe the evidence was sufficient to prove rape, they may nevertheless convict of one of a range of alternative charges.

Less frequently trials will be resolved in other ways. First, the accused may change his plea to one of guilty during the trial, in which instance no further evidence will be led and the court can move immediately to a consideration of sentence. Second, the prosecutor may desert the diet if a weakness in his case develops, or if new evidence which he is unaware of comes to light. The diet may be deserted *pro loco et tempore*, in which event fresh proceedings can be commenced at a later date. Alternatively, the diet can be deserted 'simpliciter', which in effect means that the case is abandoned altogether. As a consequence the judge will direct the jury to find the accused not guilty.

In 21 per cent of incidents in this sample an accused person was indicted to a trial. (See Fig. 4.1) It would be surprising indeed if all accused who were sent for trial after pleading not guilty were found guilty by the jury and sentenced. In this sample of sexual assault cases just less than half of those men who went to trial were convicted. The remainder were found not guilty or not proven (both of which result in a full acquittal of the offender), or in a few cases trials were abandoned before verdicts were reached.

Finally, the above discussion begs the question of how the attrition rate for sexual assault compares with that for other comparably serious crimes. There has certainly been an assumption in the literature on rape that these cases reach trial less frequently than other types of crime, but we know of no British research which has looked at this question in a systematic way. Such an assumption has certainly been challenged with respect to the situation in the USA where two recent research studies claim to have shown that the attrition rate in rape cases is comparable with rates for other crimes like homicide, burglary and assault.

However, we have already noted that, in the British context, reporting rates to the police for sexual assault may be lower than for other crimes, and there is also some evidence from unpublished criminal statistics to suggest that in Scotland a higher proportion of rape cases than of other serious crimes are dismissed at trial.

Sexual-Assault Trials

Having provided background information about what happened to the sexual-assault cases in our study, we turn now to focus on what happened at the trial. Our discussion draws from the interviews we conducted with women who had attended a court hearing and from the transcripts of the complainer's evidence.

Most women were of course anxious about going to court. For many, attending court as the principal witness was an unknown experience which in itself caused considerable apprehension and resulted in women being obviously nervous and tense in the witness box. Women were aware that they would have to go over upsetting memories about the incident in court, but most had limited knowledge of the court and of court procedures. The actual experience of the trial for the majority of women confirmed their worst expectations principally because the defence cross-examination made the complainer feel that her own character and behaviour was on trial. In addition to the defence cross-examination, women were also critical of the lack of concern shown to them by the court. For example, many spoke about the distressing experience of having to give evidence about personal details in front of a court which was predominantly male and which consisted entirely of strangers. They also drew attention to the fact that nothing had been done at the court to put them at ease.

Women were given little constructive advice and preparation prior to the trial, and this contributed to their anxiety and stress and affected their performance in the witness box. For example, nerves often affected a woman's ability to respond concisely to questions and to remember detail. Many aspects of court procedure which are considered familiar and routine by court staff are intimidating to the lay person on a first appearance in court. For example, women were confused about the role of the various personnel in the courtroom. In the absence of introductions from the judge or the prosecutor himself (in many cases no one whom the woman had met previously in connection with her case was present in court), women were left to deduce who was counsel for the defence and prosecution largely from the manner and content of questioning. Most managed to differentiate. One woman said that 'the one that was cheeky and shouting was the defence' and that the prosecution was 'more calm'. Another said that 'one treated me like a human being, the other treated me like a bit of dirt'. But, some women remarked that they were unable to tell who was who even after they had completed giving evidence.

Feelings of vulnerability in court as a consequence of having no one on their 'own side' to protect their interests at trial were frequently voiced. Women felt particularly let down by the prosecution, who they thought could have acted in a more robust way to provide protection from defence question. Women felt that they were as much on trial as the accused, yet, unlike the accused with his defence agent, they were unrepresented. In order to examine in detail the nature and content of the questioning which caused so much distress to women, we analysed official transcripts of the complainer's evidence. Some of the more important findings of this analysis are reported in the following sections.

Various legal criteria have to be established for a charge of rape to be proved. First, there has to be evidence of penetration. This can often be provided from the medical examination. In addition, there has to be evidence that the woman was an unwilling partner throughout. In cases of attempted rape and assault with intent to rape the significant criteria to be proved, in addition to the lack of consent, are the intention of the accused and the stage which the assault has reached.

Incidents of rape, as with other sexual offences, generally take place in relative privacy, often without witnesses.[4] In addition, forensic or medical evidence which might be corroborative of physical violence or force and hence lack of consent is thus very difficult. Moreover, evidence of lack of consent will not necessarily lead to a conviction, since in a rape case the question as to whether the defendant believed the women consented also arises.[5]

Thus, there are often difficulties in providing proof from purely *legal criteria* alone, and other criteria which we have termed *quasi-legal* and *extra-legal* come into play. Quasi-legal criteria are factors which are not constituent components of a legal definition of a crime but which can be used to infer or deduce the existence of legal criteria. An example of a quasi-legal factor is the degree of resistance shown by the complainer during the incident. Extra-legal criteria are factors which are extraneous to the event of the incident; these include the character and general life-style of the complainer. Both quasi- and extra-legal criteria are used to make inferences about the credibility of the victim.

Questioning and cross examination always took place in order to establish that the various legal criteria had been met. Prosecutors questioned women to show that there had been sexual penetration. If there had been no sexual penetration then a charge of rape could not be proved, although one of attempted rape could. In addition, the prosecutor had to show that the complainer could identify the accused as the perpetrator of the crime. In most cases of rape the accused admitted to having had sexual intercourse with the complainer. The prosecution thus had to show that intercourse was obtained either forcibly by producing evidence of physical injury or by proving that there had been threats of violence either to her directly or to others close to her.

The transcripts showed how sometimes even legal criteria were interpreted in different ways by the prosecution and defence. For example, signs of injury were usually taken as corroborating lack of consent, but on occasions the defence made out that the injuries had been self-inflicted in order to lend credibility to a fabricated story. The following excerpt illustrates.

Defence: Had you inflicted any injuries at all to yourself between this incident that we have been talking about and your examination by Dr ....?

Complainer:	What exactly are you talking about?
Defence:	Well, did you bite your hands, for example?
Complainer:	No.
Defence:	Sure?
Complainer:	Yes.
Defence:	If there was a bite mark on one of your hands, or indeed on any other part of your body, you wouldn't have put it there?
Complainer:	No.

In others, the defence made out in questioning that the complainer, while sustaining physical injuries, had in fact enjoyed the violence, and, in one case, that this was 'part of the love-making process' and, in another case, 'an unusual form of sexual behaviour'.

Because of the difficulties of establishing that all the legal elements of the crime were present, and particularly because of the difficulties of proving lack of consent in rape cases, the existence of the legal components of the crime could often only be inferred or deduced from what we have termed quasi-legal criteria. Quasi-legal criteria included the level of resistance displayed by the complainer and her behaviour after the incident, including such factors as promptness of complaint. It was very common for a woman to be questioned in detail about her resistance to her attacker. She was asked both about her verbal refusals and her physical actions. What she had shouted or screamed at the time of the attack was often the focus of questioning, as shown in the following excerpts. First:

Defence:	Did you not try to scream or shout?
Complainer:	I did shout.
Defence:	At the top of your voice?
Complainer:	Yes.
Defence:	What were you shouting?
Complainer:	Somebody to help me.
Defence:	Tell us the words you shouted?
Complainer:	I was shouting, 'Will somebody please help me'.
Defence:	Are these the words you shouted, 'Somebody please help me'?
Complainer:	Yes.
Defence:	And did you utter screams as well?
Complainer:	I just kept shouting that.
Defence:	You didn't scream?
Complainer:	No, I just kept shouting all the time.
Defence:	So there were no screams at that stage. Is that right?
Complainer:	Yes.

Second:

Defence:	For example, you did not start screaming and kicking up a fuss?
Complainer:	Of course I was shouting. I was saying, 'I don't want to have sex with you', I told them that. They knew damn well I didn't want to have sex with them.
Defence:	Were you screaming?
Complainer:	I was crying out loud. Not screaming as such, but crying out loud.
Defence:	Do you mean by that you were shouting or simply crying out loud?
Complainer:	Crying out loud.

Defence: Audibly, so you were not shouting?
Complainer: No.

As shown in these excerpts, it was very difficult for a woman to demonstrate her lack of consent by verbal resistance alone. The excerpts also clearly show an example of one of the defence tactics designed to fluster the woman whereby in questioning he attempts to develop a fine distinction between 'screams' and 'shouting' in the first and between 'shouting' and 'crying out loud' in the second.

In addition to being asked about the extent of verbal resistance, women were also questioned about the physical actions they had taken to repel the attack, for example whether the women had slapped or punched the offender. Often the defence questioning focused not so much on what she had done, but what she had *not* done to resist her attacker, as the following excerpts taken from one cross-examination illustrate.

Defence:	If this is what in fact happened, what you say about being dragged by the hair, *did you not attempt* to do anything about it? *Did you not attempt* to retaliate?
Complainer:	Yes, I did.
Defence:	What did you do?
Complainer:	I struggled with him to get away.
Defence:	Such as?
Complainer:	I was trying really hard to get away, but he just kept pushing.
Defence:	Did you have a handbag with you?
Complainer:	Yes.
Defence:	*Why did you not try to strike him with your handbag at that stage?*
Complainer:	It was up at my shoulder. I didn't manage to get it down off my shoulder.
Defence:	*Did you not try to punch him or strike him in any way?*
Complainer:	Yes, I did.
Defence:	*Did you not try to get up when you were pushed down?*
Complainer:	Yes, I did.
Defence:	*Did you not think of poking him in the eyes?*
Complainer:	No, I didn't think of that.
Defence:	*Did you not think that might have been a good way of repelling an attack by any man?*
Complainer:	I didn't think of that.

....

Defence:	*Did you never think of trying to grab his neck?*
Complainer:	No.
Defence:	*Or kicking him in the privates or anything like that?*
Complainer:	I couldn't very well kick him there when he was sitting on top of my legs, could I?

These excerpts are taken from a very lengthy cross-examination during which the complainer fainted and had to be taken from the courtroom to receive medical attention. They show very clearly another defence tactic whereby questioning focused on what the woman did *not* do to repel her attacker. This put her in the position of always giving negative replies, which made her feel the guilty party for not doing more to resist.

Lack of physical injuries was often interpreted by the defence as indicative of a failure to resist. Defence questioning implied that a 'real' victim would have resisted fully even if this meant being badly injured fighting back rather than suffer the 'dishonour' of a sexual attack. In the following excerpt from a cross-examination in a trial where the woman had complained of being physically assaulted and then raped by four men, the defence questioning is premised on an image of women where honour and chastity assume greater importance than safety and life. This is in marked contrast to the woman's decision not to risk injury by fighting back when she was greatly outnumbered by her attackers.

Defence: Therefore you would not be, under any circumstances, prepared to surrender your virginity to these men readily?

Complainer: Certainly not.

Defence: And would you do everything within your power to protect your virginity from these men?

Complainer: Yes.

Defence: But in fact you say that after you were taken into the bedroom you effectively did nothing whatsoever to resist any of the advances by any of these men?

Complainer: Because I was scared. I was petrified.

Complainer: I thought they were going to injure me, come after me.

Defence: What was going to be worse, if your story is true, being struck on the face perhaps or physically abused in some way or losing your virginity to four different men and perhaps five.

Complainer: At that time I did not . . . I was frightened. I didn't want to be hurt again. I just wanted to go home.

Defence: I ask you again: take your time. Tell the ladies and gentlemen what your position is. If you thought you were going to lose your virginity by being raped by four and perhaps five men, perhaps more than one, perhaps for a number of hours, are you saying you preferred that or you succumbed to that rather than the injuries you might have received by making a determined effort to get out of the house?

Complainer: Yes, but I'm not saying that I preferred to be raped. I don't know who would.

Defence: Perhaps the word 'preferred' is unfair. You succumbed, you say, to multiple rape rather than make a determined effort to get out of house?

Complainer: Yes.

Defence: That is simply not true, is it?

Complainer: Yes, that is what I said.

What a woman did after the incident was also used to throw light on the legal requirements of this crime. Often questioning assumed that women would react in a typical way to a sexual assault. A 'normal' reaction was considered to be one where a woman showed signs of hysteria and emotional distress along with a quick response to report the incident to the police.[6] Yet there were often rational reasons for the delay in contacting the police since many women, in a state of shock after the incident, were unsure about what they should do, particularly in those cases where the woman knew her attacker. In many of these cases women chose to speak to someone such as a relative or close friend for advice before deciding to report to the police.

Despite this, there seemed to be a real reluctance on the part of the legal profession to accept that for many women it was not an obvious reaction to report the incident immediately to the police. Defence questioning often used evidence of delay to throw doubts on the credibility of a woman's case. The following excerpt illustrates this.

Defence: Now you had the telephone in the house obviously because you were able to telephone Miss ....?

Complainer: Yes.

Defence: And equally if you had been all that distressed and upset by what happened, you knew I take it from part of your training (the complainer was blind) how to get in touch with the Police?

Complainer: Yes, I did.

Defence: You would dial 999, wouldn't you?

Complainer: Yes.

Defence: And that's a very simple operation?

Complainer: It is yes.

Defence: So if you had just been raped by this man as you are suggesting to the jury, you had at your disposal immediate means of contact with the police who could then have apprehended the man, is that right?

Complainer: Yes.

Defence: But you telephoned Miss .... instead?

Complainer: Well, I was distressed really, I didn't know what my next move should be.

Defence: Well, you would know would you not that for anyone to rape another person is a serious crime?

Complainer: Yes.

Defence: And the people to whom crimes are reported are normally the police?

Complainer: Oh yes.

Defence: So if what you say is correct and if you had been raped and if you wanted to report a serious crime you could have lifted the phone there and then to get the police?

Complainer: Yes.

Defence: But you never did that?

Complainer: No, because I didn't feel composed enough to do so.

Defence: But you felt composed enough to phone Miss ....?

Complainer: Well, I wasn't very composed when I phoned Miss ..... either.

Defence: And the truth of the matter is that the reason you didn't telephone the police was that you realised you had nothing to complain about in the criminal sense, isn't that right, you had never been raped that day?

Complainer: Yes, I had been raped that day.

The content of a complainer's evidence was not confined to questioning on legal and quasi-legal criteria. Frequently, questioning and cross-examination concerned factors which were clearly extraneous to the incident itself. For example, evidence was often heard on the character, sexual history and general life-style of the complainer. Although limited by rules of evidence, questioning on such topics has been justified in sexual-offence trials because it is commonly thought that such information has relevance to the issue of consent – since women, in particular those who are promiscuous, are thought to be prone to untruthfulness and are unreliable witnesses.[7]

Under the rules of evidence existing at the time of the study, it was competent for a person accused of rape or another sexual offence to seek to establish that the complainer was of bad character or associated with prostitutes.[8] In only one of the cases studied was the complainer asked directly whether she had been soliciting at the time of the incident. More common, however, was a wide-ranging enquiry into character and life-style. For example, in different cases the defence brought out that the complainer was divorced, was an unmarried mother, had a criminal record or that she was in the habit of either drinking with strangers or drinking to excess.

Personal living arrangements and general social activities were also frequent topics of defence questioning. Questioning on life-style was clearly extraneous to the crime itself and provided the court with highly selective items of information about a women, often with strong moral overtones designed both to discredit her personally and reduce the credibility of her story. For example, the following excerpts illustrates the defence scrutiny of a complainer's living arrangements and the type of company she kept.

Defence: So would I be right in saying it was fairly normal for people to come to the flat and stay and drink?

Complainer: Yes, but not all the time.

Defence: You mean sometimes people came and didn't drink?

Complainer: Yes.

Defence: Was it just alcohol that was taken or was there anything else?

Complainer: No, just cans of lager that people brought up.

Defence: Normally was it just lager?

Complainer: Yes.

Defence: When people stayed over in the flat, slept in the flat, where did they stay?

Complainer: They slept in the chair, some on the floor.

Defence: How many at the maximum would spend the night in this flat?

Complainer: Maybe about four would stay.

Defence: So sometimes there would be eight people staying in the flat?

Complainer: Yes.

Defence: Where did they all sleep on those occasions?

Complainer: They slept in chairs or on the floor. If they wanted to stay, they had to sleep there.

Defence: So they all slept in the living room?

Complainer:	Yes.
Defence:	Young men and young women all sort of sleeping together in the living room?
Complainer:	Yes.
Defence:	Was that a fairly normal arrangement? When I used the expression 'sleeping together', which you accepted, did that include some sexual intercourse during the evening.
Complainer:	No.
Defence:	That never happened?
Complainer:	No, never happened.
Defence:	So there was sometimes, you are telling us, about eight people staying in the flat, of mixed sex sometimes, more or less all sleeping in the one room, and that never happened?
Complainer:	Yes.
Defence:	That is your evidence: that just never took place?
Complainer:	Yes.

It was also very common for questions to be asked about a woman's sexual experience. In some cases a woman was asked quite explicitly whether she was a virgin or sexually experienced. In other cases questioning was more indirect and asked about the use of contraceptive methods or about knowledge of sexual terms. Some women were even asked questions about previous sexual relations with specific men, as is shown in the excerpt below, even though, at the time of research, evidence which was designed to show that a woman had on specified occasions had intercourse with men other than the accused was not permitted under common-law rules.[9]

Prosecution:	Miss ......, can I ask you, before this evening had you had sexual intercourse with other boys?
Complainer:	Oh, yes, I had, yes.
Prosecution:	In particular had you sexual intercourse with your boyfriend Robert Kaye, who you were telling us about?
Complainer:	Uh-huh.

(names are fictitious)

As can be seen from the trial excerpt quoted above, it was not only the defence who asked questions on previous sexual history. Sometimes the prosecution asked such questions in order to draw attention to the women's 'virtue', perhaps to strengthen the prosecution case. In other cases it was perhaps done in order to raise issues which the defence might have made more of if they had not been already brought out.

Defence tactics

Major contributing factors to the distress which women experienced in the witness box have been discussed in the previous section. However, in attempting to understand the complainer's experience at trial, attention should also be focused on how the defence used certain tactics to discredit a woman's evidence, and unsettle her performance in the witness box. The more frequent of these defence tactics are discussed below.

SUGGESTIONS OF BLAME-WORTHINESS

Because a woman had engaged in risky behaviour by being out alone at night or by being in the company of strangers, defence cross-examination attempted to place on her some of the blame for what had happened. For example, one woman was asked:

> *Defence:*   So you started to walk through an area of Glasgow which you did not know, which was not built-up, with someone you had just met during the course of the afternoon?
>
> *Complainer:*   Either that or I would have had to walk home. I had to get my bus fare.
>
> *Defence:*   Are you asking the ladies and gentlemen – indeed the court – to believe, Miss .... that you didn't realise when you set out on that journey that you were running certain risks?
>
> *Complainer:*   He seemed nice enough just to talk to going along the road. It didn't seem as if anything like that was going to happen.

INSENSITIVE QUESTIONING

There were cases where defence questioning seemed to be largely irrelevant to the facts of the case with the main purpose to embarrass or shame the woman. The excerpt below is taken from a cross-examination where the defence has asked about a woman's clothing on the night of the incident. He then goes on to ask:

> *Defence:*   Are you wearing tights at the moment?
>
> *Complainer:*   Yes.
>
> *Defence:*   You are wearing pants at the moment?
>
> *Complainer:*   Yes.
>
> *Defence:*   Are your pants at the moment under or over your tights?
>
> *Complainer:*   That are under just now because of . . .
>
> *Defence:*   You were starting to tell us the reasons, weren't you?
>
> *Complainer:*   Yes, because I had my periods.
>
> *Defence:*   But when you are not in that position you normally wear the pants outside the tights?
>
> *Complainer:*   Usually, sometimes, yes . . . not always, it depends.

REPEATED QUESTIONING ON DETAIL

Questioning on, for example, the exact time the incident occurred, details of the location and of the attacker's clothing, unsettled women because it was difficult to answer precisely and often had the result of making her less sure of her facts thereby reducing the credibility of her case. If a complainer is unsure of some of her facts, it is likely that the court may think twice about the reliability of her evidence in total.

PERSISTENT QUESTIONING.

A further tactic is persistent questioning on a line of evidence despite denials by a complainer. Such defence questioning had the effect of introducing the idea that there might indeed be some truth in the denied allegations. The following excerpt illustrates this.

Defence:	Had you not been a girlfriend of .... for two years before December 1980?
Complainer:	No, no.
Defence:	Had you not had sexual relations with him a couple of times before?
Complainer:	No, no.
Defence:	In back-courts?
Complainer:	The back of where?
Defence:	In back-courts?
Complainer:	No, I did not, no.
Defence:	You say you never at any time had sexual intercourse with ....?
Complainer:	I never had sexual intercourse with ....

INTIMIDATION

Intimidation by repeated reference to the seriousness of the allegations. In following this line of questioning defence counsel assumed that a woman had made up a story and that by continual references to the seriousness of the complaint she could be made to admit her false allegation. The excerpt below illustrates this.

Defence:	You understand what I am suggesting to you that you have made up a story about .... raping you, you didn't want the police in, but now that they are in you have to stick to that story, haven't you, isn't that right?
Complainer:	He raped me and that's all I can say.
Defence:	You realise, and I want you to think carefully about your evidence, that this young man can go to prison for years on your evidence. Do you realise how serious this matter is?
Complainer:	(No answer.)
Defence:	We are not playing little games out of 'My Guy' now, do you understand that?
Complainer:	Yes.
Defence:	And you realise how serious the consequences are for this man between the two police officers if you are telling lies?
Complainer:	I am no' telling lies.

Recent Legislative Changes

The foregoing analysis of sexual-assault trials in Scotland clearly indicates major weaknesses in the then existing common law rules concerning evidence admissibility. Our research findings then lend considerable weight to the arguments adduced by the Scottish Law Commission in 1983, reporting seven years after the Heilbron Inquiry, that our laws of evidence in rape and certain other sexual cases are out of touch with contemporary sexual habits and attitudes', that 'the declared law is in some respects unclear' and that 'it is apparently not always being followed in practice' (Chambers and Millar 1983: para 5.1).

Along with its report, the commission produced a draft Bill which was, after a period of consultation, incorporated with some amendments into the Law Reform (Miscellaneous Provisions) (Scotland) Act 1985 as section 36. The Act only became law at the beginning of 1986, and it therefore remains to be seen what impact it will have on the conduct of sexual-assault trials in Scotland. There are however reasons to be sceptical that the legislation will have the desired impact. Like the earlier English legislation, the Scottish Act creates a general prohibition on the admission into sexual-assault trials of certain types of evidence. In Scotland these concern character evidence relating to sexual matters; evidence of prostitution or association with prostitutes; and evidence of previous sexual behaviour which does not form part of the subject-matter of the charge.

Having established this general prohibition, the legislation then allows for a variety of situations, described as exceptions, in which the prohibitions will not operate. It can be argued that the effect of these exceptions, taken together, will defeat the purpose of the legislation. One crucial exception concerns the exclusion of evidence introduced by the Crown from the terms of the prohibition.

Our analysis of trial transcripts has indicated that there were occasions when the Crown sought to lead evidence about the complainer's character or sexual experiences. There are a number of reasons why the Crown might want to do this. One reason in the past might have been to forestall or head off more rigorous questioning on these issues by the defence. With the new legislation there is unlikely to be the same need for the prosecution to act in this way since the admission of defence evidence should be more highly controlled than in the past. But there were also occasions when evidence of sexual experience (or more often inexperience or virginity) was used by the Crown merely to boost the moral credit of the complainer by depicting her as virtuous and innocent. In such trials the prosecutor seeks to prove his case not by reference to the circumstances of the incident itself but by wooing the jury with protestations of morality. The inclusion of evidence led by the Crown in the general prohibition would lessen the likelihood of the jury making judgements derived from character assessments and focus attention instead on the facts of the case.

More worrying, however, is the exception to the prohibition that, should the Crown itself introduce 'prohibited' evidence, the defence will then be entitled to introduce contrary evidence in order to rebut or contest character or sexual history evidence introduced by the prosecutor. This could lead to allegation and counter-allegation about previous sexual experience and character which bears only remotely or not at all on the facts at issue. In order to prevent such a possibility of irrelevant evidence being introduced by the defence through the back door, it would again have seemed wiser to have brought Crown evidence within the general scope of the prohibition.

Another important exception to the general prohibition which calls into question the effectiveness of the legislation is the discretion given to judges to allow in otherwise prohibited evidence when 'it would be contrary to the interests of justice' to exclude the questioning or evidence referred to in the various categories of the prohibition. This catch-all exception clause reflects the Scottish Law Commission's concern that the general prohibition would be inappropriate in some cases 'of a kind which cannot be accurately predicted' (Scottish Law Commission 1983: para 5.17). Defence counsel are therefore to be given the right to apply to the judge for a decision to set aside the prohibitions on character and sexual history evidence 'in the interests of justice'.

What might be the likely outcome of investing in judges discretionary powers to allow in prohibited evidence? Research conducted by Adler (1982) on the operation of similar discretionary legislation in England and Wales (s. 2 of the 1976 Sexual Offences (Amendment) Act) showed that in 75 per cent of the contested rape trials where there had been an application by the defence to admit character evidence, the judge had in fact ruled to admit. She claimed, moreover, to have found widely varying judicial interpretations of the concept of 'fairness' as enshrined in section 2. Adler has come to the conclusion that giving a broad discretion to judges works against achieving a reduction in the use of sexual-history evidence because it gives scope to their personal attitudes and biases. It would seem, therefore, that the absence from the Scottish legislation of guidelines for judges as to what constitutes 'in the interests of justice' could be a major factor in undermining the progressive intentions of the legislators.

Temkin has arrived at a similar conclusion and has argued that 'rather than giving a general discretion', the cases which the Law Commission cite as being considered for eligibility under this exception 'should to some extent be dealt with by specific exceptions to the rules of exclusion' (1984: 635). In her view the interests of justice principle could be used by the defence to attempt to introduce sexual-history evidence into almost any case. She writes,

> no major improvement in the present practice of the courts is likely to result from instructing the judges that they must admit sexual history evidence in a range of situations and may do so in others. On the contrary the proposed statute will give carte blanche to those judges who believe in admitting sexual history evidence and may remove the compunctions of those who now feel that the common law constrains them from doing so.

> (Temkin 1984: 649)

The findings of Adler and Temkin and our own conclusion that consideration of character and sexual-history evidence is so entrenched in case decision-making throughout the criminal justice system that its importance cannot merely be legislated out of existence, cast doubt on claims made by legislators that the new Act will in practice make the trial less of an ordeal for women.

The trial is in many ways only the end-point of a lengthy process of case assessment, evidence-gathering and decision-making by uniformed police officers, detectives, prosecutors, doctors and other medical experts. There will have been many rehearsals of the arguments prior to a case reaching a trial and, as we have seen, many cases will have fallen at earlier hurdles. Strictly defined laws of evidence which prohibit the introduction of irrelevant evidence will have an impact on the conduct of the trial if enforced and if judicial discretion is not given free rein. What is more difficult to influence is private decision-making at earlier stages where similar criteria operate in making decisions about case progress and prosecutability. What rules, if any, apply to these earlier stages of decision-making? And how is it possible to ensure that only relevant factors are taken into account?

We noted earlier that the Scottish Law Commission had come to the conclusion that the common law rules of evidence which governed the admissibility of evidence prior to the new Act had not been adhered to. The commission itself did not seek to understand why the rules had not been followed in the past, although it could be argued that such an understanding would be essential to an assessment of whether or not the new rules are likely to have any impact or whether they would merely be ignored in the same way as the previous ones. Presumably one reason for the re-examination of the state of the law by the commission was a certain amount of uncertainty among legal practitioners as to what the rules actually were. This would of course in part be an explanation of why they were not being followed.

It also seems likely however that the rules were not being followed because consideration of 'extra-legal' factors had become such an important and normal part of pre-trial decision-making. Our own analysis of prosecution decision-making suggests two things: first, it had come to be expected by the prosecutor that illegal tactics would be employed by the defence and that nothing much could be done about this; second, in their own assessments of prosecutability and of the chances of success there was a great deal of consideration given to 'extra-legal' in addition to purely legalistic criteria. We can illustrate this latter point through a brief depiction of how prosecution decisions were taken.

The prevalence of commonsense as opposed to technical or legalistic reasoning in decision-making deserves comment [see Anne Worrall, ch. 7 below]. The very organisation of decision-making within the prosecutor's office reflects the importance of lay or common sense as opposed to legal or technical reasoning. A vast amount of the day-to-day case preparation in serious as well as routine cases is carried out by unqualified lay staff without any legal training. Our point here is not to suggest that such work is therefore carried out with less efficiency or dedication than if it were done by legally qualified staff, but rather to highlight the attributes of this lay reasoning.

What then are some of these attributes? First, the lay staff, known in Scotland as precognition officers, have the advantage over the legally qualified procurator fiscals who will be involved in the case if it comes to court, of face-to-face contact with witnesses in the case. An important part of the job is character assessment and making judgements about the sort of people prosecution witnesses are and how they are likely to perform if the case comes to trial. The conclusions of the precognition officer about the merits of a case and the credibility of witnesses are therefore treated with a good deal of respect by the legally qualified staff in the procurator fiscal's office. Indeed, on occasions we came across differences of opinion between lay staff and legal staff about how a case should be dealt with, and we observed that both sets of views went to Crown counsel, the next level in serious cases, for a decision. For example, in one case of rape there was an obvious contrast between the conclusions arrived at by the lay precognition officer based on face-to-face interaction with the complainer, and the more legalistic assessment of an assistant procurator fiscal. First, there was the precognition officer's assessment:

> At precognition the complainer conducted herself very coolly and was not in the least nervous. She is very unwilling for the matter to be taken further and went so far as to say that, although she did not wish the accused to do what they did, she did not want them to get into trouble because of it. It is a matter of opinion that had the relatives not taken some action the matter would never have been reported.
>
> A charge of rape would not prove, and in view of the complainer's attitude regarding further proceedings it is respectfully suggested that there should be no further proceedings in this case.

And then there was the assessment of an assistant procurator fiscal:

> Despite the Precognition Officer's recommendation, I respectfully recommend that the accused be prosecuted on a charge of rape. There is clear evidence from the complainer that she was forced to have sexual intercourse, and this is corroborated by the witness. The witnesses C and D also corroborate to some extent.

In fact, Crown counsel decided to mark the case 'no proceedings', perhaps because the attitude of the complainer towards prosecution outweighed other considerations such as the apparent sufficiency of corroborating evidence.

Secondly, the use of lay staff deploying a commonsense as opposed to legalistic discourse permitted an understanding of the actions of both the complainer and the accused from a moral point of view. This discourse allowed the prosecutor to apportion blame and responsibility to the various parties in the incident. The following excerpt shows how, in summing up the evidence in a rape case, the precognition officer provides for the apportionment of blame by describing the incident in moral terms:

> The first problem is the obvious one; there is a girl of 20, admittedly sexually experienced, accompanying a man into a lane in Glasgow City Centre between 1 and 2 am and there has sexual intercourse with him. There is a presumption against rape; the obvious defence is one of consent.

This particular conception of the incident allows moral blame to be awarded to the complainer thus arriving at the 'presumption against rape'. In this incident the complainer is characterised as 'precipitating' the incident by going off on her own with a man late at night. Simplifying the incident in this way means that many facts about the case are obscured or omitted in order to achieve moral clarity. These other facts will of course be available in the case papers and will have been discussed by the precognoscing officer in making a report to Crown counsel. They will however be sacrificed in order to arrive at a workable conclusion. These omissions included, for example, the fact that it wasn't an anonymous man that the complainer went off with but a man in whose company she had spent most of the evening, thus allowing a relationship of trust to develop. Obscured, too, is what actually happened 'up the lane', since the description 'there has sexual intercourse with him' could not have been the complainer's version of events.

We would say that, in making decisions about prosecutability, character assessments played as important a role as assessments of the strengths and weaknesses of the factual evidence marshalled by the prosecution. An example of the importance of character assessment is given in the following quotation from prosecution case papers. It can be seen that the writer is clearly of the view that the antecedents of the case rather than what actually happened during the incident will make the case a very difficult one to prove. We have underlined certain words in order to highlight the judgemental phraseology.

> It will emerge from the complainer's evidence that the complainer is a 20 year old *unmarried mother* with a child 3 years old, that she was having *regular sexual intercourse with her boyfriend who* at the time of the alleged incident *was in prison* and who had the very evening before the events complained of *had a chance sexual encounter with an ex-boyfriend.* It will also emerge that on the day in question she and a friend *spent the entire afternoon and the early part of the evening in a public house where they consumed a considerable amount of Super Lager and vodka* and that *she and her friend took the initiative* and joined the accused and his friend when they came into that public house. It would also appear that the complainer *quite willingly left the public house in the company of the accused.* All things considered there is much grist for the defence mill.

In our view the introduction of the legislation we have discussed above is unlikely to have a dramatic impact either on the willingness of victims to report offences to the police or an effect on making a sexual-assault trial significantly less traumatic.

First, we have drawn attention to weaknesses in the legislation itself, notably in the failure to include prosecution evidence within its ambit and in the discretion given to judges to allow in prohibited evidence. Second, we have considered how sexual-history and character evidence will probably continue to be important at the pre-trial stage of prosecution decision-making. Prosecutors will be able to justify continuing to gather and assess such evidence because of the possibility of it being considered legitimate defence evidence by the judge. This may well mean that the complainer in sexual-assault cases will still have to endure questioning on these matters by the prosecutor and possibly also by the police[10] even before the trial gets underway.

The weaknesses in the legislation are unlikely to promote the necessary changes in consciousness and ways of thinking which would undermine the presumptions automatically linking sexual behaviour with credibility. Without this change in consciousness prosecutors are unlikely to show any enthusiasm for objecting to irrelevant defence questioning. Indeed, they may even fail to recognise illegal questioning when it is pursued by the defence. At present the prosecutor's case is often undermined and demoralised by passive acceptance of what is pessimistically perceived as the inevitable impact on a jury of defence attacks on the woman's credibility.[11]

A third reason for expressing scepticism about the likely effects of the legislation on the actual conduct of trials derives from our conclusion that much of the anxiety and distress suffered by women at trial is due to pernicious and prurient lines of questioning (for the most part coming from the defence) which make no attempt to introduce factual evidence but which would appear to be mainly tactical attempts to humiliate or degrade the complainer with a view to spoiling the prosecution case. None of these tactics are covered by existing legislation in either the English or Scottish system.

Notes

1. For example, the decision of Judge Bertrand Richards at Ipswich Crown Court to sentence a man convicted of rape to a fine of £2,000 on the grounds that the victim was guilty of 'contributory negligence' (*Guardian* 6 January 1982).
2. Sections 166 and 169 (1)a of the Criminal Procedure (Scotland) Act 1975 allows for the exclusion of the public from the court during evidence by children/young persons under the age of 17 years. But, there is no Scottish provision to protect the anonymity of the complainer in a sexual-assault trial similar to that afforded by section 4 of the Sexual Offences (Amendment) Act 1976 in England and Wales. There exists an informal arrangement whereby the court is cleared of the general public during the period of the trial when the complainer gives her evidence. The press, again by an informal agreement, are allowed to remain but are asked not to disclose the complainer's identity in any published reports. The Scottish Law Commission (1983: paras 5.30, 5.31) were of the opinion that these arrangements had worked satisfactorily and that there was no need to extend the statutory regulations in this area.
3. For the purposes of the research, serious sexual assault was defined as rape, attempted rape and what in Scotland is known as assault with intent to rape. Information was also collected on incidents of indecent assault, but that data is not presented here. For definitions of sexual-assault offences in Scotland, see Gordon (1978).
4. This research found that more than half the incidents studied happened outdoors, with the greatest number taking place in a park or other public open space. More than one-third took place in a private dwelling house with the greatest number of these recorded as happening in the complainer's own home (see Chambers and Millar 1983: 18).
5. In the case of *Meek and Others HMA* (1982 SCCR: 613), it was held that an honest belief in consent can be a defence to a charge of rape. This decision was based on similar grounds to that in *DPP v Morgan and Others* (1975: 61 Cr App R136).
6. 'Interviews with complainers revealed that there was no predictable emotional reaction as a consequence of being sexually assaulted: a calm exterior often masked internal turmoil and confusion, especially in situations where women were attacked by people who were known to them or whom they trusted, and in which feelings of guilt were inevitably present' (Chambers and Millar 1983: 90).
7. This view is still commonly held by the legal profession despite the view expressed by the Advisory Group on the Law of Rape that 'In contemporary society sexual relationships outside marriage, both steady and of a more casual character, are fairly widespread, and it seems now to be agreed that a woman's sexual experiences with partners of her own choice, are neither indicative of untruthfulness nor of the general

willingness to consent. There exists in our view, a gap between the assumptions underlying the law and those public views and attitudes which exist today which ought to influence today's law' (para. 131).

8. By the time of publication of our research the rules of evidence in trials of rape and other sexual offences had been reviewed by the Scottish Law Commission, and legislation has been passed which introduces changes to rules existing at the time of the study. See Law Reform (Miscellaneous Provisions) (Scotland) Act 1985, section 36.

9. See discussion of *Dickie* v *HMA* 1897: 337 in Scottish Law Commission (1983).

10. Guidelines on the investigation of sexual-assault cases were issued to police forces in Scotland by the Scottish Home and Health Department in November 1985. These state that 'there should in general be no need to elicit information about the complainer's previous sexual history, her morals or any sexual relationship which has no bearing on the subject-matter of the charge'. We would advocate the extension of these or similar guidelines to prosecutors.

11. As an example of the pessimistic attitude which often pervades the prosecution case, we cite the following example from the prosecutor's papers in a rape case: 'This is not a case which I regard with a great deal of hope of a conviction; in fact I doubt whether there is sufficient evidence to go to a jury, for the following reasons: (1) The complainer is clearly of doubtful character at least in matters sexual and her character would be open to attack. If her credibility were to be seriously damaged the whole case would fall apart'.

5

Rendering Them Harmless: The Professional Portrayal of Women Charged with Serious Violent Crimes

Hilary Allen

Marco Jones is dead.[1] A violent death – stabbed through the heart on a Saturday night in a fight over a fifty-pence debt. He was 24 years old, a father and a husband. He was always, his widow maintains, a faithful partner and a good provider. He was also the only man she ever loved. It is with his widow that the social-worker's report is primarily concerned. She is described in this report as a sensitive and tender person, physically frail and emotionally devastated by his death. The older of their children is just 2 years old; the younger still a babe at her breast. She does not know how she will face the future without him, or how she will ever find words to explain to her children what has happened. Even though she is now living in a caring and supportive hostel, she still feels utterly alone. The report recommends that she be given psychiatric counselling to help her through this period of bereavement, public assistance with her housing and finances, and the support of a social-worker to help her rebuild her shattered life. Two independent psychiatrists concur with this recommendation, as do each of the various officials who promptly agree to put the proposals into action. By all accounts, Marco's widow is a tragic and pitiful figure. Were it not for the fact that it is she who has thrust the fatal knife into his heart, and that the occasion for these reports is her formal trial for his homicide, these compassionate arrangements might seem entirely uncontroversial.

In its own context there is little that is unique and almost nothing that is particularly remarkable about this case. At the outset of the trial, the woman is an alleged murderer who has admitted killing her husband, and thus risks a sentence of life imprisonment. By the trial's conclusion, however (by which time the offence has been reconstituted as no more than manslaughter),[2] she appears as a helpless and pitiful victim, to whom society owes all manner of compensatory benefits. In the portrayal of women charged with serious violent crimes, such transformations are so recurrent to be almost standard. And they are transformations that are systematically reflected in the treatment that is actually meted out to these women by the courts. Successive Home Secretaries and numerous pronouncements by senior judges have emphasised the need for severe custodial sentences in cases of serious violence against the person (Thomas 1979), and in the case of male offenders this policy is routinely followed.[3] In the case of *women* convicted of such crimes, however, the commonest practice is to impose non-custodial sentences, and in the severest cases – notably those involving homicide – it is common for such sentences to be accompanied by quite elaborate arrangements for medical and social support.

This chapter is concerned with the terms whereby this transformation is achieved and sustained. It takes as its material the depiction of female offenders and their offences in court reports by psychiatrists and probation officers.[4] And it illustrates the various ways in which, during the deliberations as to the proper disposal of these cases, the meanings attributed to both offenders and offences are typically manipulated, modified and reconstructed. As I shall illustrate in the main body of the discussion, professional reports can provide the court with an alternative 'frame' for the judgment of criminal cases. Like the concluding speech in mitigation (Shapland 1981), they are outside the restrictive discourse of the formal trial. As such they are free not only to introduce many considerations that would properly be excluded from the trial itself, but also to provide an alternative (and sometimes ironic or contradictory) perspective on the very issues of action and responsibility that the trial has in principle resolved.

The central assertion of this chapter is that within these reports the portrayal of female violence follows a distinct and sexually specific pattern which tends towards the exoneration of the offender and deploys discursive manoeuvres that are either absent or untypical in cases involving males. Against the bald facts of the criminal allegation or conviction, these reports counterpose a subtler and more compromising version of the case, which systematically neutralises the assertion of the woman's guilt, responsibility and dangerousness, and thus undercuts any demand for punitive or custodial sanctions. As I discuss in the final section, such treatment of violent female offenders is somewhat uncomfortable to feminist analysis. On one hand, the notions of female subjectivity that underpin this treatment are in many ways offensive to feminism; on the other hand, they sustain a logic of denial and exculpation of female crime which many feminist discussions are also engaged in promoting.

The Suppression of the Crime

Given that the occasion for the professional report is a prosecution or conviction for a serious criminal offence, it goes without saying that the unpleasant 'facts' of the case will be amply present to the court. The initial baldness of those facts may be illustrated by such documents as the offence summaries that are appended to the official court records of each case.[5] The following is a typical example:

> Victim drinking with girlfriend in pub. At closing time his jealous ex-wife comes over and stabs him in the back with knife. Defendant admits and tells police she had wanted to kill him. Victim in intensive care for 9 weeks; continuing invalid.
> (Court file, defendant charged with attempted murder.)

In suggesting that the reports on female cases may function to suppress or erase such 'facts', I am not suggesting that they typically engage in any material *dispute* with them. On the contrary, by the time the report is prepared, it is rare for the material facts to be a matter of any argument, and indeed it is common for the report to include a brief description of the commission of the crime. What these accounts typically achieve, however, is a suppression or erasure of a rather subtler kind: they acknowledge the trajectory of objects in space – the knife in the hand, the thrust of the blade into the heart – but progressively delete from that trajectory all that would mark it as an action by an intentional and culpable subject.

An important component of this suppression is the routine problematisation of the psychological aspects of female cases. Reports on female offenders almost invariably address themselves to the issue of the mental state of their subjects, and throughout these reports the discussion of both the offence and the appropriate judicial response to it is interwoven with complex observations about the female offender's mentality and inner experiences. Overall, an average of 20 per cent of the total length of reports on female offenders is occupied by statements which in some way refer to the subject's psychology (Allen 1986). This is in sharp contrast to reports on male offenders, which instead tend to focus on the more external and material aspects of the offender's behaviour, biography and life-style. Quantitatively, psychological statements occur only half as frequently in reports on males; qualitatively, such psychological observations as *are* made about male offenders tend to be perfunctory and formulaic. The following, for example, is an extract from a psychiatric report on a man who has clubbed and hacked to death a casual friend, stolen his electric kettle and a shopping bag, and then set fire to the body. The major part of the report, as is typical in male cases, has confined itself to the flat recounting of the external details of the offender's history and behaviour. The following is all that the psychiatrist has to say about the psychological background to the offence:

> The defendant is of average intelligence. I could elicit no evidence of mental disorder and he is fit to plead. He had consumed a good deal of alcohol on the day of the alleged offence, but he was an habitual drinker and there is no evidence of psychosis.
> (Psychiatric report, male accused of murder and arson)

Such desultory observations make no attempt to mitigate the material meanings of the offence, and suggest no particular reason for the offender's moral exoneration. By contrast, the attention to psychological questions which is typical of female cases allows both material and moral significances to be systematically reconstructed. Most conspicuously, the psychologisation of the case allows the question of the criminal intentions of the female offender (even if formally undisputed for the purpose of the conviction) to be reinvoked at the point of sentencing – and to be reinvoked in terms which both displace the material significance of the offence and attenuate the offender's moral responsibility for it.

The manoeuvre depends upon undercutting the formal acknowledgment of the offender's action with the assertion that at the moment of the deed she was acting without conscious volition, without comprehension or without meaning. In a few cases (as, for example, in the well-publicised cases involving pre-menstrual tension), sophisticated medical explanations are given for this curious state of mind (Allen 1984). More commonly, however, no such explication seems to be regarded as necessary; instead, there is a simple denial of the woman's mental engagement with her behaviour, as if such an unreasoning and unreasonable condition were a quite natural state of womankind, for which no exceptional cause need be sought. Thus, in the case of a woman who has strangled and suffocated a girlfriend in the course of an argument (and who is not assessed as in any way mentally ill), we are suddenly informed,

> It may well be that she was not aware that by putting a plastic bag over [the victim's] head and tying a flex around her neck that she was thereby killing her.
> (Psychiatric report, female accused of murder)

Of another, who has stabbed her common-law husband through the heart, again in the course of an argument, we are told,

> Whatever happened on the night in question causing the death of [the victim] I do not believe that [the defendant] acted with any intent to cause him harm.
> (Psychiatric report, female accused of murder)

At the very moment where these narratives seem most to require a definitive moral subject, as the responsible author of the crime, these women's status as such subjects is emphatically revoked. The psychological commentary presents them as not intending the deed, as not knowing or understanding that they are committing it, as experiencing nothing in relation to it. The following narrative expresses these ideas more explicitly and at more length. It is drawn from a psychiatric report on a woman who has gone to her lover's house, fought with his wife and killed her, then started a fire which has killed his two children.

> Olive remembers the early parts of the fight except that she does not remember having her hair pulled out. Her mind is then quite blank until she realised that Jenny had stopped fighting and was seriously wounded. This fact can easily be explained by Olive becoming totally involved in the battle and oblivious to everything around her. She was brought back to her senses, she states, by the sound of one of the children crying. She noticed that a fire had been started in the room, but does not remember starting it. In a daze she fed the child and left the house ... Her lack of memory for the events can be explained by her natural defences in protecting herself. I do not

think it at all likely that she planned to commit this crime. The crime, in all probability, developed from the original fight, and the tragic events which followed were caused by the defendant's dissociation from her own feelings, so that she was in an emotionless trance and unable to appreciate what she had done or take steps to prevent a further tragedy from occurring. At this point she could not make responsible decisions. This too was her natural defence against extreme stress. It is a well-known and typical hysterical reaction.

(Psychiatric report, woman charged with murder, manslaughter and arson).

At the heart of the crime we are offered a characteristic series of mental disjunctions, absences, dissociations. The woman is oblivious to everything around her, does not perceive even the injuries she is causing and sustaining. She is not 'in her senses', does not understand or recognise the work of her own hands. She is in a daze, dissociated, cannot appreciate what she has done. Across the whole drama there is an absence of intention, of will, of responsibility for action. The crime 'develops', the 'tragic events' 'follow', she can do nothing 'to prevent a further tragedy from occurring'.

The initial psychologisation of female behaviour thus provides the conditions for a further characteristic manoeuvre – that of the *naturalisation* of the crime. Through the suppression or denial of criminal intention, the violent deed which provides the occasion for judgment is progressively erased or redefined. Having first been displaced from a domain of *culpable* human actions, for which the subject can be held morally responsible, the crime may then, by extension, come to be displaced from the domain of human actions altogether. Instead, it is rewritten as a mere event in nature, a natural disaster in whose devastation the offender has simply been swept away, without either volition or responsibility. Conspicuously, this naturalisation of female crime will have the effect of blunting whatever moral discredit would otherwise attach to its author, and will thereby reduce the apparent need for any punitive sanction against her. And in the more extreme cases, it may even allow the offence to enter the moral calculus paradoxically. Instead of counting *against* the offender, as a morally reprehensible action for which she must be punished, the 'tragic event' of the crime may actually come to be added to the sum of her involuntary and undeserved troubles, for which, if anything, she deserves public compensation. This tendency is strikingly illustrated in the following case. The defendant's lodger has irritated her by refusing to turn off the television and come for his supper. In response she has killed him, by tossing a gallon of paraffin over him in his chair, followed by a lighted match.

It would be hard to over-estimate the effect which these events have had upon her. She is naturally, I think, a somewhat nervous and anxious person, and at times has felt quite overwhelmed by her feelings of guilt. As she has told me her history, I have felt the stage being set for this tragedy by her parents. Unloved and repressed by them, she has found herself in relationships which seem to have reinforced her feelings of worthlessness and uselessness. From her description the victim appears to have been a violent borderline alcoholic, and for much of her life she seems to have been the one who has been put upon and generally exploited, until this violent retaliation took place.

(Social inquiry report, woman charged with murder)

The terms of this presentation interrupt the attribution of personal blame. The woman has not *formed* the difficult relationship with her lodger but merely 'found herself' in it. She is not the author of her unsatisfactory life and circumstances but simply the puppet of others who have 'set the stage' for her 'tragedy'. And even the crime itself is not an act that she has perpetrated but only a series of 'events' and a 'retaliation' that has 'taken place'. The loss of the victim's life, under conditions of unthinkable suffering, seems morally incidental to this scenario and is accorded no place in the calculation of the offender's due desserts. Instead this calculation focuses only on the woman's own suffering, of which these events are significant only as symptom or cause.

Damage and Dangerousness

The same discursive manoeuvres that thus neutralise the demands for a *punitive* custodial sentences may also serve to neutralise the demands for a *protective or preventive* one. To the extent that these reports tend to obscure the past and current violence of the offender, they often allow any question of her *future* dangerousness to be simply passed over, as of no pertinence. In reports of violent males, the need for public protection is almost always taken seriously, and any recommendation of a non-custodial sentence is a matter that will require explicit justification. In female cases, on the other hand, the possibility that the offender may pose a continuing threat to those around her is seldom even addressed, and a recommendation of a non-custodial sentence is treated as unremarkable. The following, for example, is drawn from a report on a young woman with a long criminal record, now convicted of causing actual bodily harm:

> [Whilst in a unit for difficult adolescents] Gail was destructive, obstructive, aggressive, malevolent. She stole, absconded, bullied and in general absorbed an enormous amount of attention and had to be supervised constantly. Her mother died in 1971, when Gail's behaviour began to deteriorate. The violence she had shown within the Unit was extended to people outside, and there are 4 recorded examples of attacks on girls in the local area. Following these incidents it was decided that she could only leave the Unit with an adult. This did not prevent her hitting two other girls. She . . . attacked her sister's 9 year old son who narrowly escaped serious eye injury. She totally lacked remorse when she hurt anyone . . .
> [Over the next 3 years] her violent behaviour continued and in 1975 she is reported to have attacked her social worker, pulling her hair out and kicking her. Later that year outbursts of violence at her lodgings led to her emegency admission to LM Hospital, as the Social Services had nowhere for her to go. A month later she was charged with assault . . . and she was remanded to T Remand Centre. A week later she is reported to have attacked 2 members of staff and was charged with assault. Later that year she appeared before S Court and was convicted of wounding.
> (Psychiatric report, woman convicted of causing actual bodily harm.)

After such a catalogue of nastiness (which continues unabated through several more episodes of attacks and woundings), one might suppose that the dangerousness of this offender could hardly be ignored. When we arrive at the summary of the case, however, these uncomfortable details seem suddenly to evaporate:

> When interviewed she gave a background history somewhat at variance with our documents and there was an understandable tendency for confabulation and retrospective adjustment. None the less, the essential ingredients of her past life story remain unchanged, with a clear evocation of severe parental deprivation, inconsistent handling, in multiplicity of institutions, a gravitation towards petty criminality, release being sought in drug taking, impulsive and irresponsible behaviour leading to victimisation by sexual predators and a frenetic search for comfort, security and affection. She has a determined and volatile personality, and her general background, taken in conjuction with the last 4 years of institutionalisation, have left her as a severely damaged personality. As the interview progressed, she became more animated, and one was able to detect the combination of profound insecurity and defiance. Eventually she was able to talk of her fundamental striving to find some kind of a father figure, her dislike of women and her need to be cared for in terms of security. Understandably her self-image was distorted, with considerable guilt and self-denigration. She aspired to a home, husband and children, and a conventional family life, but when questioned had little concept of how to achieve such a goal.
>
> (*ibid.*)

These 'essential ingredients of her past life' do not seem to include her persistent aggression towards everyone around her. What is emphasised instead are the various privations and unhappinesses which she has herself endured. Her violent behaviours now appear only non-specifically as a gravitation towards petty criminality and impulsive and irresponsible behaviour – and even these are only accorded significance to the extent that they led to her 'victimisation by sexual predators and a frenetic search for comfort, security and affection'. Similarly, her 'volatile and determined personality' is given significance not as the origin of her repeated acts of violence, but as evidence of the damage that she has suffered at the hands of others, and as a factor disguising her inner security and 'need to be cared for'. With the more concrete and less savoury aspects of her biography thus displaced, even the woman's (arguably quite appropriate) feelings of guilt and self-denigration can then be sympathetically pathologised as merely the product of a 'distorted self-image'. So this, accordingly, is the point where the report can invoke the orthopaedic image of all that this poor creature lacks and will ultimately aspire to: a conventional home, husband, children and family life.

In Her Own Place

This fantasy of the domestication of the violent female offender provides the final link in the process whereby she is discursively tamed, sanitised, rendered harmless. The invocation of the domestic and 'feminine' positions of these women serves two complementary purposes in these documents. First, as has been discussed by Krutschnitt (1982), it gestures towards a domain of alternative social controls, which may render the formal controls of judicial sanctions redundant. A typical example is that of a mentally disordered female offender who has repeatedly threatened to kill her husband and is now convicted of setting light to the family home with intent to endanger his life. Both medical and social inquiry reports agree that penal detention would be undesirable, as it might exacerbate her psychiatric condition. But they also maintain that even the *medical* detention of the offender is unnecessary, since she can be suitably contained within the family setting:

> I would not feel that her admission to [a secure hospital] is justified. For many years she seems to have coped reasonably well when living with her family and having out-patient treatment. She is not imminently dangerous to others at present and... I think she could be satisfactorily looked after in the community.
>
> (Psychiatric report, woman convicted of arson with intent to endanger life)

This assumption that the demands of public protection can be adequately met by placing a violent offender under familial supervision seems restricted almost exclusively to cases involving women. The sexual distinction is particularly clear in cases where the violence is directed at the offender's children. In cases of serious paternal violence, the protection of the children from further violence is often treated as an automatic priority, self-evidently justifying the removal of the offender through the imposition of a custodial sentence. In cases of maternal violence, by contrast, the possibility of further danger is rarely even raised, and instead, the 'home and family' continue to be constituted as the ideal site for the offender's containment and surveillance – an arrangement that pre-empts the demand for formal custodial detention.

A second and related effect of the invocation of home and family is to place the female offender in statuses which not only entail privileged responsibilities (that would be gravely disrupted by imprisoning her as a dangerous criminal), but which also seem fundamentally incompatible with the *perception* of her as a dangerous criminal. As is illustrated graphically in the following case, the activation of the woman's alternative statuses, as housewife, mother, and spouse, seem sometimes to undermine the very *possibility* of treating her as dangerous. In this case, the woman has been convicted of causing grievous bodily harm to her baby daughter, whom she has stabbed in the back. Ever since the birth the mother has shown hostility to the child and has been under close medical supervision, with a diagnosis of puerperal depression. What is being proposed in the report is that the woman should be briefly hospitalised as a voluntary patient in a local hospital, and should then be returned to her home under the general supervision of social-workers, visiting nurses and members of her family. This is essentially a continuation of the prior and existing regime of treatment, unmodified by the fact of the attack on the child or the subsequent criminal conviction.

> [From the birth onwards] Pamela Groves clearly constituted a serious risk to her child. My department was extremely concerned that Pamela might comit suicide or infanticide. Our obvious aim was to cement as much as possible the mother–child relationship from an early stage for the sakes of both Pamela and baby Emma, for we have always held the view that the depressive disorder would resolve itself in due

course and allow Pamela to return home to care for baby Emma and her husband. This is, indeed, what happened when she was eventually discharged. She continued to receive support from her husband, her mother, and a health visitor and from my community nurse colleague Mr Woods; also her medication continued through my out-patient clinic. Throughout the first half of that year she was leading a normal life, caring for her husband, child and home. In early August unfortunately she became depressed again.

[Following the attack] baby Emma, understandably, still shows some anxiety in the presence of her mother. Mr Groves understandably is under great stress, and although he is living in the family home, he is also showing evidence of excessive anxiety when faced with coping with his new job, his child in care and his wife mentally ill in hospital. Given this very difficult situation, it is obviously important to have a clear view of the future management. Firstly our aim here is to treat Mrs Groves. One would usually then expect her to return home to care again for her family. It is still important that she should be able to reestablish her relationship with her child. It is equally important for the child that this should occur...

Now that Mrs Groves has suffered from at least two severe episodes of psychotic depression, then the risk that she may suffer in the future must be higher than for the average woman. I believe that the risks to Emma will be minimal once the child can communicate clearly verbally, and in particular once she is attending school

(Psychiatric report, woman convicted of causing grievous bodily harm)

From a strictly criminological perspective, this report and its recommendations are really quite remarkable. Here is a subject who for more than a year has been officially regarded as likely to commit homicide. The officials responsible for her management have decided that she should none the less remain in constant and close proximity to her predicted victim, and they have knowingly arranged for her to do so in a situation where for the larger part of every day she will be alone with this person, who is utterly defenceless. Such social and medical measures as have been arranged in the hope of averting the risk have then manifestly failed: the subject has fulfilled the original expectation, by stabbing the predicted victim in the back. The offender is now judged liable to make further such attacks, and as likely to remain so for a period of years. Yet the officials concerned still insist that the desirable course of action is to restore the original situation where the offender will be alone with the (still helpless) victim and made responsible for her safety and well-being. This is regarded as the optimal situation for the offender, for the victim and for all concerned.

Although all these uncomfortable criminological details are present in the report, the coherence of its recommendations is nowhere founded on any construction of the woman as a violent and continuingly dangerous criminal. Instead, what grounds the coherence of the report is the apparently overriding construction of its subject *as a woman, as a mother and as a wife*. Home and family are her proper place. Looking after her husband and child is her normal life. Tenderness towards her family is her natural emotion. The possibility of disrupting this domestic idyll by the preventive detention of the offender is simply never raised – and the recommendations of the report are accepted without demurrer by the court.

Normal Lives

Throughout, the credibility and the coherence of these documents depends on their resonance with certain taken-for-granted images of female lives and subjectivity. In the insistence on the domestic statuses of these women, this appeal to the familiar and the 'normal' is relatively unambiguous. What my discussion may have obscured, however, is the degree of normalisation that is also involved in the other manoeuvres of these reports. In my attempt to expose these manoeuvres, I sought to construct a sense of their 'strangeness' – the strangeness of presenting their crimes as impersonal misfortunes rather than personal misdeeds; of claiming that even at the decisive moment of their crimes, these adult and averagely intelligent individuals were behaving without volition, intention, understanding or consciousness. But this sense of strangeness is exterior to the texts themselves. *Within* the texts, these portrayals are treated unproblematically, as if reflecting a taken-for-granted and uncontentious perspective on the everyday reality of female existence.

Thus the 'absence of agency' that characterises the description of women's crimes is not presented in these texts as any sudden or aberrant departure from their female normality: instead, it appears continuous with even the most unremarkable moments of their existence. In the brief biographies that routinely form part of these texts, it is not simply in relation to *crimes* that there appears a reluctance to describe these subjects as intentional or active: there appears a striking paucity of references to these women doing anything intentional *at all*. The lives of *male* offenders are regularly described in simple statements in the active voice, detailing the succession of things that the offender has 'done' in his life. By contrast, the description of women's lives is everywhere hedged about with circumlocutions and grammatical inversions that constantly obscure the subjects' active responsibility and agency.[6] There is a conspicuous concern with the women's emotional responses to the material events of their lives, but little expectation that they will normally be the active authors of these events – and every readiness to conclude that they are *not*.

Rather similarly, the frequent suggestion of mental irresponsibility in relation to the commission of the crime is rarely treated as indicating an *abberation* from female normality, and at times seems to be taken as virtually *evidence* of such normality. Earlier on, for example, I discussed a case in which the offender has killed her lover's wife in a fight, and has then caused the death of his children by setting light to his house. She is described as doing so in a state of dissociation, amnesia, emotionless trance, unconsciousness of her actions and unawareness of their consequences. Even in the course of this account, this state of mind is referred to as a 'natural' and 'easily explainable' one, and as a 'well-known and typical' reaction. These hints, however, only lightly prefigure the striking statement of normality with which the report concludes:

> A pleasant straightforward girl... Open with good social skills and normal
> emotions. I could detect no sign of any mental illness or any abnormal thought

process [and she] could not be described as having a personality disorder ... *She is a perfectly normal young woman in every respect.*
    (*Psychiatric Report, woman accused of murder, manslaughter and arson; emphasis added*)

Passing Judgments

From a feminist perspective it is easy to take objection to such a conception of perfectly normal young womanhood. The image of the female sex as passive, ineffectual, unstable and irresponsible is a familiar target for criticism by feminists, as indeed is the expectation that women's social and legal existence will be governed by the restraints of domesticity and the family. Feminist analyses of the law have long recognised that the privileges and exemptions that such conceptions may allow are bought at the expense of making legal invalids of women, of excluding them from their full status as legal subjects, and of perpetuating their social and legal subordination (Edwards 1985). And in the specific field of criminal justice, feminist authors have been uniformly suspicious of the judicial 'lenience' towards female offenders which such conceptions of female incapacity can help to sustain (Anderson 1976).

On one hand, this judicial lenience can be theorised as merely compounding the initial invalidation of women's action and responsibility. The imposition of a modest or nugatory sentence, as is common in cases of violence by women, carries the public implication that the crime itself need not be taken particularly seriously. From this perspective, the lenient sentencing of violent women can be interpreted as a more or less calculated tactic of patriarchal oppression, whereby the potential power of women's action can be censored from public recognition, and the politically sedative myth of women's compliance and harmlessness can be conveniently preserved (e.g. Squire 1981). On the other hand, the accompanying preference for 'rehabilitation' of deviant women routinely involves the reinforcement of conventional sexist expectations about the 'proper' domains of feminine activity (Rowett and Vaughan 1981: 149; Rafter and Natalizia 1981; and often implies no more than the women's supervised attachment or reattachment to the informal controls of the family (Krutschnitt, 1982). From a radical perspective, any apparent gains of this approach may be dismissed as illusory: they are won only by exchanging overt coercion for a 'privileged' and 'voluntary' submission to patriarchal authority, which neither relieves women from the normal constraints of sexual oppression, nor removes the threat of explicitly coercive sanctions in the event of further dissidence.

At the level of a general critique of the law, such arguments and objections have an obvious appeal. They offer the possibility of countering any suggestion of female advantage in the operation of the law, and of assimilating the judicial treatment of female offenders to a uniform theory of women's oppression. But aside from the rhetoric and the overarching theories, there remains an obvious dilemma. The logical implication of objecting to the existing paternalism is that these violent women – reconstituted in the full dignity of responsibility, culpability and dangerousness – should be exposed to the full rigours of penal sanctions. In short, they should be punished, and in serious cases they should (as is typical with males) be imprisoned for a very long time. This is not a position that feminists find easy to espouse.

The dilemma exemplifies the fallacy of assuming that women's interests can in principle be treated as homogeneous and universal. In a general sense, the kinds of portrayal of women that I have discussed in this text may quite easily be theorised as 'contrary to women's interests'. Certainly, they reproduce and elaborate a number of unwelcome conceptions of femininity, and in relation to a 'general' field of women's interests one may reasonably object to the pattern of differential treatment of women that such conceptions underpin. But at a lower level of analysis, and in relation to the particular women concerned, the avoidance or reduction of punitive sanctions cannot easily be seen as anything but advantageous – and if the activation of these otherwise problematic notions of femininity can be of advantage to particular women, then it may seem unduly puritanical to allow generalised ideological scruples to rule them out of court.

A conspicuous feature of feminist discussions that focus directly on the interests of female offenders is thus their tendency to reproduce rather than challenge the manoeuvres that I have discussed in this chapter. In some cases this reproduction is self-conscious and more or less cynical: without ignoring the darker side of such portrayals, it is quite possible to urge their calculated exploitation, as offering both a limited opportunity for particular women to avoid the full rigours of punishment, and a point of leverage from which the general bias *against* women may to some small extent be redressed (e.g. Luckhaus 1985).

Perhaps more interesting, however, are those feminist discussions where the reproduction of these tactics is more uncritical and wholehearted. Feminist analyses are often just as ready as the reports discussed above to deny the responsibility, culpability and even the agency of female offenders, and even where the political valency of these arguments is very different from those of the court reports, their content and structure are often much the same. Thus, for example, feminist discussions are often quick to invoke the notion that the individual female offender is not herself the true agent of the offence, or at least is not to blame for it. Much like the court reports, feminist discussions are often ready to explain female offending by reference to social or economic forces, or to attribute it to the oppressive domestic and familial situations in which these women involuntarily 'find themselves' (Leonard 1982; Rafter and Natalizia 1981). Likewise, certain feminist discussions participate in the 'normalisation' of the female criminal – refusing any notion of the female criminal as in any way more irresponsible or anti-social than other women, and instead asserting that 'any woman' might react with such behaviour in comparable circumstances. Feminist arguments may also parallel the court reports in the priority they accord to the maternal roles of women offenders (Haley 1980), and in extreme cases there is the implication that a mother's right to look after her children should be given almost automatic priority over her responsibility to the law, and that the imprisonment of mothers should therefore be avoided at all costs (Lockwood 1980).

Beneath all these arguments, feminist discussions share with the court reports the underlying predisposition to view criminal women as more victims than aggressors, more sinned against than sinning, more to be pitied than blamed. The positioning of female subjects as victims rather than aggressors is to some extent a structural characteristic of *all* feminist discourse, as is the refusal to allow female subjects to appear as morally guilty or personally discreditable. The maintenance of this reassuring and sympathetic perspective tends to motivate a rather selective attention to the field. In discussions of homicide, for example, the feminist literature routinely stresses those cases of battered women who finally resort to homicide after years of their own victimisation (Edwards 1985) – something of a veil tends to be drawn over those more uncomfortable cases where the victim is a child or another woman, or where the circumstances of the offence seem more unambiguously discreditable.

The woman who commits violent crime is a disturbing figure. She cuts across many of the expectations of the judicial system, and much of the idealism of feminism also. From either perspective it is therefore tempting to detach her from the unwelcome position of violent criminal and reposition her in some other less uncomfortable status. This repositioning is all the more attractive in that the statuses typically invoked will in many cases be quite 'correct'. The violent female offender may indeed be a victim of circumstances, of social or economic pressures, of violent men or violent emotions; she may indeed be much like other women, and have similarly pressing responsibilities in such feminine domains as motherhood and the family; she may indeed be a generally harmless creature who poses little threat outside the immediate – and perhaps exceptional – circumstances of a single crime. Furthermore, the recognition of these factors may quite genuinely enlighten many aspects of the case, and their acknowledgement is by no means necessarily oppressive or illegitimate. If anything, one might argue that there is greater oppression in the general exclusion of such considerations from the deliberations concerning males – who may also be subject to personal frailties, family pressures and external disadvantages, even though in male cases the prevailing images of criminality make it more difficult for such factors to be acceptably or effectively emphasised. The disturbing aspect of the professional depiction of female offenders is thus not that these alternative statuses are invoked *at all,* but that their invocation is so sexually specific, so deeply implicated in a general judicial sexism (of potential disadvantage to offenders of *either* sex), and so often deployed to pre-empt rather than enlighten the serious examination of criminal women's actions and responsibilities. For what *is* potentially oppressive to women – criminal or otherwise – is for the frailties and disadvantages that do tend to characterise their position in society to be treated as exhaustive of their condition as social or legal subjects. There is every reason for feminist analysis to retain an awareness of those personal vulnerabilities of criminal women that are so insistently portrayed in the professional reports. The delicate task is to do so without also following these reports into suppressing the recognition that these women can also – even at the very moment of their victimisation and coercion – be conscious, intentional, responsible, and potentially dangerous and culpable subjects of the law.

Notes

This discussion is based on findings from a research project funded by the Economic and Social Research Council (Allen 1986). I am grateful to the Lord Chancellor's Department, the Inner London Probation Service and the Metropolitan Police for their help in making available the documentary material.

1. All the illustrations discussed in this text relate to cases heard in English Crown courts during the last five years. In order to preserve confidentiality, all names have been changed, and personal details likely to identify the offenders have been omitted.
2. Under English law there are a number of circumstances in which an offence initially charged as murder can be reduced to that of manslaughter – namely, provocation, diminished responsibility and lack of 'specific intent' to cause 'really serious harm' to the victim. The last of these is the most commonly invoked, and is the ground for the reduction of the charge in the case under discussion here.
3. In male homicide cases, for example, custodial sentences are almost invariably imposed, and long custodial sentences are the rule rather than the exception. The probationary treatment that is often ordered in female cases of homicide is almost never adopted in male cases. See Home Office, *Criminal Statistics for England and Wales.*
4. Medical and social inquiry reports are not read out in open court, but form part of the confidential material available to the judge or magistrate at the point of sentencing. They are almost invariably prepared in cases of homicide, and are commonly sought in any case involving serious violence – especially where a female offender is involved. The assumption that these reports both reflect and contribute to the general construction of these cases is borne out by the high correlation between their recommendations and the final decisions of the court.
5. These summaries are prepared by clerks of court at the opening of the trial usually on the basis of information provided by the police.
6. A quaint example of such circumlocution is the comment with which a report on an elderly female tramp refers to the point in her early twenties when she first left home and took to the road: 'At this point an instability developed in her living situation'.

6

The Question of Bail: Magistrates' Responses to Applications for Bail on Behalf of Men and Women Defendants

Mary Eaton

It is inevitable that the legal system should invite questions about the nature of justice. Certainly, there appears to be a basic contradiction in the position of a state apparatus which promises justice but which is committed to the upholding of the status quo, that is a society divided by class, gender and racism. In this article I will explore this contradiction as it affects the reproduction of gender differences and the operation of sexism within the criminal justice system. I will argue that sexism is manifest not in overt disparities in the treatment of men and women but through the subtle reinforcement of gender roles in the discourse and practice of courtroom practitioners.

Sexism in the Courts

Traditionally, the issue of sexism within the courts has been addressed by comparing the sentences of men and women. Much of this work is flawed and limited. It is flawed because it usually does not effectively control for factors most relevant to the phenomena being compared (e.g. sentences). It is limited because if such factors are effectively controlled, the focus is then on a narrow range of women offenders – those whose situations can be compared with men. Most women and men differ in the type of offence with which they are charged and in the number of previous convictions with which they appear before the court. Furthermore, by concentrating on the end result, or the sentence, such work

Table 6.1 Offenders found guilty at all courts by sex and type of Offence in England and Wales 1983

Offence	Males		Females	
	Number (thousands)	Percentage	Number (thousands)	Percentage
Indictable Offences				
Violence against				
the person	47.4	92	4.0	8
Sexual offences	6.4	98	0.1	2
Burglary	70.3	97	2.4	3
Robbery	3.8	95	0.2	5
Theft and				
handling stolen				
goods	179.5	80	45.3	20
Fraud and forgery	20.1	79	5.5	21
Criminal damage	11.2	93	0.8	7
Other (excluding				
motoring)	30.0	90	3.4	10
Motoring	29.6	97	1.0	3
TOTAL	398.4	86	62.7	14
Summary Offences				
Offences				
(excluding				
motoring)	390.4	83	82.4	17
Motoring	1,053.7	91	108.1	9
TOTAL	1,444.1	88	190.4	12
All offences	1,842.4	88	253.1	12

Source: Home Office (1984a), Table 5.1.

neglects the process by which it is accomplished. Official statistics record the offences with which defendants are charged and the outcome of such proceedings, but such figures can be only a starting point for a sociological analysis of the processes which give rise to these figures.

From the official statistics we can see that, officially at least, men and women differ in their criminal involvements and in the punishments they receive.

Women form a small proportion of all known criminals (about 12 per cent in 1983), and their offences are concentrated within specific areas. Given the difference in recorded offences, it is not surprising to find that men and women

Table 6.2 Type of sentence or order given to offenders over 21 in England and Wales 1983

Sentence or order	Males Number (thousands)	Percentage	Females Number (thousands)	Percentage
Absolute or conditional discharge	18.4	9	8.6	21
Probation order	13.3	6	6.8	17
Fine	100.8	47	18.6	46
Community Service order	14.3	7	1.0	2
Imprisonment: Fully suspended	24.6	11	2.9	7
Partly suspended	3.5	2	0.3	1
Unsuspended	38.0	18	1.8	4
Otherwise	3.1	1	0.5	1
TOTAL	216.2	101*	40.5	99*

*Percentage figures do not sum to 100 as they have been rounded up or down to the nearest whole number.
Source: Home Office (1984a), Tables 7.11, 7.12.

differ in the sentences they receive. Most offenders are fined, but a higher proportion of men receive sentences of imprisonment, while a higher proportion of women receive probation and absolute or conditional discharges.

This difference in sentencing has led many writers to speculate on the apparent leniency of the courts towards women. Ignoring the differences in gravity of offences and previous convictions, much has been attributed to chivalry on the part of judges and magistrates. One extreme example of this approach is Otto Pollak's work. Taking official statistics at their face value he concluded:

> One of the outstanding concomitants of the existing inequality between the sexes is chivalry and the general protective attitude of man towards woman. . . . Men hate to accuse women . . . police officers dislike to arrest them, district attorneys to prosecute them, judges and juries to find them guilty, and so on.
>
> (Pollak 1950: 151)

Others have attempted a more systematic comparison and analysis. Among the most widely cited are the studies carried out by Nagel and Weitzman (1971) and Rita James Simon (1977). Both studies, conducted in the USA, claim to compare the sentences of men and women. Both studies acknowledge their failure to control for previous conviction and gravity of offence. Yet neither study allows that such factors may throw doubt on the findings of leniency towards women defendants. Nagel and Weitzman conclude:

> These findings seem consistent with how women are generally treated in American society. There exists a paternalistic protectiveness, at least towards white women, that assumes they need sheltering from manly experiences such as jail and from subjection to the unfriendliness of overly formal proceedings in criminal ... cases.
>
> (Nagel and Weitzman 1971: 180)

In the research which does control for offence and prior record, the apparent benefits to women disappear. Meda Chesney-Lind has reviewed such studies conducted in the USA (Green 1961; Rottman and Simon 1975; Pope 1975 – all cited in Chesney-Lind 1978). In the UK one study notable for the rigour of its approach is the Farrington and Morris work on magistrates' courts in Cambridge (Farrington and Morris 1983a). Using court records, Farrington and Morris examined nearly 400 cases, including 108 women, involving sentencing for theft between January and July 1979. Carefully controlling for gravity of offence and previous convictions, they found that the lighter sentences received by women were due to the different circumstances in which men and women appear before the court. They write:

> the sex of the defendant did not have any direct influence on the severity of the sentence or the probability of reconviction. Women appeared to receive more lenient sentences ... only because they had committed less serious offences and were less likely to have been convicted previously.
>
> (Farrington and Morris 1983a: 245)

However, while Farrington and Morris found no difference in the sentencing of men and women in similar circumstances, they did find a difference in the sentencing of married and unmarried women:

> Women who were in the 'other' category on marital status (predominantly divorced or separated rather than widowed) received relatively severe sentences, as did women from a deviant family background (coming from a broken home, usually).
>
> (*ibid.*)

Such findings are similar to those of Nagel who examined the processing of nearly 3,000 defendants (338 women) in New York State (Nagel 1981). Nagel found that

> marital status had no significant effect for males and a strong and significant effect for females – married females were considerably less likely than their unmarried female counterparts to spend any time imprisoned.
>
> (Nagel 1981: 113)

What begins to emerge from careful studies of the sentencing of men and women is the significance for the court of a woman defendant occupying a traditional role, that is being a married woman. This is a point to which I will return, after describing the case study which I carried out on a magistrates' court situated in a town on the edge of the Greater London area. The work was based on observation, interviews and document analysis.

The Case Study

The period of observation consisted of one or two mornings a week during 1980 and 1981. During that time I saw a total of 321 complete cases, involving 210 men and 111 women defendants.[1] Eight men and eight women appeared as co-defendants. Three of these couples were legally represented, and thirty-two of the other men and twenty-five of the other women were legally represented. Social inquiry reports were requested for thirty-seven of the men and thirty-five of the women. Applications for bail were made on behalf of five women and three men who are not included in the 'complete cases' seen.

It was unusual to find cases in which the defendants resembled each other in all respects but sex. Most of the men had previous convictions and most of the women were appearing for the first time. Family circumstances and disposable income were rarely similar for men and women, and this affected sentence. Fines are the most usual penalty, but many magistrates commented in interview on the difficulty of fining a woman with no disposable income. The women before them were usually responsible for the care and maintenance of children, supported either by social security benefits or by such small housekeeping allowances that to deduct any amount to pay a fine would be to deprive the children.

Magistrates frequently said that they responded to the circumstances of the cases and not the sex of the defendant, and my observations confirmed this. On the few occasions on which men and women appeared in similar circumstances, they received similar sentences. This applied to defendants appearing on separate charges and to those appearing as co-defendants on joint charges. In these cases the blame was not automatically ascribed to the man or the woman, usually both were recognised as equally culpable.

The majority of cases were treated in a routine manner (£10 fine for being drunk, between £15 and £40 for drunk and disorderly, £25 to £30 for possession of cannabis). Less routine matters gave rise to discussion among lawyers and magistrates with perhaps a contribution from a probation officer. Such discussions revealed something of the criteria by which decisions are reached. Here the importance of family circumstances, together with the offence and the previous convictions, was apparent. Contained in these discussions was a model of family life and appropriate gender-roles. This model is crucial to any understanding of the reproduction of gender differences by the court. Evidence of similar treatment for the few men and women who appear before the court in similar circumstances may satisfy the court's criteria of justice, but it has little to do with the way in which the subordinate role of women is reproduced by the processes of summary justice.

The reproduction of gender differences is a subtle process accomplished not by differential sentencing but by the routine processes of the court. To understand this it is necessary to go beyond those rare cases in which men and women appear in similar circumstances and consider the ways in which most men and women are presented to the court.

Summary Justice and Familial Ideology

The language of the courtroom both reflects and reinforces the prevailing picture of the social order. It contains and communicates the attitudes and assumptions of those involved in the social construction of justice. Elsewhere I have examined pleas of mitigation and social inquiry reports to discover what they reveal of the court's expectations concerning the behaviour of men and women. (Eaton 1983, 1985, 1986). Pleas of mitigation invoke a consensual social world in which the family is the basic unit, a privileged unit and the touchstone of normality. Those whose lives conform to this pattern can more easily refute the label 'criminal' since membership of a family is recognised to involve a degree of social control. However, while the conventional nuclear family – breadwinner husband and dependant wife responsible for child-care and domestic labour – may be used in pleas of mitigation made on behalf of both men and women, the allotted roles are different. The division of labour implicit in pleas of mitigation is endorsed in social inquiry reports – not only in what they say but also in the way they are constructed. When writing a report on a woman, the probation officer would visit her at home and incorporate a description of the home in the report. When writing a report on a man, the probation officer would, where possible, visit the home in order to talk to the wife (or cohabitee) and incorporate her comments into the report. The woman's caring role is expected to extend to mediating with outside agencies which intrude into the home.

The court's concern with the playing of an appropriate gender role within the context of the family corresponds to the findings noted in the research cited above. However, while Nagel (1981) and Farrington and Morris (1983a) have noted the significance of marital status in the sentencing of women, they advance no explanation beyond the suggestion that courts may 'disapprove' of women in unconventional roles. To fully understand the reasons for the court's approval of a conventional female gender role, one must appreciate the degree of social control which is involved in that role.

The traditional role of the married woman is that of an economic dependant with no financial resources of her own and with domestic responsibilities which tie her to the home. Those who work outside the home are usually employed in the poorest-paid sector of the labour market as part-time employees. Furthermore, such employment does not lighten their domestic responsibilities, and so they are left with even less time which is not occupied by the demands of home, husband and children. Recent feminist writings have analysed the degree of control to which women are subject within the home (Krutschnitt 1982; Heidensohn 1985). This control is most starkly demonstrated when one considers the court's response to applications for bail.

Bail or Custody?

All defendants in England and Wales appear before a local magistrates' court. For the majority (approximately 96 per cent), this is where their cases are heard and their fates decided. A minority are committed for trial to the Crown court. These defendants either choose trial by jury or are charged with matters which are considered too serious to be dealt with by the lower courts. Those who are committed for trial face a period of remand, and it is the magistrates who decide whether that period should be spent in custody or on bail. In England and Wales there is no limit to the time spent on remand; although the average in the London area was thirty weeks in 1983 (NACRO 1985a), some people experience a delay of between one and two years. (In Scotland there is a limit of 110 days.) Arguments for and against bail may be put forward by the police and by the defendant's legal representative. A person held in custody while awaiting trial is, according to legal rhetoric, presumed innocent. Since the imprisonment of an innocent person is contrary to natural justice, it is deemed permissible only in exceptional circumstances set out in the Bail Act 1976. Doherty and East (1985) describe these as follows:

> Where an offence is imprisonable, bail need not be granted if there are substantial grounds for believing that, if released on bail, a defendant would fail to surrender to custody, commit an offence, interfere with witnesses or otherwise obstruct the course of justice. Bail may also be refused for the protection of a defendant, or to ensure the welfare of a defendant who is a child or young person, or where a defendant is in custody in pursuance of the sentence of a court or of any authority acting under any of the Service Acts, or where the defendant has in relation to the proceedings absconded or breached bail conditions. Finally, bail may be refused where the court is satisfied that it has not been practicable to obtain sufficient information for the purpose of making such decisions, for want of time, since the institution of proceedings against the defendant.
>
> (Doherty and East 1985: 252)

Despite the apparent safeguards of the Act, many of those held in custody are subsequently given non-custodial sentences or are found 'not guilty'. In 1982, of the 52,606 prisoners held in custody, 36 per cent (19,464) were given non-custodial sentences, and 3 per cent (1,578) were acquitted (Peckham 1985: 240). The conditions endured by remand prisoners have been described elsewhere (King and Morgan 1976). Audrey Peckham gives a graphic account of her own experience in Pucklechurch (Peckham 1985). Noting that 62,871 people were held on remand in 1982 whe writes:

> I cannot understand why so many people are remanded in custody. Of the people with whom I spent my five months on remand, it seemed to me that very few represented any kind of threat to society. Most were either ill, or inadequate, or had made one mistake. I am not arguing for the abolition of remand centres. I understand that there are some criminals who do represent a threat and should be kept in custody. What I am saying is that the population of our remand centres could be

reduced today by between 50 and 70 per cent, without anyone being adversely
affected.

(Peckham 1985: 240)

This is clearly an area in which the discretion of the magistrates operates. It is at
such non-routine points in the criminal justice process that discussion takes place
and assumptions are revealed. What emerges from a consideration of the men and
women whose applications for bail I heard, was a concern with social control and
an implicit recognition of those social arrangements, family structures, which
offer effective control. The choice for the magistrates is between the formal
controls of the prison system and the informal controls of the community, or more
precisely, of the family.

The first case concerns someone with no family ties and therefore nothing to
offer for surety of good behaviour. Neil Brown (aged 24) was charged with the
theft of several items from local shops, valued at £55.45.[2] These included three
pairs of trousers, a purse, three toy cars and cosmetics. The police objected to bail
saying that they feared the defendant would continue to offend as he had had
twenty convictions in twenty-four years; they feared he might abscond, and the
defendant had previously committed offences while on bail. Furthermore, the
defendant had left prison only three days prior to this appearance in court. Neil
Brown was legally represented, and his lawyer told the court that his client feared
that if he was immediately returned to prison he would lose what little confidence
he had gained. The lawyer added that his client had found a room to rent and was
looking for work. Bail was refused.

A similar fate awaited Joan Smith (aged 18) who was also without family
commitments. She appeared on several charges of shoplifting. The first concerned
the theft of a dress and shirt valued at £20.99, the second a pair of trousers valued at
£17.99, the third a large amount of toiletries and cosmetics. The police applied for
a renewal in order to establish the full details of the case, and they opposed bail.
They described a violent struggle which had taken place when a shop assistant had
apprehended Joan Smith, who had then given the police a false name and address.
On learning her true name and address the police found that the room in which she
lived was full of goods and correspondence, which led them to believe that she had
ordered goods from mail-order companies and moved before paying for them.
This appeared to have occurred several times since she first came to London one
year previously. The police said that they believed she would fail to appear for
trial and would re-offend if given bail. In support of their argument they cited her
five previous offences of shoplifting, which had been committed in Derby, where
Joan Smith had lived with her parents. There was also an assault on a woman police
constable and the defendant was in breach of a supervision order.

The legal representative then told the court that he had been instructed to make
an application for bail on behalf of the defendant. By using this wording rather
than beginning to make the application, or saying that he wished to make an
application, the solicitor distanced himself from the procedure and seemed to
withhold his professional involvement – he was acting merely as a mouthpiece. He
then told the court:

Miss [Smith] is prepared to help police in finding receipts and witnesses to the purchase of the goods, and she could do this better on bail when she could contact the relevant people.

Bail was refused, and the magistrates gave the reasons:

she might fail to surrender to bail, we fear she might re-offend, and there is the nature and seriousness of the offence, her character, antecedents and community ties.

The second woman in my sample offers an interesting point of comparison with the women with domestic responsibilities who are considered later. In the case of Janet Bailey (aged 21) the local mental hospital does not promise the degree of control which in another case is attributed to the institution of marriage. Janet Bailey was charged with theft and burglary, that is with taking £21.50 from a church. She gave her address as a local mental hospital, but was, at the time of her appearance, in custody. Her case was to be further remanded for medical reports on her fitness to plead. The police objected to bail and told the court that the defendant had stated her intention of going to Ireland, and had offended while on bail for another matter.

In reply, her lawyer said that at the mental hospital Janet Bailey had been receiving treatment which was not available at Holloway. However, he added that there had been no change in her circumstances since she was last refused bail. Like the solicitor in the case of Janet Smith, he seemed to distance himself from the application;[3] he was almost inviting the magistrates to repeat an earlier decision. This they did. In both cases the lawyers were unable to present their client as an acceptable family member and were unable or unwilling to find other reasons why bail should not be refused. Their lack of commitment to their cases contrasts sharply with the enthusiasm manifested by the lawyers in the next two cases. In these cases there is reason to believe that re-offending, and interfering with the course of justice, might take place. However, the lawyers use the family circumstances not only to demonstrate their clients' fitness for bail, but also to reduce the seriousness of the offences which they describe as 'family disputes'.

Brenda Cartwright (aged 39) was charged with threatening to cause criminal damage, and of going equipped to cause criminal damage. The case was to be heard by the magistrates, but since the defendant was pleading 'not guilty' there was to be a remand for three weeks. The police opposed bail. An officer told the court that the defendant was accused of going to her mother's home where her daughter, aged 18, lived with her grandmother who had adopted her. At the home Brenda had, it was alleged, threatened to burn down the flat. The objection to bail was based on a fear that the defendant would interfere with witnesses as she had done in the past.

The solicitor representing Brenda asked the police officer what they thought she would do. The officer replied that in the past there had been threats to the daughter's life and health. The solicitor then told the court:

This whole matter is really a family feud which has come before the court from time to time. On some occasions allegations were proved, on some occasions not. A recent robbery with threats resulted in the money being returned and my client was co-operative with the police.

To this the police officer replied:

She recently visited her daughter's place of work and made threats. In the past bail was allowed because there were young children in the home. These children have now been placed in the care of the local authority.

As far as the police officer was concerned, in forfeiting her role as mother, Brenda forfeited her right to bail. Her lawyer argued that his client would not interfere with witnesses. In an attempt to re-establish her identity as a respectable family member, he argued that she was on good terms with her brother (i.e. an adult male who could be seen to have some control over her) and she would keep away from the others. Bail was granted on condition that the defendant did not go within 100 yards of her mother's block of flats, and that she contacted neither her mother nor her daughter.

The second case in which the family context was emphasised to reduce the gravity of the offence concerned Wayne Ross (aged 21). He had been charged with malicious wounding and held in custody since the incident two days earlier. The police told the court that the victim had withdrawn his complaint, but papers were with the police solicitors as the matter was serious. The victim was the defendant's brother-in-law and the police considered that pressure had already been brought to bear. They opposed bail because they feared interference with witnesses.

In the application for bail, Wayne's legal representative emphasised that this was a family dispute. He told the court, 'it came within the ambit of the family. . . . The defendant is not a danger to the public . . . both sides have cooled down now'. Bail was granted on condition that Wayne stay out of the area in which his brother-in-law lived. In both cases the family context of the offence was used to mitigate the gravity of serious assault and threatening behaviour. The expectation of the lawyers using these arguments is that what happens within a family will be viewed rather differently from similar occurrences between strangers. The assumption is that less official intervention is appropriate in family matters which are privileged by privacy. The confidence of the lawyers in making such pleas is well founded – the response of the magistrates is to endorse the privileged and private nature of the family.

If the family is privileged in matters of outside interference, it is because families are expected to police themselves – that is, to be responsible for the social control of the members, especially the structurally subordinate members, like women and children. The degree of control which is expected to reside in the conventional family structure is illustrated by the court's differing responses to the three defendants in the final case.

Eileen Boyle (aged 37), Denis Green (aged 30) and Joanne Day (aged 33) appeared as co-defendants on a charge of stealing eight garments valued at £472.60p from a department store, and of going equipped to steal. (They had some of the store's bags hidden about their persons.) Eileen Boyle had no previous convictions; Denis Green and Joanne Day had several previous convictions, and histories of offending while on bail. Since their arrest the previous day they had been held in custody. The case was to be committed to trial and the magistrates had to decide what to do with the defendants in the meantime.

A police officer told the court that the three had been seen acting in a suspicious manner. The store detective called the police. When the defendants left the store they were followed by the store detective, and a police officer, who saw them put the garments into a car. When arrested, one of the women, Joanne Day, gave several false names and addresses. The police asked for a remand for a week 'to sort out identity from fingerprint evidence'. There was no objection to bail for Eileen Boyle, although there was a request that she should report daily to her local police station. She was described as a single mother of four children who lived in a neighbouring district. The other two defendants were described as 'professionals' who had come some distance to shoplift on a large scale. There were objections to bail for both of these defendants. Speaking of Denis Green, the police officer said,

> His wife claims that he no longer lives at the address he gave us, and we could find no evidence, such as clothes, of his being there. There were only bills in his name.

Joanne Day was described as someone who had come from Birmingham to shoplift in the London area, and who had given numerous false names and stories to the police. At this point a man stood up in the court, identified himself as Joanne's husband and asked if he might speak. He was invited to take the stand. He then pleaded that his wife should not be kept in custody. He said that he could not cope without her and that she could not cope with custody as she was a nervous person, and he said that there were children to look after. The senior magistrate then asked how she looked after the children and was told that she was an excellent wife and mother. Her husband added that she probably lied because she was frightened that he would leave her if it happened agin. He admitted that he had threatened to, but said that he would not do so. He assured the court that his wife would not commit another offence and that she would come to court to face the charges. The magistrate asked if he had any money with which to stand surety, and he said that he had and he was willing to take the risk. The magistrate commented that 'Children place a different complexion on it'. Having conferred, the magistrates announced their decision. Denis Green was remanded in custody. Eileen Boyle was given bail on condition that she reside at her home address and report to her nearest police station. The police had asked that she report twice a day, but this was reduced to once a day when she told the court how much of her time was spent taking children to and from school. Joanne Day was given bail on condition that she reside at her home and report twice a day to her local police station, and her husband was to act as a surety for £500.

The importance of a family in assuring the court of the stability of a defendant is apparent here. However, on the second hearing in connection with this case a further factor became apparent – that is, the role of social control exercised by the acceptable model of family (male breadwinner and dependents) but not found in other family forms (e.g. single mother and children).

On their next appearance, a week later, both women applied to have their reporting conditions lifted. Joanne Day's application was granted '... since she has four children and a surety of £500'. Eileen Boyle told the court that reporting each evening meant that her son had to babysit and this was disrupting his evening classes and his social life. The magistrate asked why she did not take the younger children with her when she reported since it would not take long. He had turned to his colleagues as she replied and did not seem to hear her say that on the previous day it had taken one and a half hours. Her bail was renewed with the existing conditions.

So at the end of the second hearing the woman who was originally represented at the more 'criminal' – Joanne Day – was subject to less formal control than the woman who was originally seen as less of a problem and for whom the police did not oppose bail. Both women had domestic responsibilities – both had four children. The difference in the court's response is clearly not due to a difference in the extent of such responsibilities since, as a single mother, Eileen Boyle could claim to have a greater degree of responsibility than the married woman, Joanne Day. However, to a court concerned with issues of social control, Joanne Day is clearly in a more secure situation. In responding as they did, the magistrates recognised the degree of social control, particularly of women, which is inherent in the traditional family. This may well explain the finding noted by Farrington and Morris, and by Nagel, that a woman occupying a traditional gender-role is less likely to be subjected to formal social control. The control inherent within a traditional form of family structure was implicitly recognised by those lawyers who seemed reluctant to support an application for bail on behalf of defendants without such family ties (cf. the cases of Neil Brown, Joan Smith and Janet Bailey above). It was also recognised by the lawyer in the case of Brenda Cartwright, where the defendant's brother was cited as an adult male who might be seen as someone with the ability to police her behaviour in the absence of her husband.

Conclusion

Throughout the process of summary justice a model of the family is employed when dealing with both men and women defendants. This model, with a male breadwinner and a dependent woman, responsible for child-care and domestic labour, is used in pleas of mitigation and social inquiry reports. The same model also underlies current legislation on taxation and benefits [see Ch. 2 above] and traditional policies in providing for and responding to the family. It is a model based on a sexual division of labour which has consequences for women in both waged and domestic labour. For many women it means deprivation and isolation.

In the labour market, men may expect to earn a 'family wage' since it is assumed that their earnings provide for others. Women find that the jobs available to them do not offer the same earnings. In 1982 the average full time wage for a woman was 72 per cent of a man's wage. Women in part-time work, who constitute two-fifths of the female labour force were even worse off; their hourly rate in 1982 was, on average, 57 per cent of the hourly rate paid to men in full-time work (Kahn 1985: 81). As part-time workers these women have fewer rights to sick pay, holiday pay or pensions. While many married women work to keep the family above the poverty line, they are usually unable to claim for dependants if they become unemployed. Domestic responsibilities bring long hours of work for most women. One survey revealed that women with young children worked an average of seventy-seven hours a week – nearly twice as long as an industrial working week of forty hours (Oakley 1974b: 33). Child-care and housework are still assumed to be the woman's work even if she has paid employment outside the home (Young and Willmott 1973). The choice facing many women is the 'double shift' of paid employment and domestic labour, or the isolation and lower income of full-time housework.

Isolation is not just the result of the social organisation of housework. It is also a consequence of the traditions of privacy which surround the family. In the cases of Brenda Cartwright and Wayne Ross, discussed above, the fact that the offence involved members of the same family was used to mitigate its gravity. The same attitude is manifest in police reluctance to respond to instances of wife assault (Dobash and Dobash 1979; McCann 1985). Those relegated to the domestic sphere are most vulnerable to the abuse of power within that sphere. Even where women do not suffer physical abuse, mental illness may be a response to the conflicting demands placed on them. Depression is more likely among women involved full-time in housework than it is among unmarried women and married women with jobs outside the home (Procek 1981; Brown and Harris 1978).

Within the family women are vulnerable to violence, depression and poverty and for these reasons it has been the subject of much feminist critique (Gittins 1985; Land 1978, 1980; Pahl 1980; Wilson 1977). Only by questioning the position of women within this structure is there any challenge to the continual subordination of women – a subordination learned and reconstituted daily within the family. Of course courts do not question the gender roles of women within the family – these are accepted as normal and natural. They are implicit in the model of family which underlies pleas of mitigation and social inquiry reports, as they are in applications for bail. But applications for bail go further than other examples of courtroom rhetoric. In applications for bail we have more than a description of an acceptable model of the family and its asociated gender roles: we have an acknowledgement that such a family structure may offer a form of control comparable to that offered by the prison system.

Notes

1. The large proportion of women defendants is the result of selecting courtrooms with cases involving women.
2. Pseudonyms are used when referring to defendants.
3. This was the second application for bail and so not subject to the decision in the Nottingham Justices case of 1980 that an application for bail need not be heard on or after the third application unless there are new circumstances to consider (NACRO 1985a: 3)

7

Sisters in Law? Women Defendants and Women Magistrates
Anne Worrall

This chapter examines the social construction of the relationship between women defendants and women magistrates.[1] Using material from interviews undertaken in 1983 (Worrall, forthcoming),[2] I will argue that women magistrates are socially constructed within a number of discourses, in such a way that they can claim to be both similar to (for the purposes of special and authoritative understanding) and different from (for the purposes of sentencing) women defendants.

Women magistrates may be located within two definitional sites. First, as women in positions of authority over other women, they may be regarded as 'wise women' (Heidensohn 1985: 167). Alongside women prison officers, women nurses and women social-workers, they stand between the demands of the patriarchal state and the mass of women on whom those demands are made, translating 'expert knowledge' into 'common sense' for the consumption of the always-already failing woman (Hutter and Williams 1981; see also the Introduction above). Second, as magistrates, they are part of the complex machinery of control (Carlen 1976; Pearson 1980) which characterises 'amateur justice' (Burney 1979). The deconstruction of the 'women judging women' complex therefore involves the excavation of a number of layers of social relations. The foundation of the relationship lies deeper than moral outrage consequent on a sense of womanhood betrayed and spotlights the interplay of class and gender issues in the courtroom.

The Ideology of Amateur Justice

Although the roots of amateur justice go back to the thirteenth-century 'keepers of the peace', the judicial aspect of justices' work did not assume the form that we know today until the nineteenth century, with the passing of the Summary Jurisdiction Act 1848 (Burney 1979). While the purpose of this Act was to formalise and regulate the power of magistrates (e.g. by establishing rights of public access and the right of the accused to be represented by a lawyer), the *experience* of summary justice has come to be characterised by the sacrifice of many of the attributes of the ideology of law, legality and a fair trial, in the interests of speed and efficiency. This sacrifice is usually justified on the grounds that magistrates deal only with 'trivial' matters, but triviality, like beauty, is in the eye of the beholder and may ultimately derive less from the nature of the offences and penalties of the magistrates' courts than from the triviality in authoritative eyes of the *defendants* (McBarnet 1981).

Despite this jaundiced view of magistrates' courts as conveyor belts for the guilty pleas which constitute 95 per cent of their caseload, it must be admitted that the appointment of lay magistrates represents an explicit statement about the need to safeguard the interests of 'the community' against the abuse of the power of the law by 'experts', whether those be legal, medical or social-work experts. Summary justice, it may be argued, is not simply a quicker, cheaper form of 'proper' justice; it has the potential to be a qualitatively different form of justice. It is based on the assumption that there exists an entity called 'the community' which, although it consists of widely differing interests, can ultimately accommodate that difference in a natural consensus, which is *reflected in* the administration of justice, rather than being *constructed by* it.

What, then, are the characteristics and qualities required of magistrates? In the course of interviewing magistrates, I was shown an 'Interview Guide' for the selection of new magistrates. In this schedule it was suggested that

> It is necessary to... ensure a good balance of representation on the Bench. For instance, there must be a spread of ages, of both sexes, of socio-economic and employment backgrounds, and even of political persuasion, in addition to geographical coverage, if the Bench is to be representative of a true cross-section of the community.

The personal qualities sought in a magistrate are those purported to reside in the 'decent honest citizen' – 'stability, a balanced mentality and *common sense*' (Burney 1979: 87 – emphasis added).

The ideology of amateur justice therefore *requires* the absence of legality and expertise. The safeguard against the naked class justice which might ensue from such an absence is the assumed existence of a quality which crosses all barriers of class, age, race or gender – the quality of common sense.

The Appeal of Common Sense

> I like to think we use our common sense.

> (Female magistrate)

Lay magistrates are unique amongst courtroom personnel in disclaiming professional expertise. Few of the magistrates I spoke to regretted the very limited nature of their formal training. They had been content to learn the job by 'sitting next to Nellie' and believed that they had at their disposal a resource more valuable than legal, medical or sociological knowledge – the resource of common sense.

Magistrates appeal to common sense in order to account for their actions. In so doing they make assumptions about 'what everyone knows' to be self-evidently true (Carlen 1976). They free themselves from any obligation to justify their actions on other, more 'professional' grounds. By using the term 'common sense', magistrates make their activities 'visibly-rational-and-reportable-for-all-practical-purposes' (Garfinkel 1968). They are, as ethnomethodological studies have demonstrated, employing a procedural device which allows them to make sense of data which has no inherent meaning or coherence. They are establishing rules for handling such material and for minimising any challenge to their handling of it.

One of the central characteristics of common sense is the assumption of a 'reciprocity of perspectives' (Cicourel 1968). As representatives of the community, magistrates take it for granted that most 'ordinary' people would have a similar experience of the immediate scene in question if they were to change places with them. Consensus about law and order issues is something which is assumed to exist amongst all decent folk, regardless of their sex, age, class or political allegiance – regardless, in short, of individual difference. Thus represented, common sense becomes the metaphor for those statements which tend to be excluded as invalid by experts and which, when uttered, tend to threaten the authority of experts. It consists of all those crude, unrefined and challenging statements which are unanswerable within expert discourse – like those uttered by the magistrate who told me that she and her colleagues 'take psychiatric reports with a pinch of salt'.

Common sense is an elusive and multifaceted construct, but its unspoken goal is singular – the *reproduction of consensus. Common* sense is sense which is not only common because it is crude but because it is purported to be held universally to be true and to be universally applicable. It is common *sense* not only because it is the opposite of nonsense and falsehood, but because it is 'sensed'. It is truth which is not accessible to rational thought or argument. On the contrary, it is intuitive, instinctive and accessible only to the senses. It has to be experienced. But this logically detracts from its universalisability, for my experience is unique, as is yours. Yet, despite this acknowledged difference, its appeal remains in its claim to be stating that which can be recognised by everyone as describing truthfully their own lived experience and which can always-already be inscribed upon the lived experience of others.

> Common-sense has its own necessity; it exacts its due with the weapon appropriate to it, namely an appeal to the 'self-evident' nature of its claims and considerations.
>   (Heidegger 1949, quoted in Burton and Carlen, 1979)

Common sense may thus be portrayed comfortably as the safeguard of the criminal justice system, the champion of freedom, the check on expert power. In a democratic society, if justice is no longer majestirial (Hay 1975), then at least it is not dictatorial. Its administration appears to have become a very practical project, a matter of face-to-face interaction and negotiation. The meaning of justice is reduced to the individual consciousness of thousands of actors who daily play the courtroom game. Conversely, the abstract concept of Justice is perceived as being no more than the aggregate of these atomistic interactions.

But the administration of criminal justice is not a game (Carlen 1976), and the rules governing it are not freely agreed upon by the participants. Certain personnel are given more authority to define than others, and certain accounts more credibility than others. The common sense which magistrates claim to be universally recognisable by all citizens is, rather, a specific discourse sanctioned by law and elevated in practice to the status of 'expertise'. In short, majestirial justice has been replaced by magisterial common sense.

Magisterial Common Sense and the Woman Defendant

Magisterial common sense is characterised by a denial of expertise coupled with a claim to authority for statements which are assumed to reflect public moral consensus. Despite explicitly disclaiming any legal, medical or sociological understanding of crime, magistrates implicitly draw selectively from all these and other perspectives in the construction of their own privileged discourse. It is a discourse within which three key myths may be identified as having important consequences for women defendants:

1. The process of *self-disqualification* enables magistrates simultaneously to deny and claim authority for what they say; the consequence for women defendants is that they are rendered *invisible*.
2. The concept of *individual merit* enables magistrates simultaneously to generalise and deny the possibility of generalisation; the consequence for women defendants is that they are rendered *intractably heterogeneous*.
3. The *privileging of personal life experience* enables magistrates simultaneously to claim and deny similarity with defendants; the consequence for women defendants is that they are rendered *like-yet-not-like women magistrates*.

Self-Disqualification and the Invisible Woman Defendant

I've dealt with very few women.

(Female magistrate)

Although women still constitute a small proportion of all defendants appearing in courts, I found only one magistrate who was aware of any increase in their numbers of recent years. On the whole, it still seems to be women defendants' scarcity that characterises their image in the minds of magistrates – they are *under-represented*. It is hard to believe, for example, that the following statement by a woman magistrate could possible be factually accurate: 'I've been a magistrate for ten years and I think I've only had three or four women appearing before me.' Other magistrates were less extreme in their estimates, but as Pat Carlen (1983a) found in Glasgow, most prefaced their remarks with disclaimers:

> I'm not very helpful on women, I'm afraid.
>   (Female magistrate with eighteen years' experience)

> For some unknown, unexplained reason, my personal dealings with female offenders have been extremely limited.
>   (Male magistrate)

Nine out of the twelve magistrates interviewed explicitly disqualified themselves from being competent to speak about women defendants. Those with relatively few years' service felt they lacked experience, while those with longer service implied that women defendants were too few to justify generalisation anyway. Thus it was made clear that whatever views might subsequently be expressed by the interviewee, these were based on no more than anecdotal evidence and were emphatically not to be taken as authoritative statements.

So the first manifestation of magisterial common sense in relation to women defendants is an expressed emphasis on self-disqualification, consequent on perceived lack of experience. That lack of experience results from limited time in the job ('I've only been doing this work for five years'), limited access to the material being studied ('I deal mainly with juveniles and domestics'), or the elusiveness of such material ('We don't see many women here'). In other words, women defendants are not recognised by magistrates because they are invisible. Alternatively, it might be argued that women defendants are invisible to magistrates because they are not recognised as being 'real' criminals. Women are 'out of place' in court (Worrall 1981) and are routinely 'not seen'. Those who do draw attention to themselves as a result of 'unusual' offences, behaviour or personal circumstances are always–already marked out as 'unfeminine'.

Individual Merit and the Intractably Heterogeneous Woman Defendant

> You can't generalise – every case must be treated on its own merit.
>   (Female magistrate)

Since so few are 'seen' by them, it follows that magistrates claim to be wary of generalising about women as a category of defendants. A further contribution to this caution is made by the sentencing principle of individualised justice (Pearson 1976; Edwards, 1984). The practice of seeking the most suitable sentence for a particular defendant has the effect of depoliticising the personal circumstances of those appearing in court. This effect becomes exaggerated in relation to women, since, as we have seen in the Introduction to this book, femininity is constructed within the private and personal confines of domesticity, sexuality and pathology. Even when women defendants are 'seen', they are not recognised as sharing, or having in common, any conditions of existence that might explain their lawbreaking activity – they are rendered intractably heterogeneous.

The process of individualisation is ostensibly gender-neutral but serves, in practice, to reinforce gender distinctions. If each case is treated on its own merits – so the argument goes – it is not possible to generalise on the grounds of age, class, education or any other socio-economic factor, including gender. Yet this is precisely what magistrates *do*. Despite their denials, they do demonstrate a sociological understanding of women's position in society and of the stereotypical role expectations of women as wives and mothers. Some magistrates are conscious of the oppressive nature of such role expectations, but they are also conscious of the contradictions between this sociological understanding and the formal gender-blindness of the law. The law does not allow for the *social* construction of *legal* subjects. In order to reconcile the contradictions between legal and social construction, the *moral* concept of *merit* is invoked. The appeal to merit is one which is seen to supercede these contradictions, for it is an appeal to the discourse of morality – of right and wrong, good and bad. These are truths which are held to be self-evident. Whether a defendant is a man or a woman, it is assumed that the qualities of goodness and badness, the notions of culpability and mitigation, free-will and determination, are also gender-blind. Moral attributes, such as selfishness, callousness, responsibleness and consideration, are deemed to be universally recognisable and consensually definable. But the concept of 'merit' is itself socially constructed within the ideologies of what constitutes 'meritorious' conduct, and these ideologies are themselves gender-related. What is seen to constitute selfish and irresponsible behaviour in a man differs widely from what is seen to constitute such behaviour in a woman. The differential tolerance of drunkenness in men and women is but one example of this (Otto 1981).

Magistrates, in common with the rest of us, are faced with the problem of induction: how and when to move from specific to general statements. The problem is exacerbated, however, because they feel expressly discouraged from using theory to bridge that gap or to redefine the problem as being one of *deduction*. The construct of 'individual merit' allows generalisations to be made at precisely the same time as the possiblity of their being made is denied. It provides the means whereby magistrates can reconcile (or close the gap between) the specificity of their own personal experience and the demands of their role. It enables them to act and speak in ways which are just and equitable – that is, generalisable. Thus the individualised, or intractably heterogeneous, woman defendant is a myth, for despite their denials, magistrates routinely generalise about the women who appear before them.

Privileging Personal Life Experience and the Feminine Woman Defendant

> I feel sad to see a woman in the dock, but I put it out of my mind.
>
> (Male magistrate)

Closely linked to the construct of 'individual merit' – indeed, it may be seen as the opposite side of the same coin – is the mechanism of 'privileging personal life experience'. Magistrates are encouraged to regard their own life experience as 'privileged' in the sense that they are expected to draw on their own experience to inform their judgments. Thus their own personal life experience is ascribed special status within the courtroom when the personal life experiences of other personnel are considered irrelevant to the task in hand.

Most magistrates were only too aware of the dilemmas posed by this expectation that they were like-yet-not-like the defendants with whom they dealt and they felt under an obligation to 'make sense' of their practices. Some (both male and female) admitted feeling personally distressed by women defendants but felt obliged to suppress that instinctive response. One magistrate implied that her own personal problems might have resulted in her responding sympathetically to such women, but she added, 'I can switch off when I go into court'. The irony of such comments is that, while magistrates are exhorted to use their common sense and trust their intuition (conditioned, as it must be, by their life experience), certain responses, nevertheless, have to be excluded, controlled or modified in the search for 'objectivity'. Thus 'objectivity', which in most discourses would be taken, of necessity, to include logical, rational argument and to exclude sensation, is somehow accommodated within magisterial common sense, without posing a threat to it. This is possible because what is being spoken of is not, in fact, objectivity but consensus. What magistrates felt the need to suppress were those responses which they perceived to be unacceptable to their colleagues. They were the responses which might detract from or threaten consensus.

The strategy employed by magistrates to accommodate these conflicting responses to women defendants was one of targeting women into two groups: those who it could be agreed merited compassion and those who did not. The binary stereotyping of women defendants is well documented, but its strategic value to magistrates has been less well examined. In order to 'live with' the contradictions in their practices, magistrates draw on their own life experience to decide whether or not they can 'identify with' or recognise the conditions which appear to explain or excuse women's criminal activity. The key components in this targeting process are (1) the extent of woman's domestic responsibilities, (2) the extent to which her appearance, demeanour and life-style accord with sexual 'normality' and (3) the extent to which her problems can be pathologised and 'treated'. In short, the woman defendant is constructed within the discourses of *domesticity*, *sexuality* and *pathology*.

DOMESTICITY

> Women are treated no differently from men, except where there are domestic circumstances – that's only natural.
>
> (Female magistrate)

Two different arguments were propounded for the consideration by magistrates of women's domestic responsibilities, although these were frequently conflated. *First*, domestic problems were seen to explain or *excuse* female crime (which, of itself, was assumed to be *unnatural*). Women might be reduced to breaking the law either directly by insufferable husbands ('Women aren't naturally criminal – it's the men that force them into it'), or indirectly by the pressures of family life:

> A married woman, and especially a mother, is the keystone of the family and is subject to great strains and tensions, particularly if in a 'one-parent family' situation or when the husband is unemployed. This could push a woman into crime particularly, in my opinion, shoplifting or attempting to obtain benefits to which she would not be entitled.
>
> (Female magistrate)

Domestic problems may also lead to alcohol abuse, which in turn was recognised as an explanation of crime – provided either that treatment was being sought (and the problem could thus be pathologised) or that the shaky hand was still rocking the cradle! (cf. Curlee 1968, quoted in Otto 1981):

> A woman stabbed her husband in a pub recently – we were lenient because she was going to have treatment for her alcohol problem.
>
> (Male magistrate)

> Alcoholism is increasing in women. We dealt with a woman who was drunk in charge of a child in a pub. I thought – it's better than leaving the baby at home!'
>
> (Female magistrate)

Second, domestic responsibilities were also important in the *mitigation* of sentence. The effect of a sentence on a woman's family was often considered more important than the effect on the woman herself. Imprisoning women with children was agreed to be a very last resort, primarily because of the consequences for the children:

> Trying and sentencing a mother has its problems for me because I look at her situation, taking into account the effect upon her family. In cases where women have in their care babies or young children, I feel that magistrates explore every possible sentence other than imprisonment.
>
> (Female magistrate)

Despite this, there are some 1,600 children with mothers in prison (NACRO 1986), and that is not, perhaps, surprising when one considers the irony of this remark from one woman magistrate:

> The governor at one women's prison told me once, 'Women should come here for at least six months, then we can train them to be good mothers and they're grateful'.

Motherhood, *per se*, does not protect women from imprisonment, and magistrates do not take kindly to women whom they perceive to be 'blackmailing' them with their domestic responsibilities (Walker 1985). The issue in question is whether or not the defendant is a *good* mother, that is, conforming to conventional, middle-class expectations or appropriate motherhood and wifeliness (Edwards 1985). Mothers who commit crimes are, almost by definition, bad mothers who need training to be good mothers. Ironically, such training may require their removal from the site of mothering to a site of punishment. In order, on the one hand, to disrupt the sequence of mothering minimally, 'punishment' should be kept to a minimum. On the other hand, to improve the technical quality of mothering, 'training' needs to be extensive. Pat Carlen (1983a) discovered that these ironies are not lost on those women who experience them, and that their typical response was not one of conspicuous gratitude.

SEXUALITY

> A woman in charge of an office who cooks the books gets no sympathy from me – I treat her like a man.

> (Male magistrate)

The corollary of marking positively (Ardener 1978) women defendants with domestic responsibilities is marking negatively those without them. Within this latter category, two groups appeared to receive little sympathy from magistrates. Young single women who committed offences in company posed a threat to conventional images of femininity and challenged magistrates' authority: 'They don't give reasons – just shrug their shoulders' (female magistrate). Such 'dumb insolence' was not expected from women defendants since it did not accord with stereotypical expectations of women as guilt-ridden and anxious to please. Defiance manifested in dress, posture or speech is typically a masculine attribute, and women who displayed such an attitude risked alienating magistrates whose personal life experience did not equip them to 'identify with' such a lack of femininity.

Similarly, older women in positions of authority in their work were unlikely to be viewed as meriting compassion. Like women magistrates, they had entered a public world dominated by men. While their aggressiveness and competitiveness were seen as more legitimate than the defiance of younger defendants, the price they had to pay for breaking the law was that of being treated (by implication more harshly) 'like a man'.

Criminal activity that could not be attributed to domestic responsibility tended to be viewed as an expression of sexuality or, more specifically, a lack of femininity. Certain crimes were identified as 'women's' crimes. Shoplifting, soliciting, social security fraud and embezzlement could be recognised as gender-role expressive (Edwards 1985). Other crimes were less acceptable:

> I think that perhaps in the past, women did receive more sympathy from courts than men, but with the increasing number of women appearing for various crimes, particularly those usually committed by men, I think their attitude is changing.

> (Female magistrate)

As Heidensohn (1985: 94) observes, 'offences which have apparently nothing to do with sexuality are – when committed by women – transformed into expressions of female sexuality or the lack of it'.

PATHOLOGY

> We ask for reports more often on women – they often have problems of 'change of life' or medication.
>
> (Male magistrate)

Closely associated with the image of women defendants as 'sexual' is a further assumption that they are 'sick'. As we have seen, magistrates are fairly sceptical about psychiatric diagnoses and, consequently, those I interviewed did not feel they had come across much 'proper' mental illness amongst women defendants. Nevertheless, the ascription of what might be described as 'sub-psychiatric' medical conditions to women defendants was widespread.

It has been argued in the Introduction to this book that, in the construction of femininity the 'normal' female body and mind are perceived as being predisposed to malfunction. Menstruation, pregnancy, childbirth and the menopause all result in 'hormonal imbalance' – a phrase which connotes that women may themselves be 'imbalanced' during those times. This principle of 'periodicity' (Luckhaus 1985) implies that there are times when the mood and behaviour of even the 'normal' woman is likely to be so adversely affected by her biology that any *subsequent* criminal activity may be regarded as at least partially a *consequence* of it and *excused* by it. The dilemma posed for lay magistrates is that of assessing the eligibility of a woman defendant for inclusion in this 'excused' category. Is this particular woman 'genuinely' unbalanced and disturbed or is she a malingerer? Because of the 'periodic' nature of her alleged disturbance, it is quite possible for any woman to *appear* 'normal' in court while claiming that she was 'abnormal' at the time of her offence. To resolve this socio-legal conundrum, magistrates have to rely on information supplied by 'experts' in medical and social inquiry reports. But magistrates reserve the right to use their common sense to evaluate the information provided by experts and even when the expert has a relatively undisputed 'authority to know' – as a psychiatrist undoubtedly does – his claims may still be weak because common sense denies any need for that particular area of knowing (Huntington 1981). Information from general practitioners and probation officers was generally accorded more respect by magistrates than that from psychiatrists:

> Older women give medical reasons, produce a doctor's certificate. We have to take that into account because doctors don't write those lightly.
>
> (Female magistrate)

> I think we pay more attention to what the probation officer says than the psychiatrist – *they* seem to state the obvious.
>
> (Female magistrate)

The discourse of pathology reinforces beliefs about the natural contrariness of women and about women being 'at the mercy of their raging hormones' (Luckhaus 1985).

Implications for Sentencing

Although magistrates believed that they tried hard not to send women to prison, they were not enthusiastic advocates of alternative disposals. Domestic responsibilities were seen to preclude most women defendants from doing Community Service, and one magistrate expressed a novel variation on that theme: 'Community Service is usually done in someone's spare time – women don't have any!' (male magistrate). This comment could be seen as reinforcing a view expressed to me by a probation officer responsible for selecting candidates for Community Service, that a woman might be rejected where it was felt that her husband would object to her being out of the home on a Sunday and thus impose additional domestic pressure on her. Alternatively, it could be seen as reflecting a deeper concern about the justice of requiring society's largest group of unpaid workers to perform even more 'voluntary' work as punishment (Dominelli 1984). Women's lack of financial competence also embarrassed magistrates (Carlen 1983a) and presented difficulties in the imposition of fines. The absence of an independent income frequently meant that a woman's fine would have to be paid by her husband, although some magistrates felt this to be no bad thing, especially in the case of television licence offences.[3]

Unsurprisingly, the sentence most favoured by magistrates for women was the probation order, since this offered the least disruption to a woman's domestic situation and enabled her problems to be individualised and pathologised. Probation was invariably advocated on 'welfare' grounds (Eaton 1985), and little consideration seemed to be given to the implications of such a sentence for a woman's position on the sentencing 'tariff'. Recent attempts by the Probation Service to raise the tariff weighting of probation orders and render them credible as direct alternatives to custody for more serious offenders (Home Office 1984b) were implicitly regarded as irrelevant to women, who were assumed to be characteristically 'one-off' offenders rather than recidivists (Pearson 1976). The consequence for women who *do* re-offend, however, may be to escalate their progress up an already truncated tariff[4] towards a custodial sentence, regardless of the severity (or lack of severity) of their offences (cf. Ch. 8 below).

Together, the discourses of domesticity, sexuality and pathology provide a complex of excusing and mitigating explanations of female crime which was accepted fairly uncritically by the male magistrates I interviewed. The women magistrates, however, appeared to experience a much greater degree of ambivalence and discomfort in relation to women defendants, and this was recognised by one or two of their more perceptive male colleagues:

> Women offenders are different physically and emotionally – more complex. I don't understand them as well as women magistrates do. But women magistrates are sometimes harder – perhaps they feel that women who offend have let the side down.
>
> (Male magistrate)

Sisters in Law?

Images of Women Magistrates

> We're told that we're representing the Queen, and I think some of them feel they
> need to look like her!
>
> (Female magistrate)

> None of us women magistrates wear hats – we're unique, I think! I won't wear one.
> I get confused in a hat. My head gets hot and I get hopeless.
>
> (Mrs Christian Annersley, quoted in Blythe 1969: 251)

It is not difficult to conjure up a mental picture of a 'typical' woman magistrate
(cf. Pearson 1980). She is white, middle-aged to elderly, middle or upper class, the
wife of a local dignitary or a retired headmistress. She may or may not have
children of her own, but she knows how they should be reared. She will invariably
have 'done good' and wear a hat! Yet, as Mrs Annersley's account of her work
indicates, this was not a totally accurate picture even twenty years ago. While the
women I interviewed could all be described as 'typical' in their age, class and
background, they were neither rigid nor ignorant in their opinions and gave the
impression of wanting to understand crime and women criminals in particular.
They recognised that their personal life experience was privileged, in the socio-
economic sense of the word, and that this sometimes restricted the usefulness of
'privileging' that experience in the sense of using it to inform their judgments.
They were certainly not incapable of sympathising and identifying with the
problems experienced by the women appearing before them, but at the end of the
day they felt obliged to regard women defendants as 'not like us' because the
consequences of any alternative interpretation were too painful to contemplate.
Those consequences would threaten the all-important notion of consensus to
which magisterial common sense is committed. Over-identification by women
magistrates with the oppression of women defendants might oblige women
magistrates to challenge the dominance of their male colleagues on the Bench. So
while a woman magistrate may be recruited to ensure a 'balance of the sexes', she
is prohibited by the imperative of consensus from fully expressing her 'femaleness'
in her practice on the Bench. The 'knowledge' about women defendants which she
is authorised to have by reason of her own status as a *woman* magistrate is rendered
inferior and inappropriate by reason of her subordination to male magistrates. If
'real' criminals are men, then 'real' magistrates are also men, and the women who
invade the public space of the courtroom in positions of power and authority are
expected to emulate the qualities of reason, 'objectivity' and *sexism* demonstrated
by their male colleagues.

What then are the conditions which determine relationships which women
magistrates have (1) with their male colleagues and (2) with women defendants?

Achieving Consensus and the Simultaneous Recognition and Denial of Difference

> We think of ourselves as a nice team.
>
>   (Mrs Christian Annersley)

Lay magistrates are selected both for their differences and for their ability to 'get on' with each other. They are, in theory at least, expected to demonstrate that they are 'moderate, fair and conscientious: decent people picked for their ability to get on with other decent people' (Burney 1979: 212). Yet precisely because magistrates are encouraged to rely on their own experiences and senses, the scope for conflict between them would, at first sight, appear to be considerable. An outsider might question the extent of material and ideological difference existing been magistrates (Hood 1962; Baldwin and Bottomley 1978), but there is a high level of 'felt' or perceived difference amongst magistrates themselves: 'We get a wide spread of occupations on our Bench' (female magistrate). This view was endorsed by most magistrates I interviewed, yet they all stressed the relative ease with which consensus was achieved, despite these differences. Difference was recognised, only to be cast aside:

> I venture to suggest that this is one of the strengths of the Bench – that it is comprised of men and women of different opinions who eventually make a *unanimous* decision.
>
>   (Female magistrate)

> We usually all agree. I've not been in a situation of real conflict.
>
>   (Female magistrate)

The point here is that while magistrates normally sit in threes – a system designed to accommodate the expression of *differing* opinions – they routinely experience the system as one of *agreement* or consensus. This is particularly significant for women magistrates who may feel prohibited from even expressing certain of their instinctive responses because they may be 'too personal' and 'too individualised' to be acceptable to their male colleagues. Such inhibition led one woman magistrate to protest (too loudly?):

> We have a wonderful relationship on our Bench – we don't mind who we sit with. There's no difference between men and women on the Bench – the women can be *just as fierce*.
>
>   (Female magistrate, my emphasis)

Thus women magistrates who can sublimate or deny their womanhood are celebrated, for magisterial common sense – the guardian of public morality – is gender-neutral. But gender-neutrality is a myth, and the imperative of consensus ultimately robs magisterial common sense of the power that might result from genuine gender conflicts. The guardians of public morality are men, or else those who will accept a male-defined consensus. The only personal life experience which is, in reality, given special status or authority in the courtroom is that of male magistrates. It is not then surprising that women magistrates exercise caution in their judgments of women defendants.

Women Defendants: Like-us-yet-not-like-us

While the male magistrates I interviewed were relatively content to attribute female crime to domestic strains and responsibilities,[5] the women magistrates tended to expect women either to accept their lot and make the best of it, or to be more 'rational' and discriminating in the remedies they sought. There was no lack of understanding of the difficulties:

> I was on a baby-battering case. With all my children, I know what a strain it must be without a supportive husband
>
> (Female magistrate)

but these were not accepted as excusing conditions. Another woman magistrate echoed the sentiment:

> I can understand a young mother without a supportive husband getting desperate – but not hitting little babies. Why don't they take it out on their husbands?'

Why indeed? One may well ask. The dilemma for these magistrates was that their own experience, on which they were relying, did not equip them fully to understand the woman defendant because *common* sense does not allow for different material circumstances. Yet they felt unable to go beyond that experience to recognise the validity of generalisable statements about power relations within the family. Magisterial common sense requires that the unspoken common condition of this contradiction that would allow for an inversion of the hierarchy of these statements (namely, power relations) be excluded, or at least only partially expressed. The power relation between mother and child is expressed, but that between husband and wife is prohibited.

Even more ambivalence was expressed by women magistrates about the attribution of the criminal activity of women to their biology. In this they were not expressing concern about the dangers for all women of the 'medicalisation' of women's behaviour, nor were they arguing that such reductionism

> impugns the integrity of the female actor, stripping her action of cultural and political meaning and anaesthetising the social and economic origin and conditions in which that action takes place.
>
> (Luckhaus 1985)

Rather, such conditions were excluded because the magistrates had not – or claimed to have not – experienced such conditions for themselves.

> Menopause is used frequently as a defence – I'm not very sympathetic. I tell my male colleagues, I'll let them know what really happens *when it happens to me*.... Pre-menstrual tension – *my girls* don't seem to suffer
>
> (Female magistrate, my emphases)

> As a woman and mother of three grown-up daughters, I believe that women have to recognise and accept any variations in their behaviour due to the menstrual cycle, and not use this as an excuse.
>
> (Female magistrate)

The ability of women defendants to touch very primitive emotions of sadness and sympathy in women magistrates is a taboo subject. It is not something to be shared and examined, but to be hidden away and denied because it is too threatening to the dominant ideologies about crime, justice and masculinity. Discussion about women defendants was thus foreclosed by women magistrates with the symbolic phrase, 'I can understand but....' The shared condition of female experience was recognised, but such a recognition represented the challenge of the Other – the disruptive intrusion of an alternative, non-legitimated mode of lived experience. Such a challenge must be confronted and controlled. So the moment of recognition passes, and the space for negotiation opened up by the challenge is reclosed. The women magistrates I spoke to were not the female equivalents of 'Disgusted, Tonbridge Wells'. They were women who felt confused about the extent to which they could claim to understand other women. They were women who often *did* understand but who did not trust their own understanding. They seemed to feel acutely that they were living in a man's world and that they must locate themselves in a symbolic universe of meanings that were empirically grounded in *male* rather than *female* experience.

Conclusions

This chapter has attempted to demonstrate that the relationship between magistrates and defendants is constructed within a discourse of common sense which, despite its inherent paradoxes and discontinuities, is represented as a consistent and coherent unity. Although magisterial common sense may appear to challenge and transgress 'expert' discourse, it is in fact a competing discourse of 'expertise'. In relation to women defendants, it is characterised by a threefold myth:

1. That magistrates can never claim to know anything about women defendants because knowledge accrues through experience and women defendants are always-already invisible and inaccessible to the senses.
2. That magistrates can never generalise about women defendants *qua* women, because the law is blind to differences of gender (as of class, age, race, etc.).
3. That magistrates can always reach a consensus about women defendants both because of and despite social, economic, political or, specifically, gender differences, these differences being hailed (at the point of recruitment to the Bench) and denied (at the point of judgment) in the interests of justice.

These judicial myths have been challenged, and it has been argued that magistrates construct the woman defendant within specific conditions:

1. They act 'as though' they have knowledge of women defendants, that knowledge emanating from cultural stereotypes of appropriate female behaviour and being reinforced by their own socially and discursively privileged personal life experience.

2. They invoke the ostensibly gender-neutral moral concept of *merit* to justify treating women defendants *qua* women differently from male defendants, since meritorious conduct in men and women is differentially defined.

It has been argued, additionally, that women magistrates suppress their empathetic understanding of women's position in society (an empathy based on shared biological experience) because, having entered the masculine world of the criminal justice system by virtue of their womanhood, their ability to sustain their authority and credibility within it is dependent on their denial of that womanhood.[6]

Nevertheless, in this chapter I have sought to demonstrate that there may exist the potential for a greater understanding of women defendants by the magistracy, if women magistrates felt more confident – and were allowed – to express their genuinely differing perspectives and opinions. The structure for such a richness and variety of contribution exists; what is lacking is the will to experience the discomfort of conflict, especially when the mechanism for achieving an apparent consensus – the appeal to, and of, common sense – is so readily available. Women magistrates, like women defendants, are socially constructed within the discourses of domesticity, sexuality and pathology. The evidence of this chapter suggests that they may indeed be 'sisters in law', subject to a common oppression but not yet able to fully recognise each other.

Notes

I am grateful to the magistrates serving the Newcastle Borough, Stoke-on-Trent and Stone Petty Sessional Divisions in Staffordshire who allowed themselves to be interviewed or who have talked informally to me about women defendants. The first year of the research was funded by a Keele University Studentship.

1. This relationship has been largely neglected by the literature about magistrates' courts, although two recent articles have intimated that it may have some special significance (Farrington and Morris 1983b; Dominelli 1984). In both articles it is suggested that women magistrates may be less lenient than their male colleagues in their sentencing of women and that this punitive disposition may be attributable to a sense of affront. Women who break the law, it is argued, are censured by women magistrates for their 'betrayal' of womanhood.

2. The twelve interviews on which this chapter is based are part of a wider study of the criminalisation of particular women lawbreakers, involving interviews with solicitors, psychiatrists, probation officers and women who had appeared in court. I had not originally expected the sex of magistrates to be a factor of any significance, but the differing responses to women defendants of the eight women and four men interviewed suggested that it might be. Although the sample is very small, the interviews took place against my background of regular contact with magistrates during eight years of work as a probation officer.

3. Most magistrates made an almost automatic link between fines and television licence offences, and several expressed concern that women were discriminated against in respect of this particular offence, since they were often the ones at home during the day

when detector officials called. Television was seen by magistrates as 'part of the family' and women tended to receive sympathy for what amounted to an additional domestic responsibility.

4. There are no Detention Centres for women and very few Attendance Centres or Intermediate Treatment schemes; young women serving Youth Custody sentences are also frequently mixed with older women prisoners.

5. In my experience as a probation officer, and during these interviews, I encountered few male *lay* magistrates who expressed blatantly sexist attitudes of the kind sometimes reported as being expressed by high court judges (e.g. Pattullo 1983). Most erred on the side of chivalry. As one solicitor put it to me: 'They are the kind of men who still give up their seats to women – if they weren't, they wouldn't have got on the Bench.' Though irrelevant to this article, the most sexist attitudes I encountered in the wider study were expressed by the 'experts' – solicitors, psychiatrists and probation officers.

6. In an unpublished paper about her study of gender, the magistracy and sentencing practice in Leeds, Dominelli (1986) argues that women are under-represented on benches, are 'relatively new to the job' and feel 'deskilled and disempowered' by being 'subjected to continuous scrutiny' by the 'Court-Establishment'. I think that this analysis is too simplistic. The process whereby women in court – both magistrates and defendants – are *muted* (Ardener 1978) is a complex one, and there is evidence from other arenas where women are the recipients of help, advice or services, that a simple increase in the numbers of women in positions of authority will not guarantee a better deal. As Dale and Foster (1986) observe, women entering traditionally male professions require tremendous courage and commitment to stand out against the barrage of institutional and cultural assumptions which face them.

Part Three

Women in Custody

8

Out of Care, into Custody: Dimensions and Deconstructions of the State's Regulation of Twenty-two Young Working-Class Women

Pat Carlen

Ever since the sixteenth-century custom of chopping off the ears of vagabonds, rogues and beggars, the British have always had some difficulty in distinguishing between poverty and crime

(Booth 1985:7)

This perennial difficulty ws exacerbated in the nineteenth century when the discovery of childhood (Aries 1973 coincided with the transformation of the 'lower orders' into the 'dangerous classes' (Briggs 1967; Radzinowitz 1966). Concern about the poor ws thereafter inseminated by a bourgeois missionary zeal to save working-class children from the moral degeneracy assumed to be associated with poverty and squalid living conditions. Young working-class women were seen to be at especial risk of moral contamination, and the ensuing state regulation of young women's sexuality and the development of conventional femininity has persisted (Smart 1981). For although only a small minority of children in the care of local authorities have been in trouble with the law prior to the imposition of their Care Orders (House of Commons, 1984: xiii), of the 3 to 4 per cent of young persons in Care on the grounds of 'moral danger', about 80 per cent are young women (Campbell 1981: 7;A. Hudson 1983: 9). In fact, girls are disproportionately admitted to residential Care for what are called 'status offences' – like running away from home, staying out late at night or being aggressive – behaviours which would not be punishable at law if engaged in by an adult 'and which would not justify a Care Order under criminal proceedings' (B. Hudson 1984: 41). Yet, whatever the official or actual reason for the Care Order, studies indicating that maybe half the population of young offender institutions have previously been in residential care (e.g. Home Office 1977) suggest, too, that disproportionate numbers of young people either go directly out of Care into penal custody – or, in some cases, into penal custody whilst still in Care. The majority of young people in Care do not, of course, acquire criminal records; but because twenty-two of thirty-nine women recently interviewed about their lawbreaking and criminalisation had also been through the Care/custody mangle,[1] an urgent task in the deconstruction of their socio-biographies was analysis of the Care factor in criminal careers.

In 1985, thirty-nine volunteers willing to talk about the causes and consequences of their lawbreaking each granted me two hours of tape-recorded discussion. Twenty convicted women were interviewed at Bullwood Hall Prison and Youth Custody Centre (the Bullwood Group) and nineteen more in private houses, mostly their own homes (the Contact Group). All twenty-two who had been or were still in residential Care (Table 8.1 and 8.2) were from working-class backgrounds. Six were black. In terms of their membership of three groups – the unemployed, single-parent families and the poor in institutions – identified by Field (1981) as being amongst the major groups in poverty, the twenty-two had been poor all their lives. Consequently, this chapter will not only try to indicate

Table 8.1 Research groupings of the women by place of interview

Bullwood Group		Contact Group	
Pseudonym	*Age at interview*	*Pseudonym*	*Age at interview*
Daphne	15	Anne	20
Della	15	Jill	21
Yasmin	16	Tara	21
Tricia	17	Donna	22
Audrey	18	Carol	27
Cynthia	19	Zoe	28
Shirley	20	Kim	28
Lena	21	Hazel	29
Norma	22	Muriel	30
Dawn	23	Josie	30
		Nadia	35
		Sally	36
Total 10		*Total 12*	

Note: The Bullwood Group were interviewed in Bullwood Hall Prison and Youth Custody Centre. The Contact group were interviewed in private houses – mostly in their own homes.

Table 8.2   Research groupings of the women by age of entry into residential Care.

	Pre-11 Entry		Post-11 Entry	
Pseudonym	Age at interview	Pseudonym	Age at interview	
Yasmin	16	Daphne	15	
Audrey	18	Della	15	
Shirley	20	Tricia	17	
Jill	21	Cynthia	19	
Lena	21	Anne	20	
Donna	22	Tara	21	
Hazel	29	Norma	22	
Muriel	30	Dawn	23	
Nadia	35	Carol	27	
		Zoe	28	
		Kim	28	
		Josie	30	
		Sally	35	
Total 9		Total 13		

how ideologies of family and femininity pave the paths from Care to penal custody. It will also attempt to show how class-biased and racist inequities in the administration of welfare and criminal law are intertwined with discriminatory typifications of gender competence. Together they have a complex but malign influence on the mode and degree of criminalisation experienced by young women in Care who break the law and/or step out of place.

Structure of the Argument

What is presented in this article is not intended to be a universal explanation of women's crime. It is an ethnographic analysis of a 'slice of life' – or, more precisely, a deconstruction of a sequence of events that occurred in the early lives of twenty-two young women who went into penal custody either while they were still in, or very soon after leaving, Care. In this article the interplay of class, racism, gender and Care factors is presented in sequential mode, a descriptive procedure entailed by a project taking 'careers' as the focus of investigation. However, what is presented as narrative was originally produced within a theoretical analysis that in turn engendered the argument structuring that narrative, a narrative made more complex by the awkward empirical fact that at different stages in the young women's careers from Care to Custody, different factors appeared to predominate. It is, therefore, to facilitate understanding of the complex interplay of class, racism, gender and Care factors and their diverse material, ideological and psychological preconditions and effects, that a summary presentation of the ethnographic analyses is given in Table 6. 3. A summary of the general argument is outlined herewith.

Argument

1. The dynamics of the process whereby a small section of working-class women are translated from Care to Custody are partly explained by that perspective in criminology somewhat vacuously known as 'control theory'.

2. The version of 'control theory' used here is based on the assumption that people outwardly conform while they perceive it to be worth their while (psychologically and materially) to do so. (However, the subjective calculation also takes into account the likelihood of apprehension and criminalisation; the white-collar criminal can rationally calculate that it is not worth his or her while to conform because even if the crime is detected, the gains accruing from the fraud (or whatever) would most likely far outweigh the disabilities arising from the punishment).

3. For working-class men in employment the major locus of social control is the workplace (Young 1975), and, therefore, while men can continue to calculate that the rewards from employment outweigh those from crime, employed men are unlikely to engage in the more easily criminalised forms of lawbreaking. Through employment and trade unions they can make the economic and political 'class deal'.

4. Working-class women on the other hand have traditionally been contained within *two* material and ideological sites of social control: the workplace and the family – though it can be argued that both sites have provided women with fewer rewards than they have men. Working-class women have therefore been doubly controlled. They have been expected not only to make the 'class deal' but the 'gender deal' too. (True, feminists have persistently constructed 'alternative' reward sites, but when women in institutions do this – and especially if they choose other women as sexual partners – it is usually taken as evidence of their essential gender deviance and is punished by the authorities.)

5. Most working-class women make both the 'class deal' and the 'gender deal' because the exploitative nature of those two deals is obscured by the ideologies of familiness and consumerism working together to engender within the women a commitment to, if not a belief in, the imaginary rewards of respectable working-class womanhood.

6. This commitment to the rewards of 'respectable' working-class womanhood is most likely to be engendered when young women are brought up in families where both psychological and material rewards are represented as emanating from either the labours or the 'love' of a male breadwinner. (Even though many households do not nowadays *have* a male breadwinner, the normative

heterosexuality celebrated in women's magazines, pop sings and the predominantly conservative and liberal mass media still represents male-related domesticity
coupled with a wage-earning job as the twin ideals to which (gender-) competent
modern women should aspire).

7. Women brought up in Care since birth or early childhood, together with
those put into Care by seemingly rejecting families in adolescence tend not to
acquire the psychological commitments to male-related domesticity, tend not to
have their class position occluded by the forms and outward trappings of bourgeois
family ideology, and yet *do* acquiesce in a commitment to consumerism that is
often the only space within which, they believe, they can make their own lives.
(There is also often a commitment to an imaginary family form. For a detailed
account of the relationships betwen identity, ideology, crime and women's
everyday lives, see my forthcoming book, *Women, Crime and Poverty,* (Carlen 1988).

8. The majority of women are *not* criminalised even if they do break the law,
because while they remain within the family they are seen to have made the
'gender deal' and to be gender-regulated. Conversely, girls in Care (by definition
beyond family control in at least the physical, and sometimes also in the
disciplinary sense) are often seen as being gender-decontrolled. Already seen,
therefore, as being *unregulated women,* once they break the law, they are also seen as
being potential recidivist lawbreakers. Their 'files' become 'records' and the
authorities act accordingly.

9. The official responses to young women in Care who get into trouble combine
with prevailing economic and ideological conditions to minimalise (or in many
cases destroy) the likelihood of them having either future opportunities or
inclinations to make either the 'class deal' or the 'gender deal'. They perceive
themselves to be marginalised and therefore, having nothing to lose, decide that
lawbreaking is a preferable alternative to poverty and social isolation.

In this article it is argued that when specified economic, ideological and
regulatory/penal practices combine as constituents of individual life-histories
they overdetermine both the lawbreaking and criminalisation of a small section of
working-class women. The narrative describes how these conditions repeatedly
combine to effect the belief (held for different reasons by both the young women
in Care themselves and by their state guardians) that life outside the Care/penal-
custody complex has nothing to offer that might either *induce* the women to
conform or *enable* them to keep out of trouble in the future.

Like all other British women, these twenty-two were born into material
conditions structured by two dominant sets of relationships: the class relationships
of a capitalist mode of production and the gender relationships of a patriarchal
system of social reproduction. Unlike the majority, they had refused to be party to
the contract that had been drawn-up for them. But their refusals had been neither
silent nor polite. The persistence of their nuisances, the violence of their
resistances and the audacity of their insouciance in face of official attempts to
control them, had gradually marked both them, their actions and their files with a
criminality that must eventually defy the best jurisprudential attempts to

represent them as victims. Nor would they wish to be so represented. What follows is a theoretical commentary on the women's own vivid accounts of how they had set about making their own lives in conditions that had certainly not been of their own choosing. Conditions, in fact, that no sane persons *would* choose.

Cautionary note: A full analysis of the social and political meanings of crime would explain not only why some people break the law but also why certain groups can continue to do so with impunity. For, while the majority of the economically disadvantaged and the powerless do not become recidivist criminals, many acts of serious lawbreaking (most, if we refer only to financial crimes) result neither from poverty nor any other kind of deprivation. It might, therefore, be instructive to the reader, as she engages with the stories of these twenty-two women, to ponder also on the very different economic and political circumstances of that larger group of lawbreakers whose crimes are seldom brought to book. I refer of course to the crimes of the rich and the powerful.

Into Care

The majority of young people in Care are there because their families are too poor to pay for alternative ways of coping with illness, bereavement, single parenthood, homelessness, and so on (cf.Freeman 1983: 148; House of Commons 1984). Further biases are accounted for by race and gender.

In 1984 the Second Report from the Social Services Committee, *Children in Care,* Volume I (House of Commons 1984: *cxix),* observed that 'ethnic minority children are disproportionately represented in the Care population'. Summarising views put to it by a number of organisations, the committee reported that 'the unnecessary removal of black children from their families' (p. *cxx*) was 'said to spring from 'Eurocentric' views held by social-workers about ideal family patterns and ideal family behaviour' (P. *cxx).* Idealisations of femininity are also operative in Care proceedings.

DHSS statistics (1984) together with a number of research studies (e.g. Casburn 1979; B. Hudson 1984; Webb 1984) support the view that

> the majority of girls do not get drawn into the complex web of the personal social services because they have committed offences. It is more likely to be because of concerns about their perceived sexual behaviour and/or because they are seen to be 'at risk' of 'offending' against social codes of adolescent femininity
>
> (A. Hudson 1985: 1)

So with the twenty-two women interviewed. Thirteen had been taken into residential Care after the age of 11 (the post-11 group) and 'status offences' accounted for the orders imposed on eight of them (even though three of the eight had been taken to court after admitting criminal offences). Two orders had been occasioned by 'family circumstances' and three by acts of lawbreaking. Yet, whatever the official reasons for the orders, it is an ironical fact that while all those admitted to residential Care before the age of 11 (the pre-11 group) held inaccurate

Table 8.3 Out of Care, into Custody: Dimensions, Deconstructions, and Dynamics

Career stage[a]	Economic and ideological conditions			Deviant or law-breaking activities	Consequences
	Class	Gender	Racism		
Entry into Care	Pre-11 Parents lack money and access to other material goods and therefore cannot meet extra financial demands.	Post-11 1. Self-referral owing to material restrictions at home. 2. Referred by parents or guardians who fear that girl's behaviour is gender-deviant.	Disproportionate removal of ethnic minority children from their homes because of 'Eurocentric' views on childrearing.	Post 11 Status offences – like staying out too late at night, truancy, general 'unfeminine' behaviour.	1. Excessive assessment and categorising leading to feelings of self-and-social estrangement. 2. Attempts to escape Care through drugs or absconding. 3. Quest for true care through development of non-institutional relationships.
'Trouble' in residential institutions	1. Developing sense of deprivation and difference – sense of being in the Care class. 2. Developing sense of lack of control over life chances. 3. But class position often not perceived because immediate material needs well provided for.	1. Castigation of women via talk. Developing feelings of guilt (about being outside 'the family') and abnormality. 2. Higher standards of behaviour expected of adolescent girls than of adolescent boys. 3. Insensitive response to girls' physical development. 4. No discussion of women and sex.	1. Children brought up as white'. 2. Racist presumption that black children in Children's Homes cause problems. 2. Racist assumption that young black women likely to be promiscuous. 4. Isolated in Children's Home from other black people.	1. Drugtaking. 2. Absconding. 3. Various petty crimes.	1. Increased sense of difference and isolation. 2. Movement from 'placement' to 'placement' and eventually to a Secure Unit. 3. Increased determination to 'escape' - absconding. 4. Drugs administered to control behaviour. 5. Placing of most troublesome young women in 'independent' accommodation while still in care.

Into crime				
1. Increased poverty once girl has absconded. 2. Once apprehended by police, no 'friendly' adults to intervene – only social-workers who have run out of 'placements' for them.	1. Girls in Care are likely to be viewed by court as already being out of their 'proper' place and therefore are dealt with more harshly. 2. Fewer non-custodial facilities for lawbreaking women. 3. Knowledge that they will be approached by male predators whilst on the run results in many women carrying a knife and then being arrested for carrying an offensive weapon. 4. Escalation of young women up the sentencing tariff for a variety of reasons.	1. Racism operative when young girl comes to attention of the police. (Home Office 1986). Reports of verbal abuse with sexual connotations. 2. Likely to be under greater surveillance in shops and public places. Greater likelihood of arrest if they do break the law.	1. Crimes committed for survival while on the run. 2. Drugs – to provide non-institutional network of friends. 3. Entry into some types of more organised crime.	1. Deviant/lawbreaking activities more likely to come to attention of police because children are in Children's Home. 2. Magistrates look doubly askance at lawbreaking women who are already in residential Care, not living with a family. 3. Custodial sentence likely if social-workers say that the troublesome young woman has already been through every 'placement' (Care and penal systems merge at this point). 4. Young women placed in independent accommodation – bedsitter or hostel.

continued

Table 8.3 continued

Career stage[a]	Economic and Ideological conditions			Deviant or law-breaking activities	Consequences
	Class	Gender	Racism		
Out of residential Care	1. Extreme poverty encountered upon leaving institution. 2. Difficulties with DHSS or supplementary benefits payments. 3. Living in hostels that do not allow residents to remain indoors during day. 4. Growing awareness of stigma and economic deprivation.	1. Women suffer disproportionately from shortage of rented housing for single people. 2. Through loneliness or hostel policies women forced to seek company in public places and are likely to be seen as violating appropriate gender behaviour by so doing. 3. Growing awareness of gender ideologies – especially 'deviance' of being apart from nuclear family.	Affects housing and employment opportunities.	1. Unauthorised removal of personal file from institution. 2. Prostitution and theft and other minor crimes both for economic survival and to carve out an independent way of life.	1. Some choose to 'live rough' rather than in unwelcoming and exploitative hostels. 2. Some become pregnant in order to acquire both family and home. 3. Institutional living has left them ill-equipped to look after themselves. 4. Once apprehended for crime, their institutional record and gender deviance goes against them in court. 5. Increase in belief that law-breaking is the only way of making a decent living.
Into custody	1. Material circumstances outside prison by now so bad that prison viewed as a refuge from men, money problems and isolation. 2. Nothing in their past histories leads them to believe that they have any chance now of making the 'class deal' and gaining even the meanest rewards for class conformity.	1. Once they have completed their sentences very few after-care facilities for women. 2. Housing situation worse for women ex-prisoners. 3. Nothing in their past histories leads them to believe that they have much chance of making the 'gender deal' and gaining even the meanest rewards for gender conformity.	Varies from institution to institution[b] but the Home Office reported in June 1986 that more than four times the expected proportion of adult women in prison are from ethnic minority groups.[c]	1. With nothing going for them on the outside, they create trouble in Youth Custody Centre in order to stay there. 2. Some invoke 'hard' girl status by tattoing; determination to gain prison reputation. 3. Some experience despair and guilt and engage in self mutilation.	1. Custodial sentence results in loss of accommodation and in loss of few possessions they have. 2. Custodial sentence results in loss of embryo family through children going into Care. 3. Women begin to fear the cumulative effects of institutionalisation but find it difficult to conceive that they have much to gain in the future by conformity.

(a) The stages are not numbered as their ordering is different for individual career patterns.
(b) See Reports of the Chief Inspector of Prisons 1983-85 and also *Breaking the Silence* (GLC 1986).

views on the normal form of the modern family (cf. Barrett and McIntosh 1982: Segal 1983) together with romantic idealisations of its functions, the majority of the post-11 group claimed that their own experiences of family life had made them initially welcome the removal from home (cf. A Hudson 1985: 8).

Once they had reached puberty many of the women had found that previously permissive parents suddenly because unduly restrictive (cf.Christina and Carlen 1985). Indeed, several had been glad to get away from the beatings suffered at the hands of relatives. Except for Sally (who at 15 had already chosen her own 'way out' by 'being into drink and drugs'), all of the post-11 group had seen 'going into [residential] Care' as an escape from difficult family situations. Their families appeared to have held similar views. Tricia's and Zoe's mothers had been the first to report their daughters to the police. (Tricia for theft from her mother's purse, Zoe for running away from home.) The fathers of Carol and Josie, Daphne's mother and Cynthia's grandmother had made repeated requests for the girls to be taken into Care. Sally had already been turned out of home before being sent to Approved School. Kim had 'cleared-off' in response to her grandmother's unjust accusations of prostitution.

Certainly, none of the post-11 group had been 'typical girls' (Griffin 1985) in terms of being 'muted' (Ardener 1978; Stanworth 1985), limiting their activities to the private spaces of their homes (McRobbie and Garber, 1976) and/or engaging in only those pursuits allowed by the conventional discourses of femininity. And as Barbara Hudson (1984) has argued, whereas much behaviour seen to be peculiar to teenage boys is legitimated by discourses of adolescence that allow 'adolescent' males a developmental space for behavioural experimentation prior to their emergence into adulthood, no such discursive leeway is allowed to girls who engage in the same behaviours. Discourses of femininity are seen to be subverted by discourses of adolescence. The young female is always an embryo woman, never a developing person (cf.Sachs and Wilson 1978). If, therefore, the discourse of femininity does indeed supercede that of adolescence, then from the accounts they gave me of their teenage activities it can clearly be seen that Zoe and the others had definitely slipped their ideological moorings.

Refusal to stay within oppressive families, schools, and (later) institutions was a distinguishing feature of the twenty-two women's careers. All said that they had truanted from day schools and/or absconded on more than one occasion from residential Care. As far as school was concerned, hostility was directed less against the teachers and more against the system of 'schooling' itself. Repeatedly women made remarks like, 'I just couldn't bear sitting down all day being told what to do', though two had provoked expulsions rather than tamely submit to the disciplinary violence of corporal punishment.

By the time they reached secondary school many young women were already feeling over-constrained by the combined disciplines of family and school or (in the case of the pre-11 group) by the combined restraints of schooling and residential institution. Those still at home often felt devalued in comparison with brothers, and with nothing on offer at home or school some of the youngsters had sought fun in public spaces outside the domestic, educational and institutional

Table 8.4 Institutional and other residential experiences of twenty-two convicted women who had spent part of their lives in Care

Pseudonym and age	Age of entry into residential Care order and duration	Summary reason for Care order as explained by interviewee	Reason given for Care order as explained by interviewee	Institutions experienced – excluding assessment and Remand Centres (CH = Children's Home; CHE = Community Home with Education; YCC = Youth Custody Centre (*indicates several different placements)
Daphne (15)	13 years to time of interview	Criminal offence	With others, set fire to, and destroyed, a school	CH; CHE* Foster parents, YCC
Della (15)	13 years to time of interview	Status offence	Poor school attendance (but taken to court for theft)	CHE, YCC
Yasmin (16)	2 years to present	Family circumstances	Unknown to Yasmin	CH*, CHE, Adolescent Unit, Special School* YCC (2) own single accommodation while still in care
Tricia (17)	13 years to time of interview	Status offence	Truancy (but taken to court for theft)	CH, CHE, Adolescent Unit, YCC (2), hostel*
Audrey (18)	2–18 years	Family circumstances	Unknown to Audrey	CH,* CHE, Adolescent Unit, Therapeutic Community hostel, single accommodation while still in Care, YCC
Cynthia (19)	13–18 years	Family circumstances	Mother (single parent) unable to care for her	CH,* CHE, Special School, hostel, YCC
Shirley (20)	birth to 18 years	Family circumstances	Unknown to Shirley	CH,* foster-parents, hostel, own single accommodation whilst still in Care, living rough on the run, YCC

Name	Age	Type	Reason	Institutions
Anne (20)	14–18 years	Status offence	Out of mother's control (but taken to court for stealing a book)	CHE,* Adolescent Unit, foster-parents, hostel, own single accommodation while still in care, living rough/on the run, YCC
Jill (21)	4–18 years	Family circumstances	Mother's illness and death (father living elsewhere)	CH,* Adolescent Unit, foster-parents,* Special School, living rough/on run, hostel, YCC
Lena (21)	7–18 years	Family circumstances	Physical abuse by mother	CH,* CHE, hostel, YCC
Tara (21)	14–18 years	Criminal offences	Fraud, forgery, theft	CHE, living rough/on the run, YCC
Norma (22)	14–18 years	Family circumstances	Physical abuse by mother	Special School, YCC
Donna (22)	2 months to 18 years	Family circumstances	Mother (single parent) unable to look after her	CH,* Adolescent Unit, Therapeutic Community, special school, own single accommodation while still in Care, living rough/on the run, YCC
Dawn (23)	13–18 years	Status offence	Running away from home	Approved school, living rough, prison
Carol (27)	12–18 years	Status offence	Father unable to cope with daughter after death of wife	CH, mental hospital, hostel
Zoe (28)	12–18 years	Status offence	Staying out late, running away from home	CH, living rough/on the run, prison
Kim (28)	12–18 years	Status offence	Running away from home	CH,* borstal, prison

continued

Table 8.4 continued

Pseudonym and age	Age of entry into residential Care order and duration	Summary reason for Care order as explained by interviewee	Reason given for Care order as explained by interviewee	Institutions experienced – excluding assessment and Remand Centres (CH = Children's Home; CHE = Community Home with Education; YCC = Youth Custody Centre (*Indicates several different placements)
Hazel (29)	6–18 years	Family circumstances	Mother (single parent) unable to care for her	Approved school, borstal, prison
Muriel (30)	6 weeks to 18 years	Family circumstances	Unknown to Muriel, who was found abandoned on Waterloo Stn., 6 weeks old	CH,* mental hospital, foster parents* approved school, hostel, living rough/on the run, borstal, prison
Josie (own name) (30)	11–18 years	Criminal offence	With others, accidentally setting fire to a row of cottages	CH,* Approved School, living rough/on the run, hostel, borstal, prison
Nadia (35)	birth to 9, then 12–18 years	Family circumstances	Original reason for being in care unknown – adopted at 9 – returned to care three years later after death of both adoptive parents	Approved School, living rough/on the run, borstal
Sally (36)	14–18 years	Status offence	Staying out late at night, drinking alcohol	Mental hospital, Approved School, hostel,* living rough/on the run, borstal prison

spheres. For as Hagan, Simpson and Gillis have stressed 'delinquency frequently is *fun* – and even more importantly, a type of fun infrequently allowed to females' (1979: 29). But, when the women's larks went wrong, retribution was swift:

> The first time I got in trouble was for abstracting electricity. Somebody betted me to make some 999 calls and I got done. I went to court and was moved to an Approved School.
> (Hazel, aged 29, temporarily out of residential Care at the time of which she is speaking).

> I was in a hostel and I used to go out and I started drinking heavily. For that I got sent to Approved School. Which I don't think was right when I'd never even committed a crime. OK, they saw me as uncontrollable but they didn't find out *why* I was uncontrollable and put that right. I ran away from one place because all they kept going on about was sex. At that time I'd only ever been with one man.
> (Sally, aged 35)

Because every one of the post-11 group had run away from home at least once, and most had roamed the town when truanting from school, they had also spent much of their time in the company of young men who, unlike young women, are seen as natural occupiers of public space. Yet only three of the post-11 group admitted to having had sexual intercourse in their early teens. The others either claimed to have had no interest in men at all at that age or, more often, merely to have wanted a share in the greater degree of freedom accorded to males (cf.Christina and Carlen 1985; Tchaikovsky 1985). For example:

> Boys are better than girls, they're more joyful. Girls are just boring. Like, girls can't climb trees for a laugh, or jump over walls. But boys can, and that's what I like doing.
> (Daphne, aged 15)

> At that time, I liked motor-bikes. I was always more interested in the bike than the fellow on it.
> (Norma, aged 22)

All the post-11 group indicated that as young teenagers they had fiercely resented the restrictions emanating from poverty, family, (cf.Jordan 1983) school and gender ideologies. Questioned about their early teenage ambitions the most frequent reply was the deceptively simple (and as things turned out, movingly innocent): 'I just wanted to lead my own life, that was all'. With their working-class situation limiting their options on alternatives to life in the family home, entry into residential Care was in prospect seen as being at least a step on the road to independence. In reality the opposite was true. Sooner or later each of those thirteen women discovered that, in terms of developing independence, life in residential Care was no life at all.

Too Much Care; Too Little care

'All children coming into Care need some degree of planned, professional diagnosis' (Home Office 1970). So reported the Advisory Council on Child Care in 1970, and given the range of residential facilities used by local authorities, it is not surprising that strenuous attempts are made to 'fit' child to Children's Home or other 'placement' (see Richardson 1969). Yet, as Foucault (1977) has indicated, assessment, categorisation and 'placing' also have hidden disciplinary functions, coercive and, ultimately, exclusionary effects that the women in this study had certainly sensed and rebelled against.

Psychological assessment had been a major element in construction of the 'outsider' status frequently invoked by the women as being partly responsible for their rebellious reactions to Care. Constant assessment, categorisation and recategorisation had led to a sense of essential difference, otherness and deviance. This in conjuction with continual movement from 'placement' to 'placement' (the implication being that for every normal child there *is* an appropriate placement) had finally resulted in their envelopment in a tenacious isolationary matrix. Psychologically manacled to their files (and the 'outsider' identities constructed therein), physically filed away behind the bars of Secure Units and Youth Custody Centres, it had seemed to many of the women that too much Care had pushed them into a disciplinary space where no one cared at all. The complex social problems that had precipitated them into Care in the first place had carefully been translated and redistributed as the individual problems of yet another batch of gender-'careless', delinquent girls.

Filing, assessment, categorisation, 'placing'

Morris *et al.* (1980) have pointed out that many children in Care 'believe that they have done wrong, especially when they later meet young offenders at the children's home and find that they are on the same kind of order – a Care Order'. Yet, even when they accept that they were taken into Care solely for 'family reasons' beyond their control, young women desperately want to know what those reasons were. It is then that 'the file' takes on such importance. What is in it? Is the record accurate?

Young people in Care who do eventually read their files are frequently surprised at the inaccuracies and prejudices they contain (see Denton Wakerley 1985). Many of the women interviewed thought that at least some of the absurder assessments stem from the pressure put on young women in Care to define and share their 'problems' (cf. Ackland, 1982: 145):

> If they'd nothing to write about you then you didn't stay there long. Sometimes they used to make things up and write them about you. I think they read these books and it doesn't really matter what you say, as long as it's got a slight link with the book. If you've got nothing to say at all, or if you have great difficulty in expressing yourself, then they're fucked.
>
> (Muriel, aged 30)

Talking about why she had always been 'on the run' from her various 'placements', Anne remarked that 'it's too hard to explain but they were always trying to get at you mentally'. Others stated more tersely that 'case conferences and reviews just do people's heads in'. The most constant complaint concerned the 'pressure to have problems', the coercive assumption of difference. What the women were talking about, in effect, was the psychiatrisation of women's deviant behaviour (cf. Carlen 1985b, 1986) and the way in which attempts are made to regulate women through redefining them and castigating them by talk (cf. Okely, 1978; Carlen, 1983a). For although only three of the interviewees had spent time in a mental hospital, the majority mentioned that they had frequently been made to feel that they were 'not quite right in the head'.

> I always felt that, being in Care, they sort of put things into your mind and make you feel as if you're all mixed up when really you haven't got a problem. It's *very* hard to explain but they make you feel that you're very special because you're in Care and that you've got problems. Really, they're just messing up with your head.
>
> (Audrey, aged 18)

Donna's account of being sent to an Adolescent Unit reveals not only her own sense of violation at the clumsy 'therapeutic' intervention but also the sexist and racist assumptions incorporated into the 'assessment' that had occasioned the move.

> They were definitely a lot stricter with girls than boys. I found out *why* because I took my file out of the office. It said how I was an attractive 13-year-old West Indian girl and that if I kept on like I was I'd soon have a couple of babies. So they sent me to an Adolescent Unit. There were bars on the windows, we were all locked up and they wanted you to join in all kinds of games. Like they wanted me to hold on to this pillow and imagine it was my mother. It was embarrassing; that wasn't my problem, my mother. They were saying I wasn't relaxing myself. I did try but it was like lying. I think that affected my life really. Coz I keep thinking back on it and I think, 'Oh, my God! How embarrassing.' I ran away from there.'
>
> (Donna, aged 22)

Difference

'Care's' emphasis on individual assessment and problem-solving was not the only cause of the overwhelming sense of difference that had assailed so many of the young women. Growing awareness of the dominance of the 'normal nuclear family' myth had also depressed several of the pre-11 group at some stage in their childhood:

> I always felt that I wanted to be with a proper family, be the same as everyone else. I didn't want to be different. But they do try to make you feel different. That's why I was against them.
>
> (Yasmin, aged 16)

A sense of difference permeated other spheres, too (cf. Page and Clark 1977, Ch. 3).

Like at the school I went to, no one wore uniform. But I had to because we came from the Children's Home.

(Shirley, aged 20)

I felt I had no control over anything at all. I had to get the social worker to sign a bit of paper even before I could go on a school outing.

(Muriel, aged 30)

Coz I was in Care a lot I couldn't mix with the others. I had to go home on a special bus. There was a definite difference.

(Nadia, aged 35)

We were always special cases at school. We were never told off if we didn't have our PE kit or if our uniform was imperfect. But if we were missing from the lesson the headmaster would straightway ring the Children's Home. You used to get some people say, 'Why are you in a Children's Home?' and then there would be the other ones who would say, '*What* are you in a Children's Home *for?*'

(Zoë, aged 28)

When you go out it seems as if you've got a name tag. People say where do you live and you say 'High Street,' and they say, 'Oh, I know that, that's the Children's Home.' And then you get questions about why you're in care. You try and forget it, but it always comes up. You try and start anew but it's always there.

(Shirley, aged 20)

It was in Care that Donna learned about racism; Josie about class differences – including the 'Care class' and poverty.

I was brought up the white way. I was only aware of colour when a kid called me a wog and I beat the hell out of him. I asked the children at the Home what it was and Uncle told me. I was bitter, angry and upset, and eventually I was proud of it.

(Donna, aged 20; cf. House of Commons 1984)

I can remember going to Marks and Spencer with a social-worker to buy clothes, and because we had a welfare grant form we had to wait while they served all the other customers. You were really made to feel small. It came to the stage where I felt that I'd rather go out and thieve it off someone's line. I didn't . . . but you know . . . This is when you realise that you're being given charity handouts, being written off as poor, put in a low bracket. And suddenly you become aware that there's people that are well off, people that are reasonably well off, and then, that you're working class. And *then* it's as if there's *another* class of people having to live on charity. That's probably when I started to become aware of class barriers.

(Josie, aged 30; cf. Stein 1983: 90; NAYPIC 1983: 24 on clothing books and voucher systems)

Isolation

Many of the women said that, independently of their actual experiences in Children's Homes, the very fact of being in Care had made them feel guilty, had made them believe that they must have done something wrong to be so 'unwanted'. Local authority social-work practices such as moving them from 'placement' to 'placement' and separating them from their brothers and sisters had aggravated that loneliness:

> I didn't like it when they used to push you about from one kid's home to another. You got attached to one kid's home and then the next minute you'd be moving somewhere else, leaving your mates.
>
> (Lena, aged 21)

For Shirley and Kim, young black women, the sense of isolation was even worse:

> The staff changed a lot so it took time to build up another relationship with another member of staff. After I'd been separated from my brother – that hurt me a lot, he was the only one I had – and moved backwards and forwards in Children's Homes, there wasn't anyone I could relate to, you know.
>
> (Shirley, aged 20)

> So I thought I was white until I went to junior school. Then the black children kept asking me why I lived with white people. So I got it both ends. Then the social-workers kept having these meetings about me, but as I was the only black person there I couldn't relate to any of them.
>
> (Kim, aged 28)

Jill, also black, had had no one to whom she could turn when sexually assaulted by her white fosterfather.

> My foster-dad put me off men because when I was a little girl he tried to attack me – sexually, you know. When that happened I couldn't tell anyone. I had no one to turn to. I was too scared. I liked my foster parents and I didn't want to be taken away from them. After that I closed myself in a little bit.
>
> (Jill, aged 21)

Fostering that didn't work' had made other women feel guilty (even abnormal) for not, as Muriel put it, 'being grateful for breathing the same air as them'. With each new move the sense of difference and isolation had increased, though Muriel (with good reason – she had been found abandoned on Waterloo Station at 6 weeks old) thought that Providence had marked her card from birth.

> I think it was sort of stamped on me from when I was a baby, you know. They could do exactly what they liked coz there was no one there to stand up for me. I had so many foster parents it was like being reconditioned every few weeks, like a car engine. Oh . . .I don't know. I felt such an outcast.
>
> (Muriel, aged 30)

For some of the women the sense of 'otherness' had gradually developed into a sense of nothingness, a void that they had to fill by building up a life amongst people who would *not* cast them out.

On top of everything else, the black women had had imposed on them a 'white' upbringing which some of them were later to question. All twenty-two women, however, complained (though for varying reasons) that in Care they had been denied opportunities to develop any modes of control over their lives, especially over their own sexuality:

> In my first kids' home I didn't go out with boys because I didn't realise that growing up *meant* I was to go out and have a good time. That wasn't what I was allowed to do. So when I met Jack things just happened [she became pregnant] between us.
>
> (Norma, aged 22)

> I knew nothing about sex. They never tell you anything. You know what? When I first started growing tits I didn't even ask for a bra. That's how much I knew. When I came on with my period I didn't know who to tell. I was petrified. What made it worse was that when I did tell the woman she only went in the office and told the man that I'd come on with my periods. They never told me nothing. I didn't even know what pregnancy was. The doctor said to me, 'Haven't you been told about these things?' I said, 'No'. He sat and explained it all to me. And I cried because I didn't know what had happened. They persuaded me to have a termination.
>
> (Donna, aged 23)

'In Care', said Zoë, 'You just don't get a chance to be your own person'; and most of the women echoed that sentiment, claiming that the peripatetic life, the lack of time, space and opportunity in which to learn to make and sustain relationships based on reciprocated trust had had lasting and painful effects. For, however much they had previously felt constrained within family relationships, *all* the women (the pre-11 group and the post 11 group) expressed views on Care that suggested that they had none the less sensed a real distinction between imaginary relationships based on notions of familial reciprocity and mutuality and relationships in Care. In their relationships with their state guardians (social-workers and social-work departments) they had sensed themselves as being constituted as debtors within an imaginary debtor–creditor relationship (cf. Wilden 1972). One result of this objectivication was that, instead of gaining an independence in personal relationships, the young women had come to fear relationships as always *threatening* independence and inducing dependency. Zoë and Jill described the effects as they were experiencing them.

> Nowadays if people help me or do something for me because they want something back they needn't bother because if I've got to be grateful I don't want to know. If social-workers do it, it's my right, they're paid for it, they're obliged to. I've been rejected by so many people that now I always break the relationship myself before they can do it.
>
> (Zoë, aged 28)

> I've been very lucky with social-workers and probation officers. I've really got on with them people. But sometimes, still to this day, I am still scared of grown-ups even though I'm a grown-up woman myself.
>
> (Jill, aged 20)

Thus, at every over-assessed step in the journey from Care to custody the twenty-two women had experienced an interplay of emergent difference and increasing isolation. Sensing that the whirlwind round of 'placements' might eventually lead to their own psychological *displacement*, the women had resisted Care's proprietary manoeuvers by engaging in the series of escapes that had eventually (and ironically) landed them in penal custody.

Into Crime

Ten of the twenty-two women claimed that their minor (and often non-criminal) early misbehaviours would never have escalated into 'criminal careers' at all had they not been in Care. Others, though reluctant to attribute their crimes to any one factor, thought that 'being in Care' had been an important influence on their lawbreaking and/or criminalisation.

As far as their juvenile misconduct or teenage lawbreaking was concerned, most of what the women said supports a formal explanation based on control theory.[3] The elements of the argument, therefore, are:

1. That the women's passage through Care had increasingly loosened those informal controls that primarily regulate by inducing conformity without recourse to the criminal law.

2. That, specifically, Care had broken their attachments to family and friends; failed to equip them with a whole range of knowledge (sexual, educational and life skills) necessary to independent adult living; stripped them of the rights, privacy and individuality constitutive of adult identity; and reared and regulated them as female public property rather than as private citizens.

3. That the women had responded by engaging in deviant behaviours born either of a desire to establish ties or contact with some person or group or of a sense that they had always-already been knocked out of the race to obtain the rewards of social respectability.

As for their criminalisation? The argument is that once they had misbehaved, their progress through the welfare and criminal control apparatuses had been escalated both because they were in Care *and* because they were female. For though it is *power* that engenders the most serious forms of *crime*, it is *powerlessness* that produces the most persistent patterns of *criminalisation*. The following ethnography of their journeys from Care to crime will demonstrate how the complex interplay between the survival strategies of young females in Care and the discriminatory social policies are ideologies constitutive of their increasing institutionalisation, swiftly translated gender-deviant working-class girls into criminal women.

From Care to Crime

Analysis of the interview transcripts suggested that one or more of three main types of situation had usually triggered off, or contributed to, the passage from Care to crime:

1. Situations in which a young woman's quest for care had resulted in behaviour that the authorities had responded to by the imposition of further restrictions.

2. Situations in which a young woman's flight from Care had almost inevitably resulted in lawbreaking behaviour.

3. Situations in which a young woman's departure from Care had precipitated her into a series of crises involving poverty, homelessness and unemployment. In each of these situations, too, discriminatory factors emanating from gender ideologies, plus the fact that the range of facilities for troublesome girls in Care is narrower than that for boys, operated to ensure that the young women were processed through the so-called 'alternatives' to panel custody at a reprehensible speed.

The Quest for care

As can be seen from Table 8. 4, most of the women had experienced several moves of residence whilst in Care. When asked about this they all gave a reply similar to Yasmin's: 'I kept getting in trouble and they couldn't cope. So I had to move on'. When questioned about their reasons for 'creating hell' in Children's Homes, and so on, the answers were more varied. Some referred to their resentment at being placed with people who had already committed crimes; others referred to an awareness of more basic injustice. Some said that they had been bored by lack of attention, were searching for friends who would appreciate them or that they had felt so derelict they had needed to make their mark upon someone or something. In short, their answers were variations on the same theme: that to create or maintain identity they had had to provoke a specific response to themselves as *individuals* rather than as clients of welfare:

> I didn't have a lot of respect for the people who brought me up. Instead of parents, I had social-workers, and I wanted parents to run my life, not social-workers.
>
> (Yasmin, aged 16)

Audrey and Muriel (amongst others) claimed that deviant behaviour had been a demanded response in all types of care institutions:

> I used to do really stupid things to get attention, make them think that I was a bit mad. But I do honestly feel that the staff used to encourage it by making you think that you did have a problem.
>
> (Audrey, aged 18)

> The worse rogue you were at Approved School the better time you had of it. They didn't take any notice of anyone who did everything correctly. It was a sort of prep. school for prison.
>
> (Muriel, aged 30)

Shirley thought that she had had particular difficulties to overcome and maybe part of her isolation *had* stemmed from the following type of racist policy towards young black people in Care:

> It seems that the presence of a large number of black children in an institution creates problems for staff and other residents . . . It has been suggested that as a result of such difficulties some institutions operate an informal quota system to ensure that no more than 20 – 25 per cent of their population consists of black children.
>
> (NACRO 1977: 21)

> In the Home I was in there wasn't many blacks or half-casts, just mainly white and you were trying to get your own friends, you wanted to get your own identity. So, you know, you tried to do something different.
>
> (Shirley, aged 20)

Getting into trouble in Children's Homes was mentioned most frequently by the pre-11 group. The post-11 group (and the pre-11 group in adolescence) had more usually responded to Care by fleeing from it, that is by absconding it. However, when absconding was made difficult other means of escape were tried, and it was incarceration in closed or secure accommodation that had provoked several first major encounters with the police:

> I had to go to an Adolescent Unit, a sort of closed one. It was like a hospital, surrounded by trees and woods. It was boredom most of all, boredom. We set fire to the woods because we knew that was the only way we could get help, for them to transfer us somewhere else. The police came in and took my fingerprints and took me down the police station.
>
> (Jill, aged 21; on secure accommodation; see Blumenthal 1985, and Freeman 1983: 176 – 7)

(Following this incident Jill was sent to a psychiatrist who said that she had set fire to the woods because she was still angry about her mother's death!)

The Flight from Care

By the time they had reached their teens the pre-11 group had realised that although bizarre behaviour would always gain them attention, 'it was the wrong kind of attention' (Audrey) and that they would have to look beyond Care for the space in which to develop as secure but independent adults. All of the post-11 group had absconded from the institutions to which they had been sent. Yet, before discussing the important part that absconding had played in their criminal careers, it is appropriate to look first at a less spectacular mode of escape, an activity often undetected by the authorities but one that, none the less, had also had consequences for some of the women. I refer to drug-taking.

Eleven of the women volunteered information that they had either taken illicit drugs or that they had started drinking heavily whilst in Care. Only one (Della) had begun her habit prior to her removal from home. Others said that drugs had been

Table 8.5 Women admitting to illicit drug usage or heavy consumption of alcohol while in Care

Name	Age at interview	Age and duration of usage	Drug involved
Della	15	14–15	Glue
Yasmin	15	15–16	Glue and other drugs
Audrey	18	15–18	15–18
Shirley	20	13–17	Glue and other solvents
Anne	20	16–19	Heroin and other drugs
Jill	21	12–13	Glue
		16–19	Alcohol
Lena	21	15–18	Glue
Donna	22	15–20	Alcohol
Dawn	23	13–15	Various drugs
Nadia	35	16–18	Various drugs
Sally	36	14–16	Various drugs
		16 to time of interview	Heroin

administered to control their behaviour (on the drugging of children in Care, see Taylor, Lacey and Bracken 1979: 80 and Freeman 1983: 172):

> I was on largactyl and I remember being on a lot at one point and feeling like a zombie. Yet we were only allowed to have one cigarette a day!
>
> (Nadia, aged 35)

> I went to this secure place. It was meant to help you sort out your life a bit better. I threw a fit the first time I went in there. Got a needle right up the bum. [Laughs.] I was out flat.
>
> (Yasmin, aged 16)

Given that the young people most likely to be drugged by the authorities were also those who were themselves seeking ways to assuage their gnawing sense of futility, it is not surprising that outside the institution they should have sought the 'fix' that they had already experienced (or heard of) within it. And, in the short term at least, drugs *had* eased their pain:

> All along the line I'd got this thing that I was a waste of time and that I was in the way. When I started taking drugs like deksies and bombers it was bloody wonderful, you know.
>
> (Nadia, aged 35)

> I was taking speed and I started getting into smack [heroin] when I was 16. It was very nice.
>
> (Anne, aged 20)

When I take drugs I enjoy myself. Acid calms me down and makes me feel good. When I'm taking acid, tripping like mad, that's the only time I enjoy myself.

(Yasmin, aged 16)

In the longer term several had found that drug usage just added to their problems:

I had nobody really. I was a very lonely person, and because I was lonely I found myself mixing with a crowd of really heavy people who dealt in drugs. I was never on heroin – other things, you know – and I was turning into a complete and utter junkie. I thought I was dying.

(Audrey, aged 18)

I was sniffing glue from the age of 13. A little section of us out of the Children's Home got glue and Bostik and then we started drinking cider, and then got on to spirits. I gave up the glue when I was 17 because it *was* a problem. I wasn't eating, I used to get the shakes and at the end, when I was 17, it had done nothing for me so I just give it up.

(Shirley, aged 20)

Only three women said at interview that they still had a drug problem, though all eleven thought that some of their crimes had been drug or alcohol related. It is likely that their drug-taking in Care had also had indirect effect on their careers. For it was frequently after official detection of illicit drug or alcohol consumption that they had been moved to securer accommodation or even locked up in a Secure Unit.

Whether the misbehaviour in Care involved violence, drug-taking, staying out late or whatever, the official response had always seemed to involve the young women in a move of residence – to more of the same but worse! Small wonder that Muriel's characterisation of the care she received in Care was echoed (though less graphically) by so many of the others interviewed.

As far as they were concerned, I was the devil itself. If I'd have been a dog they would have put me to sleep. In fact, they just tried to put a muzzle on.

(Muriel, aged 30)

To escape the 'muzzle' the young women repeatedly absconded.

Absconding

The majority of absconders are like everyone else and the absconding problem is created by the institutions through which the children pass.

(Milham, Bullock and Hosie 1978: 76)

Except for Zoë, all the women had absconded at least once, and eleven of them had 'lived rough, on the run' for considerable periods during their time in Care. Anne's and Nadia's experiences were similar to those of the eleven other girls who had been almost continuously 'on the run' and who had committed crimes in order to keep themselves (cf. Christina and Carlen 1985):

Anne: When I was 14 I ran away. I was in a squat at King's Cross, but I couldn't stay there so I went up to Oxford. I really liked it and made a lot of friends. I stayed for about five months until I was caught – and then that was my TDA [taking and driving away] with being in a stolen car. I was taken back to Middlesex Lodge again – and then – it's really confusing because I've been in Middlesex Lodge five times, Cumberlow Lodge, Lytton House (I've been so many different places I forget the times I've been). Well, it went on and on, I was running and being caught and running – I did a cheque book, and when I was 15 there was a burglary as well. . . . I did it for survival, I was pretty desperate and I didn't have any money. Then I got done for the cheque books and when I was 15 I ended up in Borstal – after going to Holloway.

Pat: But why did you keep running away from CHEs?
Anne: I didn't think they had a right to keep me there.
Nadia: I always used to finish up down the Dilly – at Playland.[4] When I went there I felt that I *did* belong. People were like me, talked like me, behaved like me. I felt accepted. The women there were strong. I mean, they were prostitutes and that as well, and doing kinky punters – and I did that myself for quite a while as years went on. Anyhow, I got picked up and had my sixteenth birthday in Holloway.
Pat: They sent you there straightway?
Nadia: I got sent to the only place that would have me. The police said nowhere else would have me, and I remember saying to 'em, 'If I had people of my own you wouldn't treat me like this'.

Other young women had absconded for short periods and then returned, but they had still risked trouble of one kind or another:

When I absconded from school I needed food so I kept nicking things so I could sell them. Coz I had no money, see?

(Daphne, aged 15)

Yasmin: I used to do a lot of absconding. I'd go up to London, I've a lot of friends up there. If I hitch it to somewhere and I don't get to their house that night I sleep in a bus shelter. I always carry a knife on me but I want to be careful in case the police stop me one day and they found it. But I would kill anyone who comes near me.
Pat: How do they get you back when you abscond?
Yasmin: They don't get me back. I go back. Because I get fed-up running you know, all the time. All my life I've been running and running and I just get fed up and feel it's doing me no good. I just go back. Then I pack my bags and go off again. And come back!

Whatever the reasons for absconding – and most were related to the way in which trouble in institutions had been responded to by the imposition of even further restrictions – once they *had* absconded the young women were frequently treated like dangerous and wanted criminals:

I ran away and got done for carrying an offensive weapon. I had a knife, cos I used to hitch-hike. It was just to carry around with me just in case . . . you can get some weirdos. Especially cos of my height, they think they can be clever. Especially these lorry drivers ... it was just for my own protection. I got picked up in Birmingham and ended up getting Borstal, Borstal re-call.

(Hazel, aged 29)

Note: Hazel's first Borstal sentence had been for 'criminal damage', that is breaking a window.

I ran away when I was in there [Adolescent Unit]. With some girls I went to Brighton and we slept on the beach. We phoned them because we wanted to see what they had done and in five seconds, as soon as we put that phone up, there was a police car there.

(Donna, aged 22)

I was strip-searched when I was 14 years old in the police-station. I was picked up and I was on my period at the time and I was really – you know – and I had to bend over, take my tampax out. And I was sort of like that, with my clothes on, and the policewoman said, 'I don't know what you're being bashful about'. And, you know, thinking about it, maybe I should have had a social-worker present.

(Anne, aged 20)

When I had my foster parents the police never used to mess me around because they [foster parents] were whites and they were standing by me. But when I ran away their [police] comments were just plain racist; they told lies and they took a lot of liberties. But you see, they were in a position to take those liberties because if you're alone and haven't got nobody, people can do with you as they feel.

(Kim, aged 28)

Research evidence suggests that young teenage women who come to the attention of the police and criminal courts are escalated up the sentencing tariff more swiftly than boys. In the minds of the young women who had been punished for absconding by incarceration in Secure Units, the distinction between 'Care tariff' and 'criminal sentencing tariff' had been eroded years before they ever set foot in a criminal court.

Escalatory Factors in the Young Women's Journey from Care to Custody

In 1983 Lorraine Gelsthrope, in her evidence to the Social Services Committee (House of Commons 1984) claimed that 'girls particularly end up being comitted to Care orders because there is really no adequate provision for them within the tariff system'. She continued;

There are about six or seven attendance centres specifically for girls in this country as opposed to around 100 centres for boys...Practitioners comment that there are many fewer provisions for girls and that the provisions tend to be dominated by, or orientated towards, providing facilities for boys, this frequently occurs in intermediate treatment schemes.

(Gelsthorpe 1983: 566)

These observations are supported by other research, good summaries of which are to be found in Campbell (1981), Edwards (1984) and Heidensohn (1985). Of particular relevance to the Care – custody axis are the following findings: of Webb (1984), that girls are made subject to supervision orders for less serious offences than those committed by boys; of Dominelli (1984), that some courts are biased against giving women Community Service orders; of Milham, Bullock and Hosie (1978) that 'several children, particularly girls can find themselves stranded in [secure] remand provision which has no long-term programme'; and of Fisher and Wilson, who found that the female residents of a probation hostel

> tended to have less serious criminal records than the males, but to be similarly characterised by behaviour worrying to social workers, probation officers, the courts and various agencies which had dealt with them since childhood.
>
> (Fisher and Wilson 1982: 137)

Hilary Walker (1985) has argued that even much probation practice is biased against the particular interests of female clients. Housing research suggests that women leaving institutions suffer disproportionately from the shortage of rented housing for single people (Department of the Environment 1982; Austerberry and Watson 1983).

In analysing the twenty-two interview transcripts, I was particularly interested in discovering if there were indications that the women themselves had been aware of escalatory factors in their own passages from Care to custody; and also if their experience in Care had had any special features directly conducive to lawbreaking and/or criminalisation. The older women had been well aware that the 'Care' factor had been influential in their early dispatch to Approved School.

> I went to this Assessment Centre and then to Cumberlow Lodge and just got assessed for this Approved School. I was actually put there for being 'out of parental control'. I didn't have any parents anyway. So I thought I was really hard done by, in a place with criminals. I was just sent there because I didn't have any parents. I thought it was mighty unjust.
>
> (Muriel, aged 30)

Yasmin was aware that she had been escalated through the system because of the narrower range of provision for women:

> The first thing they found me guilty for I was sent here [Bullwood Hall] straight away.[5] They didn't put me in a hostel, give me community service or anything like that. But boys, they go to a hostel or a probation hostel. Women – they ain't got no choice, just get slammed behind the doors.
>
> (Yasmin, aged 16)

Some women said that lawbreaking had been endemic in some (but not others) of their children's homes. Others claimed that residential social-workers had often known about their illegal activities but had turned a blind eye:

> They blank things like that. We done an off licence when I was in a kids' home and they could see us coming up the back stairs with crates and they did nothing about it.

It's a lot of hassle, a lot of paperwork, so they brush it under the carpet.

(Muriel, aged 30)

Pat: What about the Children's Home, didn't they realise you were thieving?
Yasmin: I'd just say I got them from me mate and they used to believe me. Coz I'd lose my temper with them and they just couldn't cope with that. [Laughs.]

Audrey stressed that the relationship between children in Care and social-workers is a very legalistic one; for instance, the social-workers at her Children's Home must have guessed that all her new clothes had been stolen, but as they could not have proved anything they had never commented on her extensive and expensive wardrobe. Several of the women expressed resentment at their belief that whereas residential social-workers reacted sharply to (and thereby amplified) trouble *within* the institution, they were prepared to condone illegal activities committed outside it. This was not to say that the women thought that residential social-workers should have 'shopped' them to the police, rather that they should have privately confronted them with their delinquency. Yet it seems that for children in Care there is often no space for an informal response to their lawbreaking. The escalatory effect that this might have on their criminalisation in comparison with that of lawbreaking children still protected by parents is suggested by NAYPIC's Charlie Maynard's response to a 1985 item in the London *Standard,* where it was reported that Hounslow's Director of Social Services had directed social-workers to report all children on drugs (including soft drugs) to the police if they refused to abandon the habit:

> Calling the police in is more likely to cause more problems. I don't think a natural parent would just call in the police. These young people are treated differently because they are in Care.

(Maynard 1985)

And, as the women bitterly noted, because children in groups tend to come under extra police surveillance, and because also many police officers assume that all children in Care are delinquents, their children's homes had in any case received disproportionate amounts of police attention. Any lawbreaking, therefore, had had a greater likelihood of coming to police notice than if the young people had lived elsewhere.

Finally, there was a strong conviction amongst the interviewees that because they were in Care, when they *had* appeared in court on a criminal charge, the magistrates had been mainly influenced by social inquiry reports prepared by social services departments. Furthermore, that because they were in Care, social-workers, believing that they had already exhausted all the social service provision, had recommended a custodial sentence primarily to give themselves a break from their most difficult charges. *Could* such a reason possibly explain the finding by Thorpe *et al.* (1980: 74) that (in relation to interim Care orders, Care orders, Detention Centre orders and referrals to Crown court for Borstal sentencing) social-workers make 'three times as many custodial recommendations as probation officers'?

They said to me something about Borstal training. That was never explained to me, I
didn't know what that was. Then my social-worker was going on about sending me
somewhere in Brentwood ... But you know, they weren't talking to me, they were
just getting on with it. I was sort of sitting in the background. It was just the social-
worker talking to the judge.

(Shirley, aged 20)

If anything went wrong in our neighbourhood, the police would be on our
[Children's Home] doorstep and we'd go up to court for cautions. The social-worker
would be present but, even then, my social-workers gave me the impression that if
they put me in prison or something, it was easier for them. If the responsibility was
laid on *them* they didn't want it because they'd sort of run out of places for me.

(Muriel, aged 30)

'And', said Anne, 'If you're a girl too, and you get into trouble, people think it's
worse. They don't understand'.

The Departure from Care

Lack of preparation for non-institutional living, loneliness, homelessness and
poverty have been listed as the all-embracing problems confronting young people
legally leaving Care between the ages of 16 and 19 (NAYPIC 1984; Stein and Carey
1984; Stein and Maynard 1985). The need for 'continuing care' has also been
stressed (House of Commons 1984). What has been less well-publicised is the
practice of placing some young people in their own bedsitters even before they
officially leave Care. Four interviewees had been thus placed in bedsitter
accommodation and four in hostels catering mainly for older people. They had all
seen the moves as a form of disciplinary action taken against them because they had
been 'difficult'. This interpretation is supported by NAYPIC, who in their
evidence to the House of Comons Select Committee's Inquiry into 'Children in
Care', made the following comments:

We also know of cases where young people are simply thrown out of [children's]
homes to fend for themselves for periods of time. This is obviously an unacceptable
form of control. If parents did this they would get into trouble with social services
and the courts.

(NAYPIC 1983: 15)

The majority of young people leaving Care do not commit crime. But Stein and
Carey (1984: 14) did find in their study of seventy-nine young people leaving the
care of a social services department in 1982 that at the second interview 16 per cent
had committed offences and 'a further 4 per cent were already in custody'. The
women I interviewed certainly believed that their eagerly awaited departure from
Care had been a significant turning-point for the worse in their criminal careers.

Given the volume of criticism concerning the dependency engendered by
institutional living, it might seem inappropriate to criticise social services
departments for giving troublesome young women in their care a foretaste of

independence by placing them in private, single accommodation. After all, many of them will have stated again and again that their main aim in life is to get the Care Order off their backs. Yet the biographies of the women in this study suggest that they were so placed not as part of a planned and caring programme but rather as a last resort when they had exhausted every other type of social services provision. In fact, because of their sense of difference, isolation and varying degrees of institutionalisation born of unhappy experience in Care, they were the least well-equipped to cope either financially or emotionally in the lonely isolation of a bedsitter.

The haphazard treatment of rebellious girls in Care is well reflected in Yasmin's experience. When I interviewed her in Bullwood Hall she was aged 16 and already serving her second youth custody sentence. In Care since 2 years old, she had been in continuous trouble throughout her young life. Her childhood passage through Care had been one of constant movement from placement to placement until she was eventually locked-up for several months in a closed unit. As soon as she was 16 she was, according to her 1984 social-work report, 'placed on her own in the community because of her need to attack boundaries'. After serving her first Youth Custody sentence she was placed in her own self-contained flat. The report continues, 'Her move from custody into complete fredom proved too great a shock to her system and she resorted to glue sniffing'. Unfortunately that was not all she (and others similarly treated) had resorted to, as the following accounts indicate:

> I have £57 a fortnight, right? Then I have £25 to £30 rent. Then I've got to buy my food and things for myself and things for my place. And that gets you nowhere. So then I go out stealing, don't I? I have to nick my own food. Out of here I eat hardly anything at all. Can't afford to buy new clothes, just nick 'em all. [Laughs.] I've never been caught for stealing yet but I think that eventually I will be picked up.
>
> (Yasmin, aged 16)

> Soon as I was 16 they moved me out of the Children's Home I'd been in for six years into a bed and breakfast place in a red-light district in Queensway. At the time there was girls coming in, different guys, money every night. I was getting offers of big money and I was saying, 'No' because I wasn't even sure what prostitution was. Anyway, it turned out that this was to be my way of living. I went to the clubs they went to, I had friends and, to me, this was making my life. I started doing this and ended up getting arrested for soliciting every night of the week.
>
> (Donna aged 22)

> I got beat up by one of the members of staff [at the Children's Home where she had lived for nine years], so they quickly moved me out to Bethnal Green and put me in a hostel for girls that were 18 to 20. I couldn't apply for any jobs cos I was only 14, you know, so basically it started from there . . . They never bothered finding a school. Somewhere around 9 o'clock you'd go out and weren't allowed back till 12 for dinner and out again after that. And I used to go round with this other girl and that's when I really found out about criminal things, shoplifting, nicking cars. The police used to pick me up for being missing and that's where the offensive weapon comes in. You know I was staying out all night, just trying to look after myself. I was skippering [living rough]. I went back to another Children's Home after one borstal

and they just bunged you out in the morning same as the hostel 'and don't come back till 12'. So we just used to drink and started shoplifting because we weren't getting enough money. In the end, like, it was like we were making our money in crime.

(Shirley, aged 20)

Two women had been in trouble upon leaving their Children's Home because they had taken their files without authorisation; it was Muriel's determination to know about her past that had projected her straight from Care to custody:

I didn't know my mother or my father. I was totally confused as to where I came from. I thought I'd just been created. Issue! Government issue! I was 18 and I got kicked out of Care and I wanted to know who my father was and all that. I broke in there and the next day I was arrested and so, you know, I was just put straight inside then.

(Muriel, aged 30)

Carol, after five years in Rampton became involuntarily pregnant immediately upon discharge. Zoë, who had done so well at school that she had gone away to college at 18, found that she had nowhere at all to go during her first (Christmas) vacation. She was eventually allowed to return to the Children's Home as an employee. Her story is worth telling at some length as it should dispel any notion that it is only girls who have already been in trouble who have difficulties upon leaving Care.

I was actually 18 in the May, but I stayed at the Children's Home until October. Then my social-worker took me to college and I was left. That was it, then. I had no contact with anybody whatsoever, not with the social-worker, not with anybody at the Children's Home. I wrote to them. I think I had one letter in the first year, that was all. Christmas came, the first term. I had to telephone them and ask if I could go and stay at the Children's Home because I had nowhere to go . . . I telephoned them back the next day and they said, 'We've arranged for you to come and work here'. So I actually went and worked there for my first Christmas holiday. I went back to college after Christmas and I was in a terrible state. I failed my exams and I just felt I'd had enough and I left. The Matron and the Superintendent Bursar at the College got me into the YWCA. After about six weeks the girl I shared with . . . we had a terrible argument one night and they threw us both out, so I was virtually walking the streets. I happened to be standing in a shopping centre one day and somebody said, 'I know somebody who rents rooms'. It was an old man. What they didn't say was that he was also being used for prostitution . . . After I moved in, there was a certain amount of pressure put on me. They kept saying, 'You need the money'. So I started soliciting myself . . . Then one of the girls went to London and she came back for a weekend and said, 'What you're earning here for prostitution is nothing. I'm earning 100 quid a day in London'. So I went down with her and we did very well at first. Then she got caught, I got caught

(Zoë, aged 28)

Several women had come out of local authority institutions full of hope that they could make a new start. Barriers to so doing had been:

1. *Material*. Most had come out of Care equipped with few educational

qualifications into situations of high youth unemployment and an acute shortage of housing for young single women.

2. *Ideological.* The peripaetetic and poverty-stricken lives that many were forced to lead in the poor material circumstances into which they had been precipitated made them particularly vulnerable to a custodial sentence if found guilty of a criminal offence. For, as women's place is still ideologically constructed as being most properly within the private sphere of family, domesticity and home, women outwith home and family are seen as being in need of particular surveillance and penal regulation (Worrall 1981; Carlen 1983a; Eaton 1986).

3. *Psychological.* Ill-equipped (both materially and by their previous experiences) for living on their own, many of the women had soon begun to think that crime was the only route to a decent standard of living. They had *nothing* to lose, they had *everything* to gain . . . and if they were caught? Many of their friends were already 'inside' anyway.

Closed Circle: A Home from home . . . Then Prison

I'd gone through the two years at Approved school and I was very positive – at that point the best prepared for creating a future. But people weren't prepared to forgive and forget. I went for a job in a shoe-shop and started chatting to an assistant, one of the girls I'd gone to school with. She said, 'You've just come out, haven't you?' I said, 'What's all this lot, coming out? I haven't been in prison, you know'. There really wasn't a future for me. I'd been sent to a hostel that was very squalid and run by a woman who was taking kids in Care. I was only 16. So I went back to Bath, then back to Truro. Then I went out robbing with the full intention of getting nicked. I didn't see any way of making any progress at all. Everywhere the doors were slamming.

(Josie, aged 30)

All the women stressed that anyone who had been in Care could cope with prison. Della was only 15 but already she felt that she had sussed out institutional life:

I was scared when I first went into Care and I was scared when I first come into prison. But when I got to know everyone and everything I just didn't care any more.

(Della, aged 15)

Others went further. Jill was so tired of being on the run that at 17 she had welcomed Borstal as a refuge. Nadia had also been tired of 'running' by the time she had reached 17:

I didn't mind getting Borstal. I was really made up because all the girls I knew had got Borstal. I had nothing and no one outside. I think Borstal and Approved School – really – that's when the whole thing about being in prison and feeling like a bad person started. I saw that I wasn't really going to have much of a life and the people that I identified with were all people doing crimes and a bit of villainy.

(Nadia, aged 35)

Muriel also thought that her Borstal sentence had pushed her towards a criminal identity.

> Pat: So you didn't mind Bullwood?
> Muriel: I did at first. Minded a great deal at first but after a while it come Jack-the-Lad sort of thing. You get a tremendous ego in them sort of places and actually with being released it's sort of frightening, pretty frightening. Cos it's just not like that outside. You ain't got these sort of people tripping over, sort of going arse over head to do things for you
>
> (Muriel, aged 30)

But fear of institutionalisation was also a constant theme:

> They kept me in Holloway while they were deciding what to do and it was just like being in Care. Coming in prison has made me realise that I've got to stop finding security in places like Care, because some people they get to like it in here so much they want *this* [Bullwood Hall] to be their home.
>
> (Audrey, aged 18)

> To me prison's like another Children's Home really. That's how I look at it, but in another way I don't want to look at it like that cos I don't want to get institutionalised. I want to get back out. You know, a lot of people come back and come back because they get the attention that they need, that they haven't had from Children's Homes – young girls my age. You can tell when you see them talking to officers that they need the attention. I'm settling in here but I don't want to settle in too good cos I want to get back out.
>
> (Shirley aged 20)

In fact, at Shirley's last appearance at the Crown court a letter had been received from Holloway Prison saying that it was felt she was 'a girl who was in danger of becoming institutionalised with her history of living in Children's Homes followed by the custodial sentence'. Notwithstanding this cautionary note, the judge had returned her to Bullwood once more.

At 35 Nadia looked back at her own teenage experiences and knew that the younger women's characterisations and fears of institutionalisation were neither exaggerated nor ill-founded:

> I went to Holloway [at 17] and when I went in there I remember feeling quite relieved that I'd been nicked. I was just getting scared – it was all the heavies all the time and I was getting into a lot of very sordid relationships. But then I think I started to get institutionalised. I didn't want to leave Borstal so I ended up hitting this officer so I'd get a second Borstal. I had no one to go out to. I would just have had to go back to Playland, really. I felt frightened of leaving Boarstal. I had all me mates back there and we had a good laugh. And I felt embarrassed about feeling like that, as well. I felt really ashamed that I felt like that. It's been very useful I've been able to say it, you know, be honest about it, understand it for what it is.
>
> (Nadia, aged 35; cf. O'Dwyer and Carlen 1985)

At 16 Yasmin does not look forward to anything. Already she engages in self-injury so that she can stay longer at Bullwood Hall, putting off the day when she once more has to face life in her lonely bedsitter. Listen:

Yasmin: Last time I was here I cut my throat and my wrists and everything. I think
            about the past, what kind of life I've had and I just take it out on myself cos
            I like hurting myself. I like it when I bleed, know what I mean? I like to see
            my own blood because I feel good that I've taken it out on myself.

Pat: Do you have any visitors when you're in here?

Yasmin: You're joking, joking. Who'll ever come to visit me? I don't have visits
            except for my social worker. I haven't got no one on the outside. I've got
            no one. When I was out I used to think of all them girls inside. We really
            had a laugh, really had a laugh with the officers. Funnily enough, when
            I'm in a Children's Home I think that all I've got is my social-workers to
            look after me, then when I go to prison that's all I've got, them officers to
            look after me. But I miss 'em a lot and I really wanted to come back to be
            here with them. But I'll tell you what, I'll probably lose all my remission
            this time cos it's coming to when I should go. I've lost 21 days so far and I'll
            probably lose the rest because I don't want to go. You can't refuse to go
            out of here cos they force you out. But it's worth a try. I'm quite happy in
            that room with my radio. I could spend my life behind that door.

Pat: Is that the life you like?

Yasmin: It's the life I know, that's all.

Conclusion

The analyses of this chapter suggest that the paths from residential Care to the women's penal institutions are trodden most frequently by gender-deviant working-class women. Having already suffered either family breakdown or familial oppression, they are then further alienated and isolated both by Care's physical and ideological confines and by the psychological brigandry of its pseudo-scientific procedures of assessment, categorisation and 'placing'. Determined to be neither 'put away' nor 'filed away', spirited young women in Care repeatedly abscond, 'cause trouble' and come to the attention of the police. The authorities' response is to speed up the rebels' progress through the tariff of increasingly restrictive 'placements'. Those who 'cannot be contained' anywhere are finally seen as being 'beyond Care'. Isolated in bedsitters, they are, in effect, told to care for themselves. Even those who remain in Care are often convinced that, in fact, no one cares. Uncared for and depressed, it is at this stage that many begin to think that since no one has ever cared for them, they really 'couldn't care less' about themselves either. Marginalised by both poverty and isolation from family, friends and other non-institutional associations, catapulted out of Care into extremes of poverty and existential chaos, many young women also begin to believe that they have nothing to lose (and maybe something to gain) by engaging in criminal activity. Once they involve themselves in the crime that provides a better standard of living, an outlet for their energies and talents, and a network of non-judgemental friends, the custodial machinery is soon reactivated. Picked up for some minor crimes the still very young women are once more presented to the courts for 'disposal'. In court, their rumbustious careers through Care, together

with their post-Care poverty and apparent social isolation are taken as being
evidence of an essential gender deviance (cf. Farrington and Morris 1983a, 1983b;
Carlen 1983a). Imprisonment is thereafter seen as an acceptable and inevitable
sentence. The prematurely institutionalised women who once hoped that Care
might provide an alternative Home from home subsequently recognise each other
in penal institutions all over the country. Another generation of state-raised
working-class women has passed from Care to custody.[6]

Notes

The research reported here is part of a larger study of women's criminal careers
funded by the Economic and Social Research Council.

   I should like to thank Ms U. McCollum, Governor of Bullwood Hall Prison and
Youth Custody Centre for allowing me to interview the women in the Bullwood
Group, and Jenny Hicks, Moira Honnon, Helen Kent and Josie O'Dwyer for
putting me in touch with the women in the Contact Group. Thanks also to: the
twenty-two women on whose experiences the article is based; Charlie Maynard of
NAYPIC for drawing the relevant publications to my attention and for arranging
a discussion with NAYPIC members in Bradford; and all the other women and
men who have discussed with me their experience of residential Care.

1. With the exception of Carol, who had not served a custodial sentence.
2. Norma, Donna, Jill and Carol had become pregnant while still in Care.
3. An exposition of control theory is to be found in T. Hirschi, *Causes of Delinquency* (1969).
   A brief summary is provided in the following quotation from Kornhauser, who writes,
   'Social controls are actual or potential rewards and punishments that accrue from
   conformity to or deviation from normal. Controls may be internal, invoked by the self,
   or external, enforced by others . . . indirect internal controls are represented in the self
   by stakes in conformity, which consist of (a) the rational awareness of interests and (b)
   sentiments or attachments, both products of rewarding social relations' (1978:).
4. Playland was an amusement arcade that used to be situated in Coventry Street, just off
   Piccadilly Circus, London.
5. In fact Yasmin was sent to Bullwood after her third conviction. She had previously been
   fined and had a deferred sentence, but her general point, that the range of provision for
   the young women is narrower than that for young men, is correct.
6. The length and focus of this chapter does not allow me to discuss 'what is to be done'
   about the 'Care factor' in women's criminal careers. This question will be discussed in
   my forthcoming book, *Women, Crime and Poverty* (Carlen 1988). For a bibliography on
   gender and juvenile justice, see Gelsthorpe (1986).

9

Women in Prison: The Treatment, the Control and the Experience

Elaine Genders and Elaine Player

An axiom of penal policy since the pioneering efforts of Elizabeth Fry in the early nineteenth century has been that separate and different treatment should be provided for men and women in prisons. The development of penal systems in this country has represented primarily a response to deal with male delinquency and crime, and only later have measures been introduced to differentiate particular categories of offender, such as women, children and the mentally ill. Heidensohn (1985) has pointed out that women's prisons have consequently developed by adapting a model originally designed for men.[1] The purpose of this paper is to examine some of the adaptations which have been made in contemporary prison regimes for women and to consider how these adaptations relate to the experience of women prisoners. The argument presented suggests that there is a mismatch between the treatment and control of women in prison and the day-to-day experience of women prisoners, and that this lack of fit creates certain ironies and contradictions.

The first part of the paper looks at some of the ways in which contemporary prison regimes have been adapted for women inmates, and considers four aspects of treatment and control: education and training programmes; the aesthetics of women's prisons; the introduction of the Youth Custody policy; and the prescription of psychotropic drugs. Many of these adaptations may be interpreted as the benevolent paternalism of the Home Office seeking to make imprisonment a less painful experience for women and more appropriate to their needs. The congruence or dissonance between what the Prison Department *perceive* women to need and what the women themselves *feel* they need, provides the focus for the second part of the paper. Drawing upon research conducted in five female

161

establishments over a two-year period between 1982 and 1984, women's own accounts of their experiences in prison are discussed. Particular attention is paid to the nature of their problems, how the prison organisation responds to these and what consequences this has for the women concerned.

Treatment and Control

There are inevitable differences in contemporary regimes for male and female prisoners which may be attributed to variation in the size of the prison systems for men and women. Women currently represent less than 4 per cent of the total prison population and occupy only eleven penal establishments (Home Office 1985a). Given these limitations, the degree of specialisation found in male prisons, such as the gradations of security or the range of training options, would be organisationally impracticable for the women's system. But the differential treatment of men and women in prison rests not only upon practical expedience but also upon a system of ideas which justifies and rationalises treating women differently from men. This tradition draws upon evidence that the female prison population differs markedly from the male prison population. First there is disparity in the recorded rate of their offending and in the nature of their offences: in 1984 women accounted for only 15 per cent of all sentences passed in the magistrates and Crown courts; they tend to be convicted and imprisoned for less serious offences than men; they have fewer previous convictions and they serve shorter sentences (Home Office 1985a). Second, women's behaviour in prison is said to differ discernibly from that of men. Women prisoners are stereotypically perceived as a highly disturbed population who adjust far less well than men to being in prison. They are consistently recorded as committing about twice as many disciplinary offences as men and as consuming disproportionately high quantities of mood-controlling drugs (Home Office 1985b). Finally, different treatment is considered appropriate because women are biologically, psychologically and socially different from men.

Since the establishment of separate facilities for women prisoners, the adaptation of regimes has continued to be dominated by forms of patriarchal control. In the late nineteenth century the work performed by women prisoners revolved around the upkeep of the prison and the provision of laundering and other services for men's prisons. The main purpose of education and training in women's prisons was disciplinary and limited to imparting rudimentary skills. According to the superintendent of one women's prison, education should

> awaken the minds of the prisoners, and improve their natural comprehensions, to make them more docile, more easily brought to see the value of cleanliness and order, and to inspire them with a considerable self-respect
> (Carpenter 1864, quoted in Dobash, Dobash and Gutteridge 1986)

This orientation is still evident in penal work and training programmes today. As recently as 1971, vocational training in women's prisons was envisaged as domestic cooking, laundering, use of domestic appliances, home decorations, domestic dress-making and soft furnishings...all these subjects will provide useful skills to women who have been unable to make an ordinary home for their families and some will help them to obtain employment on release

(Faulkner 1971, quoted in Dobash, Dobash and Gutteridge 1986)

While there have been important changes in the development of work-related training and education in contemporary women's prisons, in particular the setting up of office skills and computer courses, the major emphasis continues to be placed upon the teaching of traditional 'women's subjects', such as home economics, child-care and other domestic skills. During our research, education officers consistently expressed the view that their job was to improve levels of skill and knowledge amongst the women and to provide them with the opportunity to gain formal qualifications. Most of the education staff admitted, however, that the probability of improving the employment prospects for the majority of women was extremely low. In practice many thought that the primary role of their department was to assist in the process of building self-confidence and self-esteem in the women, and to help them develop sufficient motivation to adopt a positive approach to their problems. This is not to suggest that one of the primary goals in education departments in male prisons is not the building of self-confidence and the development of feelings of self-worth. We would suggest that the difference is one of emphasis. In prisons for men there was greater confidence that the skills training courses, such as in painting and decorating or in bricklaying, would have a positive impact upon inmates' future employment prospects. In general the education and training offered to male prisoners focus upon work-related skills outside of the domestic sphere, whereas for women prisoners the emphasis continues to be placed in the opposite direction.

Another feature of regimes for women has been the emphasis placed upon the aesthetic qualities of female establishments, albeit that the nature of this emphasis has shifted over time in accordance with changing values and perspectives of women's criminality. In the late nineteenth century the cutting of women's hair followed by the issuing of a plain and simple uniform distinct from normal apparel was seen to reduce, or even eliminate, individuality and vanity, which were considered by the prison authorities as sins that led to crime (Dobash, Dobash and Gutteridge 1986). Contemporary regimes for women place a qualitatively different emphasis upon the aesthetic qualities of establishments, although the principle of its value remains unchanged. Today, obvious signs of security are often low, and rooms are sometimes 'feminised' by colourful curtains, bedspreads or rugs. There is also a distinct lack of prison vocabulary. Women are invariably called by their first names as opposed to their surnames or prison number; their cells are often referred to as rooms; prison wings are called units or houses; and association areas tend to be described as sitting rooms or television rooms. But perhaps most importantly, unlike men, women are allowed to wear their own clothes in prison, and are permitted to keep in their possession their own personal hairdryers and cosmetics. Indeed, the *Report on the Work of the Prison Department 1968* stated that 'This change [the abolition of prison uniforms for women] has undoubtedly improved morale and the general appearance of the female population in custody' (Home Office 1969). In short, there has been an attempt to reduce the regimentation and institutional nature of women's prisons and to make establishments more akin to normal domestic situations.

The introduction of the Youth Custody policy in the Criminal Justice Act 1982, is one of the most recent examples of the ways in which penal policy has been adapted for women. The 1982 legislation abolished the indeterminate sentence of Borstal Training and introduced sentences of Youth Custody which are of a determinate length.[2] Previously, the courts could sentence young offenders over the age of 17 to imprisonment for either less than six months or more than three years, or to over eighteen months if they had previously served a term of Borstal Training. This restriction has been removed, and the courts may use their discretion in determining the length of custody. In effect, anyone under 21 deemed by the courts to warrant a custodial sentence will now receive a sentence of Youth Custody, usually for a minimum period of four months, and a maximum of twelve months on any single offence if the offender is under 17.

Important distinctions, however, have been made in the way in which these changes have been introduced in the male and female systems (see Genders and Player 1986). First, whereas there are detention centres for boys to provide a 'short sharp shock' for a determinate period of between three weeks and four months, there are no such centres for girls. The lack of detention centres for girls results in certain adaptations. For those under 17 a short custodial sentence cannot be imposed by the courts: the minimum is four months and the maximum twelve months. For young women over 17, however, there is a new minimum sentence of three weeks, equivalent to the minimum period of detention for boys. In other words, there is a short sharp shock, a 'taste' of custody, for women over 17 but not for those under 17. Unlike their male counterparts, girls aged between 14 to 16, if deemed to warrant a custodial penalty, will serve a minimum Youth Custody sentence of over four months.

Not only are there differences in the sentencing structure, there are also differences in the provisions for males and females to serve sentences of youth custody. Young male offenders who are serving Youth Custody sentences of up to eighteen months are normally required to be held separately from adult prisoners. Indeed, most of the Youth Custody Centres (YCCs) for young men are not part of an adult prison. In the case of women the policy is completely reversed. All of the YCCs for women and girls are also sites for adult prisons. Far from keeping Youth Custody trainees (YCTs) apart from the supposed contaminating influence of adult prisoners, a clear aim of the policy has been to mix the YCTs with 'selected' adult women.

There is an obvious practical justification for the policy of age-mixing in women's prisons. The new power to mix women of all ages under the same roof has effectively opened up the system and introduced a new level of flexibility to the process of allocation. It has enabled a more efficient use of prison space and has also made possible, at least in theory, the allocation of women to establishments nearer their homes.

Pragmatism was not, however, the only force shaping the way in which the youth custody policy was to be implemented in women's prisons. There was also, at the time of our research, a pervasive view within the Prison Department, that mixing women prisoners of different ages would have positive and beneficial consequences for both the young offenders and the adult women. The idea, which was largely based upon the experiential evidence of senior prison staff, was that the adult woman would provide a stabilising influence within the establishments by providing the younger women with help and advice in respect of their outside lives and by exerting a degree of control over their disruptive behaviour within the institution. The adult women, it was suggested, would also benefit, in that it would give them a sense of personal responsibility and a recognition of their own maturity (Emmins 1982: 13). Thus the theory of contamination which continues to permeate policy in male prisons, namely that young male offenders will be corrupted by older men, appears to be reversed when dealing with women. A completely different set of assumptions has been put into operation.

The prescription of psychotropic drugs provides the final illustration of the ways in which prison regimes have been adapted for female inmates. Between January 1984 and March 1985, more than 145,000 doses of anti-depressants, sedatives and tranquillisers were dispensed to women in prison – proportionately five times as many doses of this type of medication as men received in prison (Home Office 1985b). Considerable caution, however, should be exercised in extrapolating from official statistics. These data raise more questions than they answer. For example, they provide no information about the size of the dose; nor about how many women are consuming the drugs; over what time period individual women are receiving such medication; and why they are prescribed. Information is required which would shed light on how and why women in prison begin and continue to take these drugs. Our own research suggests that it is a complex and uneven picture with different prescribing practices operating in different establishments. At one prison, for example, any kind of medication was difficult to acquire. As one inmate summed up:

> If you want an aspirin for a headache, you have to book to see the doctor. By the time you see the doctor it's the next day and the headache has gone.

There were, however, common themes which did emerge. From interviews with prison medical officers and nursing staff it was made plain that although medication was prescribed for women who were considered to be suffering from mental disorder, many prescriptions were issued for women who were not diagnosed as being 'sick' or suffering from a pathological condition. Instead, the women were described as having 'normal' difficulties in coping with problems associated with their imprisonment, and medication was seen as helping to alleviate some of the more acute pain they were suffering.

The Experience of Imprisonment

It has been suggested so far that the Prison Department's adaptations of penal policy for women and girls continues to be based upon gender specific assumptions about women's role in society and about the behaviour and needs of women in prison. In this section of the paper the relevance of these assumptions will be examined in the light of the women's experience of imprisonment.

Prior to any discussion of the women's accounts of their difficulties in prison, the first questions to be considered are: who are the women in prison, and to what extent do they fit within the conventional gender-specific roles ascribed to them? Apart from the criminal background of women prisoners, the Prison Department has little systematic data about the female prison population. It is not known, for example, what proportion of the women in prison are mothers of dependent children; how many are usually in employment; or even what social class they belong to.

During the course of our research we interviewed a total of 254 women prisoners and Youth Custody trainees, and looked at a number of aspects pertaining to their backgrounds and the lives they led outside of prison. In line with the national picture, over half of the women we interviewed were in prison for the first time, although most had had previous convictions. The majority had received their prison sentence for property offences, and in only a quarter of the cases was there any element of violence. It is, however, noteworthy that the Youth Custody trainees were significantly more likely to have been convicted for a crime of violence: almost half of those interviewed were serving their current sentence for such an offence.

Almost two-thirds of the adult women and a quarter of the Youth Custody trainees had dependent children, yet two out of every three of these women did not live within a traditional nuclear family setting, that is with their children and with either a husband or a male cohabitee described as long-standing. The family lives of the women tended to be characterised by divorce and separation, two-thirds of those interviewed having experienced broken marriages.

Given that the adaptations of penal policy represent conventional ideas about gender-appropriate behaviour, it is worth considering how far the women in our research conformed to a 'conventional' life-style outside prison. A category of 'non-conventionality' was devised based upon a number of criteria, including frequent and brief marriages or relationships with men; the existence of children from a number of different paternities; separation from children; the occurrence of serious family violence; alcoholism; in-patient psychiatric treatment; and attempted suicide. In order to be rated 'non-conventional', a woman had to qualify on at least three criteria. In the event, over half of our sample, including six in every ten who had dependent children, fell within this category, and most women qualified on four or more of the criteria.

The picture of 'non-conventionality', however, was not limited to the women's current life-styles but was also reflected in their childhood experiences. This was particularly evident amongst the Youth Custody trainees: almost half had not been raised within a conventional nuclear family; over half had spent time in the care of the local authority; and as children seven in ten had experienced circumstances which fell within the 'non-conventional' category.

The picture may be clarified by the portrayal of two not atypical cases. Anne, aged 19, who was of no fixed address on arrest, had a 3-year-old illegitimate child who was being brought up by her boyfriend's parents. She had never been employed, had a history of prostitution, alcohol abuse and convictions for minor violence, and had made two suicide attempts by taking drug overdoses. Her parents were divorced when she was very young, and she was brought up by her father and stepmother with twelve other children in overcrowded conditions. She attended a school for the educationally subnormal, and later left home to live with her mother but was rejected by her and had lived a nomadic life since her mid-teens.

The second case is that of Jackie, a 38-year-old divorcee. Heavy drinking, drug-taking and violence formed a staple part of her life, together with a history of suicide attempts, psychiatric care and financial debts. She had two adult sons, both of whom had criminal records, and a long-standing common-law relationship with a man currently serving a thirteen-year prison sentence for seriously injuring her in a knife attack. Her childhood had also been unsettled: her mother died soon after her birth, and she lived alternately with her father and an older sister, with intermittent spells in various children's homes and ultimately a period in an approved school.

This discussion is not intended to be an invidious comment upon these women's lives but aims to explore what evidence exists to justify the assumptions which underlie the treatment of women within the prison system and the expectations placed upon them to play gender-specific roles.

Judged from the perspective of conventional middle-class standards, this profile of women in prison presents a picture of marked personal failure. Standards which ascribe status to women in terms of how closely they conform to the feminine stereotype as non-violent, non-criminal, attentive to personal appearance and with their identity rooted within monogamous relationships and the nuclear family, ensure that these women are accorded a derogatory position in the social hierarchy. Viewed from this perspective, the treatment of women in prison which reinforces traditional female roles would appear to be entirely appropriate in that it provides them with the opportunity to rehabilitate themselves as women.

The compelling quality of many of the women's individual problems can, however, deflect attention from the similarity of their structural location in society. Typically, the class and gender position of the women denies them the power to control their own destiny even at the most mundane level [see Ch. 8 above]. For many of the women who took part in our research their lives were characterised by great uncertainty. They did not have a regular and predictable income; they routinely experienced the interference of official agencies, who made decisions on their behalf over such matters as where they will live, whether they will have their children living with them and even whether they will be responsible for paying their own bills.

It was also a life-style which involved a high degree of personal risk. Partly because of the areas in which many of the women lived, they were at risk of being the victims of property offences. A considerable number of the women we interviewed had their homes burgled while in prison or had suffered acts of vandalism, such as broken windows. The women were also at risk from the men they lived with, both in terms of physical violence and in terms of becoming caught up in their criminal activities. But most significantly they were at risk from their own lack of knowledge and from the state. Women we interviewed were confused about their entitlements to social security [see Ch. 2 above], they were unfamiliar with their legal rights over their children, and they were unaware of their legal rights to protect themselves against the men they lived with.

It is perhaps stating the obvious, but none the less important to note, that imprisonment serves not only to magnify existing problems but also to create new ones. Our research indicated that the problems women faced on arrival in prison had the same underlying features as those they identified later in their sentence, namely the class-related and gender-specific responsibilities they had left behind in the outside world. The concerns of most of the women related to emotional and practical problems outside of the prison, most typically to the well-being of their children: whether their children were missing them; whether very young children would forget them; or whether they should receive visits from their children. They feared for the fidelity of their partners and for their ability to manage the household in their absence. They were often concerned about ageing parents. And they worried about the safekeeping of their property and the consequences of non-payment of rent and outstanding debts.

In trying to understand the experience of imprisonment for women and to synthesise the accounts the women gave of their own situation, we borrowed the framework developed by Gresham Sykes in his study of the New Jersey State prison, in which he identified what he called the major pains of imprisonment for men (Sykes 1958). For the purposes of this paper three major pains of imprisonment for women will be discussed: the loss of liberty; the loss of possessions; and the loss of autonomy.

Loss of Liberty

The women felt their loss of liberty less in relation to restrictions placed upon their physical movement, more in terms of the difficulties of maintaining relationships with people outside. It has to be remembered that for many of them their freedom of movement was already strictly curtailed by restricted finances and domestic responsibilities. Even for young offenders with few domestic ties, the loss of liberty was more acutely felt in terms of their reduced contact with their social and emotional environments. Youth Custody trainees spoke of missing their parents, their friends and their round of social activities. When this was discussed in more detail it emerged that their concerns focused upon the possibilities of permanent loss, namely that their parents would reject them and that their friends would lose interest in them. Amongst women with children, loss of contact often lead to the very real fear that they might lose their children permanently into the care of the local authority or, in the case of very young children, that their attachment might be weakened and the child forget about them or not recognise them.

The worries which women in prison experience are not groundless fears based upon their own insecurities but realistic assessments of their vulnerability. The problems they expressed not only tended to endure throughout their sentence but became more complex over time. Ruth was interviewed several days after receiving a three-year sentence for drug offences. She expressed concern for both her husband, a heroin addict who had been co-charged and had received a two-year prison sentence, and for her 16-year-old son who was currently living alone in their house. Twelve months later Ruth was awaiting a parole decision. Her husband had been released and had filed for divorce. Her son's whereabouts had been unknown to her for several months until she was informed that he had been charged and convicted of theft.

It is clearly ironic that while much of the treatment and training in women's prisons focuses upon improving the domestic and maternal skills of the women and that adult prisoners are encouraged to take on maternal roles towards the Youth Custody trainees, one of the most devastating consequences of their loss of liberty may well be the damage caused to relationships with their own children and even the appropriation of their parental rights by the state.

Set against this, however, is the argument that imprisonment does provide, for some women at least, a welcome release from their relationships with people outside. It should be borne in mind, however, that this opportunity to break away from difficult situations, and perhaps to have time to reflect and reassess, takes place within a context which affords very little privacy and opportunity to be alone. Again, it is ironic, given the attention which is paid to the aesthetics of women's prisons, that so little provision is made for women prisoners to have any degree of privacy.

The Loss of Possessions

Implicit in the organisation of women's prisons is the recognition that personal possessions are important to women. Women are not totally stripped of their personal identity when taking on the status of prisoner. They are able to wear their own clothes and to keep with them certain items of jewellery and wear cosmetics. In addition, certain items such as photographs, radios and hairdryers can be brought into the prison by application. Not all women, however, are equally able to take advantage of the allowances for personal property. Access to a radio, for example, is obviously dependent upon, first, the possession of a radio outside and, second, upon having someone willing and able to bring or send it to the prison.

The greatest deprivation concerning the forfeiture of personal property, however, does not relate to the possessions the women do or do not have with them inside prison. For the women who took part in this research the impact was felt in the loss of property outside, either through the repossession of goods by hire purchase companies, by burglary or other theft, or by damage caused by friends, relatives or squatters using their homes. The extent of the loss which some women experienced was considerable. In some cases it included the loss of tenancies on rented accommodation and the total dispossession of their household goods. Very few women had their property insured against theft or vandalism, some of the women felt that their losses were irreplaceable. Few escaped incurring any property loss at all during their period of imprisonment. Even women who did not have a fixed address and who could be described as already dispossessed in a consumer society, nevertheless had possessions in the form of clothes and records which were typically scattered amongst various friends, acquaintances and relatives. In these cases, the unsettled nature of the women's life-styles and the tenuousness of their relationships with the caretakers of these goods, made it likely that items of property would be either untraceable or irretrievable on their release.

The Loss of Autonomy

Much of the treatment and control of women in prison is premised upon the individualisation of the women's problems. The women are typically characterised as having in some way 'failed' in their adult responsibilities. Although staff recognised that many of the problems experienced by the women were endemic to their social situation outside prison, they argued, perhaps quite reasonably, that there was very little they could do about the wider social problems of poverty, inadequate housing and unemployment. On the other hand, they stressed that a number of the problems presented by the women reflected personal limitations which could be effected by staff intervention, either by means of education and training or by personal interaction and informal counselling. An objective shared by all of the staff groups in the prisons studied, was to encourage a degree of self-confidence amongst the women and to help them cope with the difficult decisions they faced in their outside lives.

There is, however, an inevitable contradiction here in that the ordered regimes governing prison life inevitably deny women choice over even the most trivial aspects of day-to-day living. They are told what time they will get out of bed, what time they will take their meals, when they will read, write letters or watch television, and at what time they will again be in bed with their lights out. Indeed, there are few areas of prison life in which the women are encouraged, or indeed able, to take responsibility for making decisions. Regardless of their age, women prisoners are designated the status of a schoolgirl. This is powerfully brought home by the practice in some establishments of calling all women 'girls', irrespective of their age, and of addressing members of staff as 'miss'.

The dependant status of women in prison is further reinforced by the practice of prescribing psychotropic drugs to inmates who are not diagnosed as 'sick' but seen to be suffering from 'normal' difficulties associated with imprisonment. Underlying any benevolent wish on the part of medical staff to reduce the level of pain experienced by women in prison is the idea that the nature of the relief provided denies the women responsibility for their problems, confirms their dependence upon outside sources of support and denies their capability of being able to look after themselves. Medical staff forcibly argued, however, that women prisoners asked for drugs and expected this type of assistance, either because they had previously been prescribed sedatives by their own GP or because they were encouraged by the experience or advice of other prisoners. It is a curious anomaly that credence is given to women's requests for psychotropic medication and yet, according to the complaints of women prisoners, little credibility accorded to their ability to make judgements for themselves in other areas of their lives.

The lack of autonomy, however, is most apparent to the women and most keenly felt, when faced with their impotence to cope with problems which exist outside of the prison. Although many of the women's outside lives were characterised by the intervention of welfare agencies which assumed much of their decision-making responsibility, their level of dependency upon others to sort out their problems was unsurpassed in the prison setting. The reliance upon bureaucratic mechanisms to send messages, receive information and to seek specialist advice, created situations of considerable anxiety and frustration. From the outset the woman was reliant upon someone outside of the prison, a member of her family, friend or outside social-worker, to provide her with accurate information about the nature of the problem. She would then make an application for an appointment, usually with the probation officer in the prison, who would, if necessary or appropriate, liaise with outside welfare agencies, local councils or solicitors. Frequently, problems required the involvement of more than one outside agency, and as a result the flow of communication back to the prisoner was often circuitous, confused and agonisingly slow. Most women we spoke to described the waiting as the most painful part of the process.

This is not intended to be a criticism of the efficiency or competence of probation services in the prisons. Complex problems inevitably took time to sort out. And virtually all of the probation officers in the prisons studied were heavily burdened by the volume of work confronting them. Many of the applications dealt with by the probation service, however, did not always require the skills of a probation officer, in that they were often basic queries which a telephone call could resolve, indeed a telephone call which the woman herself could make.

Perhaps one of the greatest ironies of contemporary penal regimes for women, however, and one which was identified by Carlen (1983a) in her study of Cornton Vale Prison in Scotland and corroborated in our research, is the emphasis which continues to be placed upon the teaching of traditional 'women's subjects' to a population whose social circumstances dictate other priorities. Most of the women in our study were either single parents and thus the sole breadwinners for their children, or totally dispossessed of any home and family. The emphasis upon the inculcation of domestic skills and the relative lack of realistic education and training in skills relevant to the job market serves to reinforce the women's own feelings of entrapment as well as their practical dependency upon the welfare state and the men who pass through their lives.

Thus we would argue that there is a fundamental mismatch between the treatment and control of women in prison and the experience of women prisoners. At one level, prison organisation encourages the development of self-confidence and independence in coping with adult responsibilities. At another, it denies adult status and removes from the women virtually all control over those areas of their lives which they hold most dear.

Self-Help

It would be misleading to suggest that the experience of imprisonment for women is dominated by a passive acceptance of pain. The women in our study developed their own resources for mitigating the most painful effects of imprisonment. Three particular areas of self-help will be discussed here: the process of problem-sharing; the exchange of goods and services; and the exchange of criminal knowledge.

Virtually all inmates during their reception interview were advised to approach members of staff with their problems and not to indulge in the homespun wisdom of other inmates. Despite this advice, however, our research showed that two out of three women who had problems chose to discuss their difficulties with fellow inmates.

While the problems which the women brought to the attention of the staff and those they discussed amongst themselves were not mutually exclusive, there were qualitative differences. Women tended to approach prison staff with their problems when they expected the staff to be able to offer them practical assistance. Frequently, the decision to talk to staff was taken after the women had consulted their friends, and in many cases a clear view was held about what action they wished and expected the staff to take on their behalf. Claire had received a letter from the woman she lived with informing her that their landlord was repossessing their flat because of rent arrears. Claire was shocked by this news because she had left sufficient money to cover the rent in her absence. Her suspicion was that this money had been used for other purposes, probably to buy drugs. Her friend currently faced a prosecution for smuggling drugs into a male prison during visits, and Claire feared the woman would receive a prison sentence for this offence. After having discussed her concerns with other inmates she made an application to see the governor in order that she might be granted home-leave for one day. Her intention was not to discuss her worries about her friend with the governor but to focus upon the financial and practical issues.

This is not to suggest that the women never discussed their personal or emotional problems with the staff, but that there tended to be a qualitative difference in the specific details and degree of intimacy which was exchanged in the conversations the women had amongst themselves and those they had with the staff. The sort of problems which the women talked about amongst themselves tended to be issues which were shared, primarily concerns about their children and their relationships with men. Because these discussions required a degree of empathy and even some level of mutual experience, the groups of women who confided in one another tended to be of roughly the same age. There was little evidence, despite the assumptions inherent in the Youth Custody policy for women and girls, that young offenders were confiding in the older women or seeing them as mother-figures.

In addition to sharing problems, women in prison also share certain possessions and exchange criminal knowledge and expertise. Women in all of the prisons studied had developed a system of economic exchange designed to lessen the inconvenience and discomfort of prison life such as tobacco, food, clothes and small personal favours such as letter writing. It seemed that very few women did not participate in the prison economy. The transactions of goods and services worked largely on the basis of trust. Scarce resources tended to be allocated according to an inmate's need and not according to her ability to repay. The assumption was that inmates would put back into the system what they could, when they could.

While prison friendships functioned as a means of mutual support, both emotionally and economically, they also served more generally to help prisoners pass the time. From the very beginning of a woman's sentence, crime provided a common topic of conversation which helped to break down the initial barriers between prisoners. They would talk about the details of their own crimes; about the advantages and disadvantages of particular types of crime; and they would fantasise about their future criminal prosperity. There were, however, certain taboo areas. Women convicted of serious violent crimes did not tend to participate in this type of leisure activity. For these women, where discussion about their offences did occur, it tended to be limited to small groups of close friends.

Although the network of mutual support which develops in women's prisons is incapable of compensating for the prisoners' loss of liberty and possessions, it can soften the pains of imprisonment by restoring some degree of autonomy. The discussion of personal problems, for example, enabled the women to learn from the experience of others. It facilitated the discovery of how to limit bureaucratic delays in getting help with problems; who to approach and who not to approach; and what to reasonably expect. Occasionally, the women themselves were able to offer practical assistance. In one case a woman made a telephone call on behalf of a friend to clarify a family problem while she was on a period of temporary home-leave. On other occasions women would pass messages for their friends during their visits and receive information back in the same way.

The exchange of material goods and services also facilitated a degree of autonomy by permitting the women some degree of control over the few possessions they had. The fact that the women were able to pool their resources enabled them to offset certain shortages as well as to improve their standard of living. For example, women collectively purchased jars of coffee and drinking chocolate which individually they might not be able to afford. Ironically, most forms of sharing were officially prohibited by the establishments on the grounds that it would lead to extortion.

The exchange of criminal knowledge, while largely a means of entertainment, provided the women with opportunities to learn new skills of offending. While this did little to change their lack of autonomy in the prison, it did supply fresh options for coping with some of their chronic financial problems outside. Almost three-quarters of the women in our research said that they had learnt new offending skills and for some these represented realistic, and often more attractive, alternatives for coping with life outside prison than those currently on offer to them in the prison training and education programmes.

What the women's support network enabled, however, perhaps more than anything else, was the reduction of feelings of isolation and hopelessness. An awareness of 'being in the same boat as a good many other people' was of crucial importance in reducing the acute impact of the major pains of imprisonment.

Conclusion

The purpose of this chapter has been to examine the relationship between how women are treated and controlled in prison and how women experience the fact of their imprisonment. The argument which has been presented suggests that despite very real efforts in some prisons to establish constructive regimes, the greatest pains of imprisonment remain largely unresolved and may even be exacerbated by organisational intervention.

If, however, present regimes are unsatisfactory, then what should be done that is not already being done? It is obviously an easier task to stand on the sidelines and find fault than to offer constructive suggestions for change. But restoring to the women some level of control and responsibility for their own problems would at least go some way towards addressing the major difficulties which women experience in prison.

Purely practical measures might, for example, include the expansion of education and training programmes which would provide women prisoners with realistic work skills relevant to the job market outside. Another suggestion could be the provision of payphones. Certain categories of telephone calls could be paid for by the women from their prison wages, others from their private cash and others from prison funds. The installation of the telephones would incur a relatively low financial cost which could be offset against the time currently spent by probation officers running errands which the women themselves are perfectly capable of dealing with. The argument which is typically offered against this suggestion is that it represents a security risk and would be abused by the prisoners. The number of women who present a genuine risk to prison security, however, is extremely small. And the fear that such provision would be improperly used is surely an argument which could be employed against any resource design to assist the prisoner. It would seem unreasonable if concerns which relate to a small minority of the population were used to prevent the introduction of facilities which could produce considerable benefits to the majority.

A third practical measure worthy of consideration would be the introduction of legal advice centres in prisons. These could be run by local solicitors and Citizens Advice Bureaux to provide inmates with direct and immediate information and advice about possible courses of action available to them. It could be argued that such a scheme would be expensive to run and that it would provide prisoners with better access to legal resources than many women have in the outside community. A similar argument is often voiced about the provision of education and training courses in prison. Such a claim, regardless of whether it is true or false, should be set in the context of the problems which beset women in prison and the potential costs, measured both in personal relations and in personal property, which individuals and their families risk being forced to pay. It could also be argued that the pains of imprisonment which women experience are justifiable punishments and one of the functions and purposes of imprisonment. In response to this, two points should be made: first, it is well to remember that this so-called punishment often extends well beyond the prison sentence itself, and second, the severity of this punishment is independent of the severity of any crime a woman may have committed.

Discussion of proposals for change in the women's prison system, however, is predicated upon the presumption that there is some agreement about the purpose of imprisonment for women and about the categories of female offender for whom prison is an appropriate sanction. A common understanding of this kind, however, is not apparent. The only common view which does seem to prevail is that there are large numbers of women currently in prison who should not be there. As has already been mentioned, women are more likely than men to be imprisoned for their first offence, they tend to have committed less serious offences than male prisoners and to have fewer previous convictions. In addition, over half of the women remanded in custody in 1983 did not eventually receive a prison sentence, whereas the reverse was true for the male population. Clearly, different assumptions are being employed by the courts in their use of imprisonment for men and women. Yet there has never been a major review of the women's prison system. Instead it seems to have continued to evolve by a process of piecemeal adaptation to policies and practices primarily designed for the custody of male offenders. A tenet of this chapter has been to suggest that such adaptations produce their own tensions and contradictions and that an examination of first principles is called for in order to produce new directions for change.

Notes

1. Except those detained at Her Majesty's Pleasure under the Children and Young Persons Act 1933.

10

Women's Imprisonment in England, Wales and Scotland[1]: Recurring Issues

Josie O'Dwyer, Judi Wilson and Pat Carlen[2]

Since 1977, when the Inquiry into the British Penal System (May 1977) managed to fill 374 pages without discussing women and girls in prison, and 1982, when a book on gaol deaths (Coggan and Walker 1982) omitted any mention of deaths in British women's prisons (see Benn and Ryder-Tchaikovsky 1983), the situation of women prisoners has become more visible. This has mainly come about through the efforts of the campaigning group Women in Prison (WIP), founded in 1983 – though specific campaigns in relation to Durham Prison's 'H' Wing and Holloway's C1 psychiatric unit have involved other organisations, such as the National Council for Civil Liberties (NCCL) National Association for Mental Health (MIND) and National Association for the Care and Rehabilitation of Offenders (NACRO).

The bulk of the initial publicity concerning the conditions in the women's prisons stemmed from the campaigning, theatrical and literary productions of women ex-prisoners themselves. The successful plays of the female ex-prisoners' Theatre Company 'Clean Break' repeatedly highlighted the numerous abuses in the women's prisons, while books by ex-prisoners Yolande McShane and Audrey Peckham detailed the evil regime of Styal's Bleak House (McShane 1980), and the grinding boredom and debilitating tension of Pucklechurch Remand Centre (Peckham 1985). In 1985 Josie O'Dwyer herself published a chilling account of her experiences in Bleak as well as memorable descriptions of life in Bullwood Hall, Holloway and Cookham Wood (O'Dwyer and Carlen 1985). Newspaper accounts of the custodial experiences of women gaoled for demonstrating against the siting of cruise nuclear missiles at the American airbase at Greenham Common also added to the growing public awareness of the plight of imprisoned women, a concerned awareness which provoked a number of official and semi-official inquiries into women's prisons.

In 1980 the Scottish Office funded research into women's imprisonment in Scotland (see Carlen 1983a) while throughout the 1980s the Home Office has continued to conduct its own research into various aspects of women's imprisonment in England (see, for example, the preceding chapter by Genders and Player). In 1985 public disquiet aroused by ex-prisoners' accounts of the treatment of disturbed women in Holloway Prison resulted in publication of the reports of two inquiries: *The Report of the Holloway Project Committee* (Home Office 1985c) and the report to MIND and NCCL by Professor Anthony Clare and the Right Reverend Jim Thompson (MIND and NCCL 1985). A more comprehensive inquiry sponsored by the Howard League published its report *Women in the Penal System* in 1986 (Seear and Player 1986), and in the same year a book based on authoritative academic research in six women's prisons in England provided detailed, independent and overwhelming evidence to support ex-prisoners' claims that the disciplinary regimes in the women's prisons actually provoke the tension, violence and disturbances that they are purportedly designed to contain (Mandaraka-Sheppard 1986; cf. Carlen 1983a, 1985).

Recurring Issues

It is evident, both from the information provided in the aforementioned publications and from our own extensive experience of the women's prisons, that despite recent publicity there still remain many causes for concern about the processes, practices and politics of women's imprisonment. In this chapter we will first give an overview of the many problems that are specific to women's imprisonment (as opposed to men's), and then we will discuss four issues that we see as being of primary importance.

Britain's gaoled women are held in six closed and three open prisons, two Youth Custody Centres and three Remand Centres. Their combined daily population is around 1,600. Of all receptions, approximately a quarter will be remand prisoners, of whom only between 25 and 30 per cent can expect a custodial sentence. Of sentenced prisoners, approximately 30 per cent of all receptions will be for fine default, the majority of sentenced prisoners having been convicted of some relatively minor property crime. Less than 10 per cent of all receptions will have a conviction for violence (Home Office 1985a). Healthwise, it is as likely today as it was at the time of Professor Gibbens's 1967 study that at least 15 per cent of the women will have a major physical ailment and 20 per cent a major mental health problem (Gibbens 1971). A sizable number will have either been brought up in institutions since infancy or put into custodial care in their early teens. [cf. Ch. 8 above; Mandaraka-Sheppard 1986].

The majority of British women prisoners have not been gaoled because of the seriousness of their crimes but because of either their aberrant domestic circumstances or less than conventional life-styles (Worrall 1981, Carlen 1983a; Farrington and Morris 1983a, 1983b); the failure of the non-penal welfare or health institutions to cope with their problems (Matthews 1981; Carlen 1983a; Smith

1984); or their own refusal to comply with culturally conditioned female gender-stereotype requirements. These sentencing practices, combined with academic and popular theories that have repeatedly implied that women criminals and prisoners are either mad, masculine, menopausal or maladjusted (to conventional female roles) have resulted not only in it being denied that they are 'real' women, real criminals and 'real' prisoners but also in the claim that the women's prisons are not '*real*' prisons. Nothing could be further from the truth.

Women in prison suffer all the same deprivations, indignities and degradations as male prisoners. Additionally, they suffer others that are specific to them as imprisoned women. Educational, work and leisure opportunities in the women's prisons are more limited, disciplinary regimes more rigid. A particular focus for criticism by women prisoners in England is the Prison Medical Service (PMS).[3] For, although the PMS operates in both male and female penal establishments, many women have felt that prison doctors have been particularly unsympathetic to them about both gynaecological problems and the many nervous ailments related either to their present domestic circumstances and/or their previous socio-biographies as daughters, wives and/or mothers. While there is a PMS that is separate from the National Health Service, it is likely that many prisoners will agree with prison inspector Mary Gordon's 1922 claim that in English prisons 'the prisoner does not consult the doctor, the state pays the doctor and consults him about the prisoner' (M. Gordon 1922: 233–4).

It is not only in the women's Youth Custody Centres that there is a high degree of tension and violence. There is much violence in the adult women's closed prisons at Holloway and Styal (Mandaraka-Sheppard 1986). Some violent episodes are started by women who cannot cope with their tension and anxiety in any other way; some are provoked by officers who wind-up already disturbed women. Some violence is precipitated by young women who, in order to maintain their self-respect, are determined to fight the system (O'Dwyer and Carlen 1985).

To understand why some women prisoners are so vulnerable when confronted with the harshness of the prison regimes, it is necessary to remember that throughout the 1980s public expenditure cuts resulted in health, welfare and housing authorities increasingly refusing help to the destitute, the homeless, those with drink and heroin problems, the mentally ill and those suffering from a myriad of psycho-social ills too complex to be easily defined. Many prisoners have no one on the outside who cares about what happens to them in prison. Prisons are the only places that cannot refuse to take those for whom neither the health nor the welfare services will take responsibility – even though the women's very minor crimes are but symptomatic of the syndrome of acute deprivation in which many of them have already been imprisoned since birth.

Prisons are *not* equipped to cope with the problems from which every other agency is copping out. Prison officers are not trained as surrogate parents, mental nurses, drug counsellors, social-workers or domestic science teachers. They are trained as discipline officers, and the high number of discipline charges levelled against female as compared with male prisoners (Fitzgerald and Sim 1979; Smith 1984; Home Office 1985a) result both from regimes that aggravate and multiply the problems that many women already have when they go to prison and from discriminatory social ideologies that, in general, demand higher standards of behaviour from women than from men. In plain words, women prisoners get nicked for trivial offences which would be overlooked in the men's prisons.

Public expenditure cuts resulting in actual staff shortages, together with the prison officers' dispute with the Home Office about 'manning' levels within the prisons, increased the tension and violence within the women's prisons. Women, already cooped up and tensed up beyond endurance, are increasingly being pushed to breaking point when, because there are not enough staff on duty to supervise them in association with other prisoners, they are locked in their cells for up to twenty-three hours without being allowed out at all. It is particularly unpleasant for women at the time of their periods to be locked in for so many hours with their chamber pots and soiled sanitary towels. A walk around the walls of a women's closed prison or Youth Custody Centre will often reveal several used sanitary towels that have been hurled out of the windows by women desperate to maintain the standards of cleanliness which they had held outside prison.

Regular cell searches, strip searches, the many petty rules, the constant 'putting down' of prisoners, very restricted visiting hours (under extremely restrictive conditions) are further sources of tension. The only official remedy is the offer of tranquillisers. The official statistics on the high doses of drugs administered in the women's prisons bear witness to the large numbers of women who get through their sentences on official dope. It is a well-known (and not surprising) fact that the official doses are supplemented with illicitly obtained drugs. When drugs fail, some women either engage in the most horrendous self-mutilations or smash-up their cells (O'Dwyer and Carlen 1985). Unofficial responses to women prisoners' violence include beatings and kickings from both male and female prison officers. Official responses range through forced injections, restraint in special, stripped and padded cells; restraint by body belt, canvas jacket, handcuffs and ankle straps; long periods of solitary confinement in the punishment block; and loss of remission on time to be served. Women who commit trivial offences are punished by confinement to cell, loss of wages or privileges (Prison Reform Trust 1984). Prisoners at Holloway have often been sent to the psychiatric wing as a punishment, a punishment known to inmates as 'getting C1s'.

The official portrayal and treatment of women prisoners as disturbed women needing training in domesticity, motherhood or conventional behaviour patterns is shot through with contradictions. Take, for instance, the woman prisoner with children. According to NACRO (1985a) over 1,600 children under the age of 16 had mothers in prison in 1982. Yet although one of the stated (and patently absurd) official claims is that imprisonment aims to reintegrate prisoners into their communities, women in prison constantly complain that communication with their families is routinely obstructed through censorship of letters and monitored and restricted visits. Imprisoned women whose children are in care report that it is often difficult to get news of their families and that social-workers visit the prison only to put pressure on them to have their children adopted. Women who are allowed to have their infants in prison with them are sometimes made anxious because they cannot develop their own routines with the babies. In 1985 a 17-year-old prisoner was separated from her 8-month-old child for the remainder of her sentence because of some minor disciplinary offences (NCCL, 1985a). In fact, mothers in prison either fear that through loss of remission on time to be served they will be separated from their children for even longer, or that as a result of their sentence, their children will be taken into care for good. All in all, children are used as disciplinary controls on women prisoners (O'Dwyer and Carlen 1985) and, as one woman at Cornton Vale said, 'If women have kids outside they'll take any amount of stick off anybody' (Carlen 1983a: 85).

The justification of the rigid disciplinary regimes on the grounds that many of the women are disturbed, is also questionable. Despite the fact that many women see the life of loneliness and isolation which they have led outside as being one source of their present troubles, a current trend is towards isolating women prisoners from each other (Carlen 1983a; O'Dwyer and Carlen 1985). Women prisoners have told how genuine attempts to help other women are too often interpreted as offences against discipline. Furthermore, any show of affection between women in prison is in danger of being reported as a 'lesbian activity'. Discouraged thus from any form of mutual self-help, already distraught women finish up on large doses of drugs or in solitary confinement. From all accounts of Holloway's psychiatric unit and Styal's Bleak House it might be difficult to envisage how any woman remains sane in such conditions – though from personal experience we know that in fact they do! And, even though it was originally intended that the so-called jewel in the crown of the English penal system, Grendon Psychiatric Prison (!) should have a women's wing, neither at Grendon nor anywhere else have specialised 'therapeutic-community' type facilities been provided for women prisoners on a permanent full-time basis.[4]

Women describing their experiences of contemporary life in the women's prisons transmit an overwhelming sense of the tension and violence that pervades those institutions. Even in prisons such as Cookham Wood, a prison with a previously good reputation for regular association, there are reports of an increasing number of lock-ins of up to twenty-three and a half hours. Josie in particular has reason to know the deleterious effects that solitary confinement can have on one's subsequent social behaviour (see O'Dwyer and Carlen 1985: 160). Yet, even leaving aside the extreme situation of solitary confinement, it is difficult to think of many aspects of women's prisons' regimes that do not contribute to an increase of tension in prisoners! In the remaining space, however, we shall limit our discussion to four major issues: (1) the Prison Medical Service, (2) the disciplinary systems of women's prisons, (3) the proposal for 'mix nicks' and (4), by way of conclusion, the lack of support for released women prisoners.

The Prison Medical Service

The PMS is not only responsible for the general medical care of prisoners but also for 'fitting'[5] women for punishment in solitary confinement. Hardly a promising start to a doctor-patient relationship! But there are many other disturbing dimensions to prison medicine, and in recent years a particular focus of debate has been on whether or not it is desirable for the PMS to remain separate from the National Health Service (NHS) (see Smith 1984; Prison Reform Trust 1985; NACRO 1986a). The issues specifically affecting women have concerned (1) the large doses of drugs prescribed in women's prisons, (2) women's gynaecological and obstetrical needs and (3) the scandal of Holloway's C1 psychiatric unit (see also NACRO 1986b).

As we have discussed the complex question of drugs in women's prisons elsewhere (Carlen 1983a; O'Dwyer and Carlen 1985; Carlen 1985), we will not discuss it again in detail here but instead merely note Stephen Shaw's comment that '*The question of medication levels amongst women prisoner-patients seems related to a now outmoded medical/psychiatric model of female criminality*' (Shaw 1985: 5, emphases added). For we believe that in that comment lies the key not only to prescribing practices in the women's prisons but also to repeated complaints from women prisoners that they do not feel that their illnesses are taken seriously. And, as several studies have suggested, this apparent refusal to take women's illnesses seriously is not peculiar to prison doctors (see Roberts 1985; Doyal 1985). It is therefore doubtful whether the widely recommended integration of the PMS with the NHS would in itself be reform enough as far as medical services in the women's prisons are concerned.[6] What we would like to see for women prisoners is an NHS provision modelled on the Well Woman Clinics. Such provision would involve only doctors especially interested in all aspects of women's health and give every prisoner a choice as to whether she is treated by a female or male doctor.

The Well Woman Clinics outside prisons have been developed specifically to counter the tendencies of some doctors to pathologise, psychiatrise or trivialise women's gynaecological and obstetrical aches and pains. Similar provision in the women's penal system might reduce a major source of tension in women prisoners. In the meantime it is worth describing once more the conditions in Holloway's C1 psychiatric unit. For although two recent reports (Home Office 1985b; Clare and Thompson 1985) have recommended far-reaching changes in the unit, neither report describes conditions from the prisoners' viewpoint. To fill out the picture from the inmate's side, therefore, we will conclude this section with a very brief description of what it was like to be a prisoner in C1 in the early and mid-1980s. We would like to hope that by the time this book is published the conditions we describe will have gone forever.[7]

In early 1986 the medical wings in Holloway house a mixture of medically unfit prisoners who range through sick junkies, pregnant women, those with minor mental disturbance, and others suffering from physical ailments.[8] The more severely disturbed are put in the C1 unit, the wing which has been described as Holloway's Bedlam. The constant screams, bangings, and self-mutilations leave damaging psychological scars even on the mentally stable women who, from time to time, get allocated to C1 because of prison overcrowding or some failure of prison administration. Yet, ironically, it is precisely because it has been used for prisoners for whom it was not intended that the scandal of C1 was brought to public attention in 1985, when some of Holloway's ex-C1 prisoners publicised their experiences. Those women (and Josie herself is an ex-C1 inmate) still provide the only persistent voices raised on behalf of the long-term, psychiatrised, institutionalised and totally forgotten women who are constantly shuttled around the various penal and psychiatric establishments. If these 'already written off' women do not create too many problems for the prison authorities, they will most probably remain on the prison/mental-hospital circuit, but if they cause trouble, then the ultimate dustbin for the more recalcitrant prisoner is Broadmoor. To be forgotten in Broadmoor is to be forgotten for a very long time indeed.

Holloway's C1 women are often locked in cells for weeks at a time, their only human contact being made via a twelve- by ten-inch hatch through which they get their food and medication. If they smoke, they get their light only after they have taken their medicine. They are kept in what is known as 'strip conditions'. To get in 'the strips' they would probably have been dragged, stripped and restrained by a number of prison officers, some of whom might have been male. They might or might not have had a forced injection. Strip conditions mean just that: a mattress on the floor. partitions across the windows, the sink and toilet blocked off and a plastic chamber pot on the floor. Prisoners' own clothes are confiscated, the only replacement being a heavy canvas or tough nylon strip dress.

Reports of self-mutilation on C1 have been horrific. One woman gouged out her eye, another tried to cut off a breast. Josie has seen women who have cut themselves deeply from their wrist to their armpit, others with so many scars from different outbursts that they have looked like burn victims.

The following extract from an official censored prison letter well summarises the real pain of disturbed women in prison:

> You made me feel really embarrassed telling me to pull up my sleeves and show you the cuts I'd done. I hate looking at them, I feel ashamed for doing it now, but at the time it's the only way to let out the way I feel. I just slash them without thinking. I don't feel the pain at the time. It's later when I can't stand it. The cuts start to swell after a while so by the time the doctor gets here they're really sore and tender. They didn't use an anaesthetic, so it's agony. The last time I had them stitched I went all dizzy, my ears were buzzing and I couldn't see. I felt terrible. I know it's stupid to do it in the first place, but I'd rather leave it open than get it stitched and go through all that pain over again.

Following this incident, the woman was prescribed large doses of largactyl and kept in solitary confinement. Classic prison 'treatment'!

Disciplinary Regimes

There is, unfortunately, no escape from some sort of disciplinary procedure during the course of a sentence. Even if women are quiet and wish to do their time with the least possible friction, prison officers make this difficult to achieve. Not only are prisoners never informed of any rules from the time they enter prison (cf.

Mandaraka-Sheppard 1986: 76), but the crime of 'offending against good order and discipline' bridges any gap that might have been overlooked by the rule-book. Punishable offences have been known to include running up stairs, walking on the grass, possessing one T-shirt too many, having a slice of bread in a cell, and feeding squirrels (O'Dwyer and Carlen 1985: 159; Mandaraka-Sheppard 1986: 91). As prison officers are taught during training that the inmate will routinely lie, cheat, make false allegations and use serious violence against staff, it is hardly surprising that even at the start of their careers many officers' general attitude is one of animosity towards prisoners, an animosity which over the years in some of them hardens into a festering, embittered and unconcealed hostility. When even the 'model prisoner' is seen as being 'devious' and 'manipulative', it is not surprising that *no one* will get a hassle-free ride through prison.

It is in professional character for prison officers to be 'forgetful', and they complicate and obstruct things as much as possible by withholding letters or parcels, delaying or holding-up visits, 'forgetting' to unlock women for exercise and 'forgetting' to ask if anyone on the wing wants to go to the gym (O'Dwyer and Carlen 1985). In fact, many women prisoners believe that prison officers frequently goad women into confrontation so that they can exercise their physical power through sheer force of numbers. Mandaraka-Sheppard (1986: 85), for instance, reports in her study of six English women's prisons that at Styal:

> The writer was told that if... prisoners resisted going to the 'Bleak House' they were forced by male officers and as soon as they turned the end of the alley leading to the punishment block (so as not to be seen by inmates from the houses) they were smacked in the face and kicked on the legs.
>
> (Mandaraka-Sheppard 1986: 177)

Overall, her analyses led her to conclude that 'the approach of Styal's administrators to discipline was more punitive than in similar closed prisons' (pp. 77–8).

For some prison officers a 'scrap' is the highlight of their day! Josie has experienced the 'heavy mob' at first hand, and many other prisoners have seen officers return to a wing red-faced and excited, boasting about their performance during a struggle, comparing and cataloguing their injuries. Later still they have heard them laughingly conferring together as they have prepared statements for the Board of Visitors (BOV). In fact, in any consideration of prison discipline, both prison rules and the BOV need special words of explanation and comment.

It is nowadays recognised that in all institutions rules are used according to the so-called discretion of their authorised interpreters who are licensed to fit the formal rule to the specific circumstances. It is, however, also a feature of democratic institutions that those who interpret the rules are expected to be accountable to authorities independent of the institution. At every level in the penal system Home Office administrators, governor-grade staff and discipline officers have unusually wide powers of discretion (see Maguire, Vagg and Morgan 1985a). They are seldom called to account for their rule usage. This lack of accountability results not only in multiple instances of gross injustice but also in much of the trouble that occurs in all prisons and especially in the women's prisons, where inmates are more likely than are their male counterparts to be disciplined for trivial offences. Indeed, after studying six women's prisons Mandaraka-Sheppard was convinced that rigid disciplinary regimes *provoked* bad behaviour:

> The lengthy discussions the author had with inmates in different prisons gave her an insight into the spiralling effects of severe punishment. Inmates perceived the process of reporting and punishments – particularly in Styal – as an aggravating circumstance which induced further friction and defiance.
>
> (Mandaraka-Sheppard 1986: 88)

Every prison has a BOV, whose job it is to act both as a watchdog over the treatment of prisoners and as the adjudicatory body that presides over the hearing of the most serious charges of offences against prison discipline (se Vagg 1985; Maguire 1985). For years this dual role has been the focus of criticism by commentators who have argued that the BOV that claims to be the 'prisoner's friend' cannot also act as judge and jury in disciplinary hearings. Additionally, and as Mandaraka-Sheppard noted, 'governors tend to direct the BOV during the adjudications; ... [so] their punishments reflect the orientation of the institution towards discipline' (1986: 175). In October 1985 the *Report of the Committee on the Prison Disciplinary System* (Home Office 1985d)[9] announced that forthcoming changes would result in BOVs losing their adjudicatory powers on the most serious offences and that in future these powers would reside with three-person tribunals consisting of two lay members under a legally qualified chairperson. However, while prison governors are allowed such wide powers of interpretation of the prison rules it is unlikely that prisoners will perceive the system to be just. It also has to be remembered that 95 per cent of prisoners' offences will still be dealt with by the governor sitting alone (NACRO 1986a). If the new disciplinary tribunals do indeed turn out to be a first step towards reforming the prisons' disciplinary structure, Josie O'Dwyer's experience of one governor's administratively convenient usage of the prison rules leads us to suggest that a second major step towards increasing justice for prisoners would be achieved by greater regulation of the governors' discretionary powers:

> In 1982 I was charged with gross personal violence to an officer and put in a prison punishment block. The following day I had my charge read to the Board of Visitors. As the reporting officer was off sick my case was adjourned and I was kept in the block on rule 48 pending adjudication. After I had made several protests it was decided my case would be taken to outside court. I was produced at a magistrates' court charged with assault causing actual bodily harm (a long way from grievous bodily harm, which would have been the equivalent of gross personal violence). The magistrate remanded the case, giving me bail. I was already serving a two-year sentence. On my return to the prison I was again taken to the block. The following day I saw the Deputy Governor and asked him under which rule I was being kept in the punishment block. He said 'Rule 48'. I objected to this as I was now no longer waiting for a Board of Visitors and I had been charged and given bail for the incident involving the officer. Next day the Governor told me I was to remain in the block under rule 43 because I was 'unstable'. Eventually my case was dealt with by a judge

and jury at Crown Court, where after a five-minute retirement the jury returned a not-guilty verdict. Had I been dealt with by the Board of Visitors I firmly believe that they would have found me guilty as charged (gross personal violence) and that the punishment would have been heavy. As it was, I had already spent six weeks in solitary, covered of course, by the Governor's discretionary Rule 43!

Rule 43: (1) Where it appears desirable, for the maintenance of good order and discipline or in his/her own interests, that a prisoner should not associate with other prisoners, either generally or for particular purposes, the governor may arrange for the prisoner's removal from association accordingly.
(2) A prisoner shall not be removed under this rule for a period of more than 24 hours without the authority of a member of the Board of Visitors, or the secretary of state. An authority given under this paragraph shall be for a period not exceeding one month, but may be renewed month to month.
(3) The Governor may arrange at his/her discretion for such a prisoner as the aforesaid to resume association with other prisoners, and shall do so if in any case the medical officer so advises on medical grounds.

The wording of rule 43 alone is a brilliant example of the catch-all nature of rules for the maintenance of prison discipline![10]

The Question of 'Mix Nicks': Gaols Shared by Male and Female Prisoners

The main conclusion of the Howard League's 1985/86 Inquiry into Women in the Penal System (Seear and Player 1986) was that imprisonment is an inappropriate sentence for most of the 1,600 women held in British prisons. Yet if custodial sentences were to be imposed only on those found guilty of very serious crimes, the existing women's prisons would cease to be economically viable. A small centralised unit would be claustrophobic and isolate women from their families while there would be too few prisoners to make it possible to provide the separate but adequate facilities that would enable women to remain close to their homes. Hence the proposal for 'mix nicks', a proposal that would most probably have astonished early prison reformers John Howard and Elizabeth Fry (who campaigned for separate prisons for women) as much as it did us and the many others with whom we have discussed the matter.

The major objection to mixed prisons is that women in prison have problems enough without adding men to them. A prison officer spelled this out when she commented

So many women have been physically and sexually abused that prison gives them a breathing space away from men. Those who do have good relationships with male partners could encounter other problems. Jealousy from the chap outside – maybe even an unwanted pregnancy. All inmates would have to be under much closer supervision to avoid sexual harassment.

An officer at a men's prison foresaw difficulties in selecting the male volunteers:

'A majority of male prisoners are extremely sexist – and that's putting it mildly. So they wouldn't be suitable. Others who might be OK would probably have wives or girlfriends who'd object to them going to a mixed prison.' A probation officer agreed: 'It would make *our* job more difficult, too. First they separate families by sending people to prison, then they tell us that we must keep the families together, and now they propose mixed prisons which could make the partner outside wild with jealousy – however unfounded.' An ex-prisoner had a different worry and cynically foretold that relationships between men and women in prison would suffer the same fate as lesbian relationships: they would cause trouble between inmates and be used by officers as additional disciplinary levers wherewith to exercise control over prisoners.

In the report the difficulties are recognised but glossed over. Living arrangements in the mixed prisons would remain separate. No woman would be forced into association with male prisoners. But, and here's the real logic behind the recommendation for 'mix nicks', the report's authors assume that *mixing with men is in any case a good thing for women*. Or, as they put it, 'friendships between members of the opposite sex could be of value in helping to create a psychologically healthier environment'. Not necessarily so. Mixed day-centres and ex-prisoner hostels are already rejected by women who require space to be independent of men. Such women would be grossly disadvantaged in mixed prisons. 'Mix with men. Or forego a whole range of work and recreational facilities.' What kind of choice would that be?

Yet because there is much in the report that *is* to be welcomed, we would not wish to reject outright a proposal that is a serious attempt to resolve the problem of how best to contain a minimal prison population of women and, eventually we would venture to hope, a minimal prison population of men too. So what can be said for 'mix nicks'?

Mixed prisons should only be introduced on a closely monitored and experimental basis. We, ourselves, would prefer the alternative of a centralised unit for women only, with travel grants for frequent visits by prisoners' families, adequate facilities for private sexual activity with visiting partners of either sex, increased and better facilities for children's visits and closer involvement of the women's prison with community groups of the prisoners' choice. Having said that, we are also prepared to recognise that 'mix nicks' *might* work – though only under certain conditions. These conditions must be: (1) that exactly the same facilities are available to women who do not want to mix, (2) that the 'psychological benefits' of friendships between women are also recognised and lesbian activity ceases to be an offence against prison discipline; and (3) that the whole experiment is monitored by an independent equal opportunities' assessor. Without such safeguards mixed prisons could worsen the plight of women in custody. Conditions in the single-sex prisons are bad enough, but they do at least provide women prisoners with a refuge from men.

Lack of Support for Women Ex-Prisoners

Prison is not only damaging during the course of a sentence. Coming out has its own problems, and the snowballing effects of imprisonment are felt long after release. Women are often let out of prison very early in the morning not knowing where to go, or even in which direction. They may have the equivalent of one week's rent with which to find accommodation. They will have nothing for fares, food, fags and finding friends. Too many women will have entered prison as a direct result of being homeless and unsupported. Others will have had drink and drug-related problems together with mental and emotional difficulties. A majority will have had histories of institutionalisation [see Ch. 8 above]. When they leave prison their prospects of survival are disgustingly dim.

The limited resources and support available for women leaving prison actually cater for very few. The Creative and Supportive Trust (CAST) offers knitting and pottery workshops, a means of earning some money and, most importantly, a meeting place where women can get together and discuss both their prison experiences and their post-release difficulties. For instance, a high proportion of women prisoners have children in care, placed there because of their mothers' imprisonment. Regaining custody can be a new battle, one that becomes increasingly debilitating as released prisoners struggle to prove themselves to be 'fit mothers'. Frequently, this struggle occurs in circumstances where all the odds – especially the financial ones – are against them. Indeed, their crimes will have often been occasioned by their having had insufficient money to feed, clothe and educate their children in the first place. Once imprisonment has resulted in loss of their homes, their chances of ever getting their children back are considerably lessened. These are the mothers who are told either that their children will be better off with foster parents, or even that they should be placed for adoption. Many, ignorant of their legal rights and without support to fight their cases, simply give up the battle – and lose legal control of their children for good

Whether or not released women have children, they are all likely to have problems with the DHSS and, additionally, a host of general fears and anxieties resulting from their imprisonment. Yet women in custody are not informed of any outside support either before, or upon, release (see also NACRO 1986b). CAST's existence is not publicised even at its local prison, Holloway! Because of the isolation experienced by women after their release, most who come to CAST have only heard about the project through word of mouth or by pure chance.

By contrast with CAST, the Women Prisoners' Resource Centre (WPRC) has succeeded in gaining access to almost every women's prison in the country, though their work is severely restricted by lack of funds and staff in proportion to the needs they attempt to meet. Formerly funded by the GLC Women's Committee and by NACRO, WPRC's long-term future is uncertain.

Most of the women seen by WPRC are still in prison, though there is also a drop-in referral facility at their office. Their main aim therefore is to prepare women for release by dealing with at least some of the practical problems that frequently overwhelm a woman if she has no one to turn to. Most of their referrals (about 70 per cent) are concerned with housing and future accommodation. They have been successful in gaining nominations for women ex-prisoners from housing associations and councils that had previously not acknowledged any special need. WPRC also attend to enquiries concerning DHSS benefits, family problems (divorce and child-custody cases), drugs and alcohol abuse, training and education. The WPRC information pack contains many useful addresses and contacts.

Probably WPRC's greatest achievement is in having introduced pre-advertised in-prison 'surgeries'. These are organised from outside the institution and are therefore viewed by prisoners as being both independent and accessible. It should, however, also be noted that the women who might most benefit from this new service are not encouraged by prison staff to attend WPRC pre-release meetings, nor to apply to see somebody during 'surgery' hours. In other words, the least independent, most institutionalised prisoner, the one in fact who is desperately in need of outside help, is still unlikely to be aware of these resources and how they might be of help to her.

While various hostels *are* prepared to take women ex-prisoners, vacant places are not always readily available, and again, too often women in prison are unaware even of the hostels' existence. The only hostel in London catering exclusively for women ex-offenders is Stockdale House, which holds about thirteen residents. The length of their stay varies according to their need for support. This hostel receives nominations from housing associations and usually provides flats when residents are ready to move on. There is twenty-four hour supervision and the staff allow for the inevitable explosive behaviour changes experienced after imprisonment (O'Dwyer and Carlen 1985: 179). Stockdale is prepared to accept offenders whom other hostels reject either because of their reputation or their past record of violence. And, unlike most hostels, it makes places available for mothers with children.

At Stockdale House there is no strict regime or curfew, each woman has her own single room, pleasantly decorated and furnished. The residents are given a degree of encouragement, help and support that both surpass that of any other hostel and at the same time allow women their independence.

It is our opinion that there should be more hostels catering specifically for women ex-prisoners. The special needs of so-called 'hopeless recidivists' must be recognised so that many more of them get a chance to break out of the penal system and its institutionalisation. Only then will they be able to experience a life of their own making, a life outside the institutions that for so many have been 'home' since early childhood.

At present, women come out of gaol to a world that has even less to offer than the prison itself. Depressed and alone, some then sink into a despair in which they become careless of what happens to them. They re-offend and the circle repeats itself again and again. People who advocate stiffer prison sentences should, therefore, note that prisons feed off their own product. Today's so-called 'new admission' will too often be yesterday's so-called 'released' prisoner!

Address

CAST
34a Stratford Villas
London NW1 9SG

Tel: 01 485 0008

Women Prisoners' Resource Centre
Room 1
1 Thorpe Close
Ladbroke Grove
London W10 5XL

Tel: 01 968 3121

Stockdale House (Griffin Society)
56–58 Crowndale Road
London NW1

Tel: 01 380 0611

Notes

1. We have excluded discussion of Northern Ireland only because not one of us has had experience of Armagh Prison. However, it should be noted that in recent years there has been particular criticism of the frequent strip-searching of women on remand in Armagh Prison, and further information on this issue can be obtained from an NCCL report *Armagh Strip Searches* (NCCL 1985b). An account of the constant strip searching of two young Irish women awaiting trial in London's Brixton (men's) Prison is given in a GLC Women's Committtee's Report (GLC 1986). Wales is included in the title to indicate that we are covering the experience of Welsh women, even though there is no women's prison in Wales.
2. Josie O'Dwyer and Judi Wilson provided the inside knowledge of prisons and imprisonment, Pat Carlen supplied the academic references. The arguments put forward here have been jointly developed by all three authors.
3. For discussions of the Prison Medical Service in general, see Smith (1984); Prison Reform Trust (1985); NACRO (1986b) and Carlen (1986). For a discussion of women, mental illness and imprisonment see Carlen (1985).
4. Small units that are intended to be therapeutic and, especially for women with psychological and/or emotional problems, do exist in some women's prisons, though they usually provide facilities for only a very small and select group of prisoners.
5. Stating that a woman is medically 'fit' to be punished.
6. According to the director of the Prison Medical Service, already 'about two-thirds of all the actual medical work done in prison establishments is carried out by doctors whose principal employment is with the NHS' (Kilgour 1984: 1603). He does not specify how this affects provision in the women's prisons but goes on to say, 'while many establishments have all their medical cover provided in this way, all establishments including those to which full-time prison medical officers are posted have some of their cover provided by NHS medical staff'.

7. In this context it is worth putting on record part of the answer of the then Home Secretary Leon Brittan to a question about the future of Holloway from Mr Charles Irving MP for Cheltenham on Wednesday 17 July 1985: 'I acknowledge the desirability of re-siting C1 unit in purpose-built accommodation in a different part of the establishment and have asked for an urgent assessment of whether that is feasible. But C1 cannot be built overnight. Immediate steps will be taken to improve conditions in the unit. Particular attention will be paid to improvements to the fabric, the replacement of potentially dangerous fittings, and the provision of more space for association. High priority will be given to improving the regime on C1 so that the prisoners there can take full advantage of the specialist training and therapeutic facilities available.

8. The 1984 report by HM Chief Inspector of Prisons on HM Prison Holloway contained the telling comment: 'The hospital accommodation was barely distinguishable from that of the rest of the prison' (Hennessy 1984: 18).

9. See Morgan, Maguire and Vagg (1985), 'Overhauling the Prison Disciplinary System: Notes for Readers of the Prior Committee's Report' The question 'Who runs the prisons?' is raised each time the POA (Prison Officers' Association) is in dispute with the Home Office. The Home Office claims that *it* does and has expressed determination that the Prison Department and not the POA will decide staffing levels within prisons. Experienced prisoners claim that the discipline officers rather than the governor-grade staff run the prisons, and this claim seems to have been borne out in 1986 when it was reported that the recently appointed liberal governor of Styal Prison had been moved to another post after prison officers had complained about his attempts to liberalise the regime (Davies 1986). Space does not permit us to discuss the struggle for control of the prisons in this article, but until all parties (Home Office, Prison Department, governor grades, prison officers and medical staff) are forced into a greater accountability for their actions, prisoners will continue to be the main victims of the battle for power by prison personnel as the following example, provided by Josie O'Dwyer
indicates: 'When I was in a prison punishment block in 1982 an eighteen year old woman in the cell next to me had spent many months in solitary confinement and was having her Board of Visitors that day. After hearing her case the Board of Visitors awarded her two hours extra work. She returned to the Wing. Two days later she was back in the cell next to me. The nursing staff had threatened to walk out of prison because they thought she had been dealt with too leniently. (Her charge had concerned an assault on a nursing sister.) She remained in the block for many weeks.'

10. As we conclude this article (June 1986) another new book has been published on women in prison. It gives an interesting historical analysis of the ways in which the interplay of the gender and penal ideologies of the past have shaped today's penal regimes for women. See Dobash, Dobash and Gutteridge (1986).

Bibliography

Ackland, J.W. (1982). *Girls in Care*. Aldershot, Gower.

Adams, P. (1983). 'Mothering', in *m/f* 8, 41–52.

Adler, Z. (1982). 'Rape: The Intention of Parliament and the Practice of the Courts', *Modern Law Review* 45, 664–75.

(1985). 'The Relevance of Sexual History Evidence in Rape: The Problem of Subjective Interpretation', *Criminal Law Review*, December 769–80.

Allatt, P. (1981). 'Stereotyping: Familism in the Law', in B. Fryer *et al.* (1981).

Allan, D. (1982). *One Step from the Quagmire*. Aylesbury, Bucks, Campaign for Justice in Divorce.

Allen, H. (1984). 'At the Mercy of Her Hormones: Premenstrual Tension and the Law', *m/f* 9, 19–44.

(1986). Psychiatric Sentencing and the Logic of Gender', unpublished PhD thesis, Department of Human Sciences, Brunel University.

Anderson, E. (1976). 'The "Chivalrous" Treatment of the Female Offender in the Arms of the Criminal Justice System: A Review of the Literature', *Social Problems* 23 (3), 49–57.

Ardener, S. (1978). *Defining Females*. London, Croom Helm.

Aries, P. (1973). *Centuries of Childhood*. Harmondsworth, Allen Lane.

Atkins, S. and Hoggett, B. (1984). *Women and the Law*. Oxford, Basil Blackwell.

Auld, J., Dorn, N. and South, N. (1986). 'Irregular Work, Irregular Pleasures: Heroin in the 1980s', in R. Matthews and J. Young (1986).

Austerberry, H. and Watson, S. (1983). *Women on the Margins*. London, City University, Housing Research Group.

Baldwin, J. and Bottomley, A. (1978). *Criminal Justice*. London, Martin Robertson.

Bankowski, Z. and Mungham, G. (1980). *Essays in Law and Society*, London, Routledge and Kegan Paul.

Barrett, M. and McIntosh, M. (1982). *The Anti-Social Family*. London, Verso.

Barry, K. (1979). *Female Sexual Slavery*, New York, New York University Press.

Barry, K., Bunch, C. and Castley, S. (eds) (1984). *International Feminism: Networking Against*

Female Sexual Slavery. International Women's Tribune Centre, 777 United Nations Plaza, New York.

Beattie, J.M. (1975). 'The Criminality of Women in Eighteenth-Century England', *Journal of Social History*, 72, 80–116.

Becker, J. (1977). *Hitler's Children*. London, Michael Joseph.

Beltram, G. (1984). *Testing the Safety Net*. London, Bedford Square Press/NCVO.

Benn, M. and Ryder-Tchaikovsky, C. (1983). 'Women Behind Bars', *New Statesman*, 9 December.

Beveridge, W. (1942). *Social Insurance and Allied Services*, Cmnd. 6404. London, HMSO.

Birke, L. (1986). *Women, Feminism and Biology: The Feminist Challenge*. Brighton, Wheatsheaf Books.

Blair, I. (1985). *Investigating Rape*. London, Croom Helm.

Blumenthal, G. (1985). *Development of Secure Units in Child Care*, Aldershot, Gower.

Blythe, R. (1969). *Akenfield*. London, Allen Lane.

Booth, A. (1985). *Life on the Margins*. London Communist Party.

Bottoms, A. (1986). 'Intermediate Treatment', Address to the British Society of Criminology.

Bowker, L.H. (ed.) (1978). *Women, Crime and the Criminal Justice System*. Lexington, Mass., D.C. Heath and Co.

Box, S. and Hale, C. (1983). 'Liberation and Female Criminality in England and Wales', *British Journal of Criminology* 23, 35–49.

Boyson, R. (1971). *Down with the Poor*. London, Churchill Press.

Bracey, D.H. (1983). 'The Juvenile Prostitute Victim and Offender', *Victimology* 8 (3–4).

Brake, M. (1980). *The Sociology of Youth Culture and Youth Subcultures*. London, Routledge and Kegan Paul.

Briggs, A. (1967). 'The Language of "Class" in Early Nineteenth Century England', in A. Briggs and J. Saville (1967).

Briggs, A. and Saville, J. (1967). *Essays in Labour History*. London, Macmillan.

Brook, E. and Davis, A. (eds) (1985). *Women, the Family and Social Work*. London, Tavistock.

Brophy, J. and Smart, C. (eds) (1985). *Women in Law*, London, Routledge and Kegan Paul.

Brown, G.W. and Harris, T. (1978). *Social Origins of Depression*. London, Tavistock.

Bujra, J.M. (1982). 'Women Entrepreneurs of Early Nairobi' and 'Postscript: Prostitution, Class and State', in C. Sumner (1982).

Burney, E. (1979). *J.P.: Magistrate, Court and Community*. London, Hutchinson.

Burton, F. and Carlen, P. (1979). *Official Discourse*. London, Routledge and Kegan Paul.

Calvert, J. (1985). 'Motherhood', in E. Brook and A. Davis (1985).

Campbell, A. (1981). *Girl Delinquents*. Oxford, Basil Blackwell.

    (1984). *The Girls in the Gang*. Oxford, Basil Blackwell.

Campbell, B. (1984). *Wigan Pier Revisited*. London, Virago Press.

Carlen, P. (1976). *Magistrates' Justice*. London, Martin Robertson.

    (1980). 'Radical Criminology, Penal Politics and the Rule of Law', in P. Carlen and M. Collison (1980).

    (1983a). *Women's Imprisonment*. London, Routledge and Kegan Paul.

    (1983b). 'On Rights and Powers: Some Notes on Penal Politics', in D. Garland and P. Young (1983).

    (1984). 'Justice: Too Important to Be Left to the Judiciary?', *The Abolitionist* 16 (4), 8–10.

    (1985). 'Law, Psychiatry and Women's Imprisonment: A Sociological View', *British Journal of Psychiatry* 46, June, 18–21.

    (1986). 'Psychiatry in Prisons: Promises, Premises, Practices and Politics', in P. Miller and N. Rose (1986).

(1988). *Women, Crime and Poverty*. Milton Keynes, Open University Press.

Carlen, P. and Collison, M. (eds) (1980). *Radical Issues in Criminology*. London, Martin Robertson.

Carlen, P., Hicks, J., O'Dwyer, J., Christina, D. and Tchaikovsky, C. (1985). *Criminal Women*, Cambridge, Polity Press.

Casburn, M. (1979). *Girls Will Be Girls*. London, Women's Research and Resources Centre.

Central Statistics Office (1984). *Annual Abstract of Statistics No. 121*. London, HMSO.

Central Statistics Office (1986) *Social Trends No. 16*, London, HMSO.

Chambers, G. and Millar, A. (1983). *Investigating Sexual Assault*. A Scottish Office Research Study. Edinburgh, HMSO.

(1986). *Prosecuting Sexual Assault*. A Scottish Office Research Study. Edinburgh, HMSO.

Chambers, G. and Tombs, J. (1984). *The British Crime Survey, Scotland*. A Scottish Office Social Research Study. Edinburgh, HMSO.

Chapman, J.R. and Gates, M. (1978). *The Victimisation of Women*. London, Sage.

Chesney-Lind, M. (1973). 'Judicial Enforcement of the Female Sex Role: The Family Court and the Female Delinquent', *Issues in Criminology* 8 (2). 197–223.

(1978). 'Chivalry Re-examined: Women and the Criminal Justice System', in L.H. Bowker (1978).

Child Poverty Action Group (1982). *Briefing on Social Security Bill*. London, CPAG.

Christina, D. and Carlen, P. (1985). 'Christina: In Her Own Time', in P. Carlen *et al.* (1985).

Cicourel, A.V. (1968). *The Social Organisation of Juvenile Justice*. New York, Wiley.

Civil and Public Services Association (1984). *Policing Welfare: Benefits under Attack*. UCW Cardiff Conference Report, London, CPSA.

Clare, A. and Thompson, J. (1985). *Report on Visits Made to C1 Unit Holloway Prison*. London, National Council for Civil Liberties.

Coggan, G. and Walker, M. (1982). *Frightened for My Life*. London, Fontana.

Cohen, A.K. (1955). *Delinquent Boys*. London, Free Press.

Cohen, S. (1972). *Folk Devils and Moral Panics*. London, MacGibbon and Kee.

(1985). *Visions of Social Control*. Cambridge, Polity Press.

Cousins, M. (1978). 'The Logic of Deconstruction', *Oxford Literary Review*, 3, 2.

Coward, R. (1984). *Female Desire: Women's Sexuality Today*. London, Paladin.

Cowie, J., Cowie, V. and Slater, E. (1968). *Delinquency in Girls*. London, Heinemann.

Criminal Law Revision Committee (1982). *Working Paper on Offences Relating to Prostitution and Allied Offences*.

Criminal Law Revision Committee 17th Report (1986). *Prostitution: Off Street Activities*, Cmnd. 9688, London, HMSO.

Crites, L. (1978). *The Female Offender*. Lexington, Mass., D.C. Heath and Co.

Dale, J. and Foster, P. (1986). *Feminists and State Welfare*. London, Routledge and Kegan Paul.

Dalton, K. (1964). *The Premenstrual Syndrome*. London, William Heinemann Medical Books.

Dalton, K. (1978). *Once a Month*. London, Fontana.

Datesman, S. and Scarpitti, F. (eds) (1985). *Women, Crime and Justice*. Oxford, Oxford University Press.

Davies, N. (1986). 'Prison Officers Force Out "Too Soft" Governor', *Observer*, 23 February.

Deacon, A. (1980). 'Spivs, Drones and Other Scroungers', *New Society*, 25 February.

Deighton, J. (1983). *Camden Council Women's Committee Report: Policing in the Argyle Square Area*, in *Observer*, 21 January.

Denton, G. (1984). *For Whose Eyes Only?* Bradford, National Association of Young People in Care.

Department of Employment (1985). *Gazette* 93 (3) S2.1, London, HMSO.

Department of Environment (1982). *Single Homeless*, London, HMSO.

Department of Health and Social Security (1983). *Circular FIG (Fraud Investigators' Guide) 21,1982*. London, HMSO.

(1984). *Personal Social Services: Local Authority Statistics*. London, HMSO.

(1985a). *The Reform of Social Security* (Green Paper), 15 June, Cmnd. 9518. London, HMSO.

(1985b). *The Reform of Social Security* (White Paper), 16 December, Cmnd. 9691, London, HMSO.

(1986). *Prevention and Detection of Evasion of National Insurance Contributions and of Social Security Benefits*, Cmnd. 102, 1983/4. London, HMSO.

Dobash, R. and Dobash, R.E. (1979). *Violence Against Wives*. London, Open Books.

Dobash, R., Dobash, R.E. and Gutteridge, S. (1986). *The Imprisonment of Women*. Oxford, Blackwell.

Doherty, M.J. and East, R. (1985). 'Bail Decisions in Magistrates' Courts', *British Journal of Criminology* 25 (3), 251–66.

Dominelli, L. (1984). 'Differential Justice: Domestic Labour, Community Service and Female Offenders', *Probation Journal* 3 (3), 100–103.

(1986). 'Familial Ideology and Sentencing Practice', *Wise Heads*, unpublished Community Service Newsletter.

Donnison, D. (1982). *The Politics of Poverty*. Oxford, Martin Robertson.

Donzelot, J. (1979). *The Policing of Families*, London, Hutchinson.

Downes, D. and Rock, P. (1982). *Understanding Deviance*. Oxford, Clarendon.

Doyal, L. (1985). 'Women and the National Health Service', in E. Lewis and V. Olessen (1985).

Eaton, M. (1983) 'Mitigating Circumstances: Familiar Rhetoric', *International Journal of the Sociology of Law* 11, 385–400.

(1985). 'Documenting the Defendant', in J. Brophy and C. Smart (1985).

(1986). *Justice for Women? Family, Court and Social Control*. Milton Keynes, Open University Press.

Edinburgh Rape Crisis Centre (1981). *First Report*, Edinburgh Rape Crisis Centre.

Edwards, S.S.M. (1981). *Female Sexuality and the Law*. Oxford, Martin Robertson.

(1984). *Women on Trial*, Manchester, Manchester University Press.

(ed.) (1985). *Gender, Sex and the Law*. London, Croom Helm.

(1986a). 'Fighting Organised Prostitution: The Criminal Law Revision Committee's 17th Report', *Justice of the Peace*, 5 April, 216–18.

(1986b). 'Evidential Matters in Rape Prosecutions from "First Opportunity to Complain" to "Corroboration" ', *New Law Journal*, 28 March, 291–3.

Ehrenreich, B. and English, D. (1973). *Complaints and Disorders*. London, Writers and Readers Publishing Cooperative.

Eichenbaum, L. and Orbach, S. (1983). *What Do Women Want?* London, Michael Joseph.

Emmins, C. (1982) *A Guide to the Criminal Justice Act 1982*, London, Financial Training Publications.

Esam, P., Good, R. and Middleton, R. (1985). *Who's to Benefit? A Radical Review of the Social Security System*. London, Verso.

Evans, M. (ed.) (1982). *The Woman Question*. London, Fontana.

Fairbairns, Z. (1985). 'The Cohabitation Rule: Why It Makes Sense', in C. Ungerson (1985).

Fairweather, E. (1982). 'The Law of the Jungle in Kings Cross', *New Society*, 2 December,

138–9.

Farrington, D. and Morris, A. (1983a). 'Sex, Sentencing and Reconviction', *British Journal of Criminology* 23 (3), July, 229–248.

(1983b). 'Do Magistrates Discriminate Against Men?' *Justice of the Peace*, 17 September, 601–603.

Field, F. (1981). *Inequality in Britain: Freedom, Welfare and the State*. London, Fontana.

Finch, J. and Groves, D. (1985). 'Community Care and the Family: A Case for Equal Opportunities?' in C. Ungerson (1985).

Fisher, R. and Wilson, C. (1982). *Authority or Freedom?* Aldershot, Gower.

Fitzgerald, M. and Sim, J. (1979). *British Prisons*. Oxford, Basil Blackwell.

Fitzgerald, T. (1983). 'The New Right and the Family', in M. Loney, O. Boswell and J. Clarke (1983).

Foster, P. (1983). *Access to Welfare*. London, Macmillan.

Foucault, M. (1977). *Discipline and Punish*. London, Allen Lane.

Franey, R. (1983). *Poor Law*. London, CHAR, CPAG, CDC, NAPO and NCCL.

Fraser, D. (1984). *The Evolution of the British Welfare State*. 2nd ed., London, Macmillan.

Fraser, L. and Cameron, D. (1986). *The Lust to Kill: An Investigation of Sexual Murder*. Cambridge, Polity Press.

Freeman, M. (1983). *The Rights and Wrongs of Children*. London, Frances Pinter.

Fryer, B., Hunt, A., McBarnet, D. and Moorhouse, B. (eds) (1981). *Law, State and Society*. London, Croom Helm.

Furnham, A. (1985). 'The Determinants of Attitudes Towards Social Security Recipients', *The British Journal of Social Psychology*, February, 19–27.

Garfinkel, H. (1968). *Studies in Ethnomethodology*. New York, Prentice-Hall.

Garland, D. and Young, P. (eds) (1983). *The Power to Punish*. London, Heinemann.

Gates, M. (1978). *The Victimisation of Women*. London, Sage.

Gelsthorpe, L. (1983). Evidence Given to House of Commons Social Services Committee Enquiry *Children in Care*. London, HMSO.

(1986). *Gender Issues in Juvenile Justice: An Annotated Bibliography*. Lancaster, Information Systems.

Genders, E. and Player, E. (1986). 'Women's Imprisonment: The Effects of Youth Custody', *British Journal of Criminology*, October, 357–71.

Gibbens, T.C.N. (1971). 'Female Offenders', *British Journal of Hospital Medicine* 6, September, 279–86.

Gittins, D. (1985). *The Family in Question: Changing Households and Familiar Ideologies*. London, Macmillan.

Goffman, E. (1968). *Stigma*. Harmondsworth, Penguin.

Golding, P. and Middleton, S. (1982). *Images of Welfare*. Oxford, Martin Robertson.

Gordon, G.H. (1978). *The Criminal Law of Scotland*. Edinburgh, W. Green and Son.

Gordon, M. (1922). *Penal Discipline*, London, John Lane, Bodley Head.

Greater London Council Women's Committee (1986). *Breaking the Silence*. London, GLC.

Green, E. (1961). *Judicial Attitudes in Sentencing*. London, Macmillan.

Gregory, J. (1986). 'Sex, Class and Crime: Towards a Non-Sexist Criminology', in R. Matthews and J. Young (1986).

Griffin, C. (1985). *Typical Girls*. London, Routledge and Kegan Paul.

Hagen, J., Simpson, J. and Gillis, J.R. (1979). 'The Sexual Stratification of Social Control: A Gender-Based Perspective on Crime and Delinquency', *British Journal of Sociology*, 30 (1). 25–38.

Hahn Rafter, N. and Stanko, E. (eds) (1982). *Judge, Lawyer, Victim, Thief, Women, Gender*

Roles and Criminal Justice. Evanston, Northeastern University Press.

Haley, K. (1980). 'Mothers Behind Bars: A Look at the Parental Rights of Incarcerated Women', in s. Datesman and F. Scarpitti (1985).

Hall, R.E. (1985). *Ask Any Woman: A London Inquiry into Rape and Sexual Assault*. Bristol, Falling Wall Press.

Hall, S. and Jefferson, T. (eds) (1976). *Resistance Through Rituals*. London, Hutchinson.

Harrison, P. (1983). *Inside the Inner City*. Harmondsworth, Penguin.

Hay, D. (1975). 'Property, Authority and the Criminal Law', in D. Hay, P. Linebaugh and E.P. Thompson (1975).

Hay, D., Linebaugh, P. and Thompson, E.P. (eds) (1975). *Albion's Fatal Tree*. London, Allen Lane.

Hayes, J. (1985). *My Story*. Brandon Kerry.

Heidensohn, F.M. (1968). 'The Deviance of Women: A Critique and an Enquiry', *British Journal of Sociology* 19 (2), 160–73.

(1985). *Women and Crime*. London, Macmillan and New York University Press.

(1986). 'Models of Justice: Portia or Persephone? Some Thoughts on Equality, Fairness and Gender in the Field of Criminal Justice', *International Journal of the Sociology of Law*.

Hennessy, J. (1984). *Report by H.M. Inspector of Prisons on H.M. Prison Holloway*. London, Home Office.

Hirschi, T. (1969). *Causes of Delinquency*. Berkeley, University of California Press.

Hollway, W. (1981). ' "I Just Wanted to Kill a Woman", Why? The Ripper and Male Sexuality'. *Feminist Review* 9, 33–40.

Holman, R. (1978). *Poverty: Explanations of Social Deprivation*. London, Martin Robertson.

Home Office (1969). *Report on the Work of the Prison Department, 1968*. London, HMSO.

(1970). *Care and Treatment in a Planned Environment*, Advisory Council on Child Care. London, Home Office.

(1977). *Fifteen and Sixteen Year Olds in Borstal*, London, Young Offenders Psychology Unit. London, Home Office.

(1979). *Marriage Matters*. London, HMSO.

(1982). *Prison Statistics for England and Wales 1981*, Cmnd. 8654. London, HMSO.

(1983). *Prison Statistics for England and Wales 1982*, Cmnd 9027. London, HMSO.

(1984a). *Prison Statistics for England and Wales 1983*, Cmnd. 9363. London, HMSO.

(1984b). *Probation Service: Statement of National Objectives and Priorities*. London, Home Office.

(1985a). *Prison Statistics England and Wales 1984*, Cmnd. 9622. London, HMSO.

(1985b). *Report of the Work of the Prison Department 1984/85*. London, HMSO.

(1985c). *Report of the Holloway Project Committee*, London, Home Office.

(1985d). *Report of the Committee on the Prison Disciplinary System*. London, HMSO.

(1986). *The Ethnic Origins of Prisoners*. London, HMSO.

Hood, R. (1962). *Sentencing in Magistrates' Courts*. London, Stevens.

Hough, M. and Mayhew, P. (1983). *The British Crime Survey: First Report*, Home Office Research Study No. 76. London, HMSO.

(1985). *Taking Account of Crime: Key Findings from the 1984 British Crime Survey*, Home Office Research Study No. 85. London, HMSO.

House of Commons (1984). *Second Report from the Social Services Committee on Children in Care*, Vols. I, II and III. London, HMSO.

Hudson, A. (1983). 'The Welfare State and Adolescent Femininity', *Youth and Policy* 2, 1, Summer. 5–13.

(1985). 'Troublesome Girls: Towards Alternative Definitions and Policies', paper presented to European University Conference, Florence.

Hudson, B. (1984). 'Femininity and Adolesence', in A. McRobbie and M. Nava (1984).

Huntington, J. (1981). *Social Work and General Medical Practice*, London, Allen and Unwin.

Hutter, B. and Williams, G. (eds) (1981). *Controlling Women*. London, Croom Helm.

Iles, S.C. (1985). 'Women Terrorists and the Press', paper presented to the British Sociological Assocation.

(1986). Patriarchal Therapeutism, unpublished PhD. thesis, University of Kent.

Jaget, C. (ed.) (1980). *Prostitutes, Our Life*. Bristol, Falling Wall Press.

James, J. (1978a). 'Motivations for Entrance into Prostitution', in L. Crites (ed.) (1978).

(1978b). 'The Prostitute as Victim', in J.R. Chapman and M. Gates (1978).

Jordan, B. (1983). 'The Politics of "Care": Social Workers and Schools', in B. Jordan and N. Parton (1983).

Jordan, B. and Parton, N. (eds) (1983). *The Political Dimensions of Social Work*. Cambridge, Polity Press.

Joseph, Sir Keith (1974). *Speech at the Grand Hotel Birmingham on 19th October 1974*. London, Conservative Central Office.

Kahn, P. (1985). 'Unequal Opportunities: Women, Unemployment and the Law', in S. Edwards (1985).

Katz, S. and Mazur, M. (1979). *Understanding of the Rape Victim*. New York, Wiley.

Kilgour, J. (1984). 'The State of the Prisons', *British Medical Journal* 288, 26 May, 603–5.

King, R.D. and Morgan, R. (1976). *A Taste of Prison*. London, Routledge and Kegan Paul.

Klein, D. (1976). 'The Aetiology of Female Crime: A Review of the Literature', in L. Crites (1976).

Kornhauser, R. (1978). *Social Sources of Delinquency*. Chicago, University of Chicago Press.

Krutschnitt, K. (1982). 'Women, Crime and Dependency', *Criminology* 19 (4), 495–513.

Land, H. (1978). 'Who Cares for the Family?', *Journal of Social Policy* 7, 257–84.

(1980). 'The Family Wage', *Feminist Review* 6, 55–77.

(1985). 'Who Still Cares for the Family?: Recent Developments in Income Maintenance', in C. Ungerson (1985).

Lea, J. and Young, J. (1984). *What Is to Be Done about Law and Order?* Harmondsworth, Penguin.

Lees, S. (1986). *Losing Out: Sexuality and Adolescent Girls*. London, Hutchinson.

Leonard, E.B. (1982). *A Critique of Criminology Theory: Women, Crime and Society*. New York and London, Longman.

Lewis, E. and Olessen, V. (1985). *Women, Health and Healing*. London, Tavistock.

Lockwood, K. (1980). 'Mothers as Criminals', *Women's Law Review* 9, 78–86.

Lombroso, C. and Ferrero, W. (1895). *The Female Offender*, with an introduction by W.D. Morrison. London, T. Fisher Unwin.

London Rape Crisis Centre (1982). *Third Report*. London, Women Only Press.

Loney, M., Boswell, D. and Clarke, J. (eds) (1983). *Social Policy and Social Welfare*. Milton Keynes, Open University Press.

Luckhaus, L. (1985). 'A Plea for PMT in the Criminal Law', in S. Edwards (1985).

Lynes, T. (1985). *The Penguin Guide to Supplementary Benefits*, Harmondsworth, Penguin.

McBarnet, D. (1981). 'Magistrates' Courts and the Ideology of Justice', *British Journal of Law and Society*, 8, 2, 181–197.

McCann, K. (1985). 'Battered Women and the Law: The Limits of Legislation', in J. Brophy and C. Smart (1985).

McLeod, E. (1982). *Women Working: Prostitution Now*. London, Croom Helm.

McRobbie, A. and Garber, J. (1976). 'Girls and Subcultures', in S. Hall and T. Jefferson (1976).

McRobbie, A. and Nava, M. (1984). *Gender and Generation*. London, Macmillan.

McShane, Y. (1980). *Daughter of Evil*. London, W.M. Allen.

Maguire, M. (1985). 'Prisoners' Grievances: The Role of the Boards of Visitors', in M. Maguire, J. Vagg and R. Morgan (1985).

Maguire, M., Vagg, J. and Morgan, R. (eds) (1985). *Accountability and Prisons*. London, Tavistock.

Mandaraka-Sheppard, A. (1986). *The Dynamics of Aggression in Women's Prisons in England*. London, Gower.

Marshall, K. (1985). *Women and the Family in Thatcher's Britain: Moral Panics and Victorian Values*. Revolutionary Communist Party. London, Junius.

Matthews, J. (1981). *Women in the Penal System*. London, National Association for the Care and Resettlement of Offenders.

Matthews, R. and Young, J. (eds) (1986). *Confronting Crime*. London, Sage.

Maynard, C. (1985). Comment reported in *Standard*, 13 September.

May Report (1979). 'Committee of Inquiry into the United Kingdom Prison Services', Chairman the Hon. Mr Justice May, Cmnd. 7673. London, HMSO.

Milham, S., Bullock, R. and Hosie, K. (1978). *Locking Up Children*. London, Saxon House.

Miller, J.B. (1976). *Towards a New Psychology of Women*. Harmondsworth, Pelican.

Miller, P. and Rose, N. (1986). *The Power of Psychiatry*. Cambridge, Polity Press.

Millman, M. (1982). 'Images of Deviant Men and Women', in M. Evans (1982).

Mishra, R. (1984). *The Welfare State in Crisis*. Brighton, Wheatsheaf Books.

Mitchell, J. (1974). *Psychoanalysis and Feminism*. London, Allen Lane.

Moore, P. (1981). 'Scroungermania Again at the DHSS', *New Society*, 22.1.1981. 375–7.

Morgan, R., Maguire, M. and Vagg, J. (1985). 'Overhauling the Prison Disciplinary System: Notes for Readers of the Prison Committee's Report' in Maguire, Vagg and Morgan (1985).

Morris, A., Giller, H., Szwed, E. and Geach, H. (1980). *Justice for Children*. London, Macmillan.

Morris, A. (ed.) (1981). *Women and Crime*. Cambridge, University of Cambridge Institute of Criminology.

Mukherjee, S.K. and Scutt, J.A. (1981). *Women and Crime*, Sydney, Allen and Unwin.

NACRO (1977). *Children and Young Persons in Trouble*. London, National Association for the Care and Resettlement of Offenders.

(1985a). 'Bail and Remand in Custody', *NACRO Briefing*, London, National Association for the Care and Resettlement of Offenders.

(1985b). *Mothers and Babies in Prison*. London, National Association for the Care and Resettlement of Offenders.

(1986a). *NACRO News Digest No. 37*, February, London, National Association for the Care and Resettlement of Offenders.

(1986b). *They Don't Give You A Clue*. London, National Association for the Care and Resettlement of Offenders.

Nagel, I. (1981). 'Sex Differences in the Processing of Criminal Defendants', in A. Morris (1981).

Nagel, S.S. and Weitzman, L.J. (1971). 'Women as Litigants', *The Hastings Law Journal* 23 (1), 171–98.

NAYPIC (1983). *Sharing Care*. Bradford, National Association of Young People in Care.

NCCL (1983). *Rights* 7 (4), London, National Council for civil Liberties.

(1985a). *Civil Liberty*. London, National Council for Civil Liberties.

(1985b). *Armagh Strip Searches*. London, National Council for Civil Liberties.

Oakley, A. (1974a). *Housewife*. London, Allen Lane.

(1974b). *The Sociology of Housework*. Oxford, Martin Robertson.

O'Dwyer, J. and Carlen, P. (1985). 'Surviving Holloway and Other Women's Prisons', in P. Carlen *et al.* (1985).

Ohse, U. (1984). *Forced Prostitution and Traffic in Women in West Germany*. Edinburgh, Human Rights Group.

Okely, J. (1978). 'Privileged, Schooled and Finished', in S. Ardener (1978).

Orbach, S. (1978). *Fat Is a Feminist Issue*. Middlesex, Hamlyn.

Otto, S. (1981). 'Women, Alcohol and Social Control', in B. Hutter and G. Williams (1981).

Page, R. and Clark, G. (1977). *Who Cares?* London, National Children's Bureau.

Pahl, J. (1980). 'Patterns of Money Management within Marriage', *Journal of Social Policy* 9, part 3.

Parker, H., Casburn, M. and Turnbull, D. (1981). *Receiving Juvenile Justice*. Oxford, Basil Blackwell.

Pattullo, P. (1983). *Judging Women*. London, National Council for Civil Liberties.

Pearson, R. (1976). 'Women Defendants in Magistrates' Courts', *British Journal of Law and Society*, 265–73.

(1980). 'Popular Justice and the Lay Magistracy: Two Faces of Lay Participation', in Z. Bankowski and G. Mungham (1980).

Peckham, A. (1985). *A Woman in Custody*. London, Fontana.

Pollak, O. (1950). *The Criminality of Women*. Philadelphia, University of Pennsylvania Press.

Pope, C.E. (1975). *Sentencing of California Felony Offenders*. Washington DC, Criminal Justice Research Centre.

Prison reform Trust (1984). *Beyond Restraint*. London, Prison Reform Trust.

(1985). *Prison Medicine*. London, Prison Reform Trust.

Procek, E. (1981). 'Psychiatry and the Social Control of Women', in A. Morris (1981).

Radzinowitz, L. (1966). *Ideology and Crime*. London, Heinemann.

Rafter, N. and Natalizia, E. (1981). 'Marxist Feminism: Implications for Criminal Justice'. *Crime and Delinquency* 27, 81–91.

Reiman, J.H. (1979). 'Prostitution, Addiction and the Ideology of Liberation', *Contemporary Crises* 3, 53–68.

Report of the Advisory Group on the Law of Rape (1975). Cmnd. 6352. London, HMSO.

Richardson, H.J. (1969). *Adolescent Girls in Approved Schools*, London, Routledge and Kegan Paul.

Roberts, H. (1985). *The Patient Patients*. London, Pandora Press.

Rottman, D.B. and Simon, R.J. (1975). 'Women in the Courts', *Chitty's Law Journal* 23 (52).

Rowett, C. and Vaughan, P. (1981). 'Women and Broadmoor: Treatment and Control in a Special Hospital', in B. Hutter and G. Williams (1981).

Russell, K.V., Frey, V.H. and Reichert, L. (1981). 'Prostitution Business and Police: The Maintenance of an Illegal Economy', *Police Journal*, July, 239–69.

Russell, K.V. and Owen, C. (1984). 'Prostitution: Women, Clients and the Law', *Police Journal*, January, 68–97.

Sachs, A. and Wilson, J. (1978). *Sexism and the Law*. Oxford, Martin Robertson.

Scottish Law Commission (1983). *Report on Evidence in Cases of Rape and Other Sexual Offences*, SLC Report No. 78. Edinburgh, HMSO.

Seear, N. and Player, E. (1986). *Women in the Penal System*. London, Howard League for Penal Reform.

Segal, L. (ed.) (1983). *What Is to Be Done About the Family?* Harmondsworth, Penguin.
Shacklady Smith, L. (1978). 'Sexist Assumptions and Female Delinquency', in C. Smart and B. Smart (1978).
Shapland, J. (1981). *Between Conviction and Sentence.* London, Routledge and Kegan Paul.
Sharpe, S. (1984). *Double Identity: The lives of Working Mothers.* Harmondsworth, Penguin.
Shaw, S. (1985). 'The Case for Change in Prison Medicine', in Prison Reform Trust (1985).
Simon, R.J. (1977). *Women and Crime.* Lexington, Mass., D.C. Heath and Co.
Smart, C. (1976). *Women, Crime and Criminology: A Feminist Critique.* London, Routledge and Kegan Paul.
  (1981). 'Law and the Control of Women's Sexuality', in B. Hutter and G. Williams (1981).
  (1984). *The Ties that Bind*, London, Routledge and Kegan Paul.
Smart, C. and Smart, B. (eds) (1978). *Women, Sexuality and Social Control.* London, Routledge and Kegan Paul.
Smith, R. (1984). *Prison Health Care.* London, British Medical Association.
Society of Civil and Public Servants (1984). *Note of a National Conference on DHSS Fraud* (SCC), 24 September 1984. SCPS, London.
Southgate, P. and Ekblom, P. (1986). *Police Public Encounters,* Home Office Research Study 90. London, HMSO.
Squire, C. (1981). 'Indescribable Tension', *The Leveller,* 11 December, 16–18.
Stang-Dahl, T. (1986). *Women's Law: Methods, Problems and Values.* University of Oslo.
  (1987). 'Women's Law: Methods, Problems and Values', *Contemporary Crises* 10 (4).
Stanko, E. (1984). *Intimate Intrusions.* London, Routledge and Kegan Paul.
Stanworth, M. (1985). 'Just Three Quiet Girls', in C. Ungerson (1985).
Stein, M. (1983). 'Protest in Care', in B. Jordan and N. Parton (1983).
Stein, M. and Carey, K. (1984). 'A Study of Young People Leaving Care', in NAYPIC, *Leaving Care – Where?*, Bradford, National Association of Young People in Care.
Stein, M. and Ellis, S. (1983). *Gizza Say: Reviews and Young People in Care.* Bradford, National Association of Young People in Care.
Stein, M. and Maynard, C. (1985). *I've Never Been So Lonely.* Bradford, National Association of Young People in Care.
Stone, M. (1985). 'Policy and Practice', paper delivered to Conference on *Gender and Justice,* London.
Sumner, C. (1982). *Crime, Justice and Underdevelopment.* London, Heinemann.
Sykes, G. (1958). *Society of Captives: A Study of Maximum Security Prisons.* Princeton NJ Princeton University Press.
Taylor, I., Walton, P. and Young, J. (1975). *Critical Criminology.* London, Routledge and Kegan Paul.
Taylor, L., Lacey, R. and Bracken, D. (1979). *In Whose Best Interests?* London, Cobden Trust and National Association for Mental Health.
Tchaikovsky, C. (1985). 'Looking for Trouble', in P. Carlen *et al.* (1985).
Temkin, J. (1984). 'Evidence in Sexual Assault Cases: The Scottish Proposals and Alternatives', *Modern Law Review* 47, 625–49.
Thomas, D. (1979). *Principles of Sentencing.* 2nd edn, London, Heinemann.
Thomas, W.I. (1923). *The Unadjusted Girl.* Boston, Little, Brown and Co.
Thompson, E.P. (1971). 'The Moral Economy of the English Crowd in the 18th Century', *Past and Present* 50, 76–136.
Thorpe, D., Smith, D., Green, C. and Paley, J.H. (1980). *Out of Care: The Community Support of Juvenile Offenders.* London, Allen and Unwin.

Townsend, P. (1979). *Poverty in the United Kingdom*. Harmondsworth, Penguin.

Ungerson, C. (ed.) (1985). *Women and Social Policy*. London, Macmillan.

Vagg, J. (1985). 'Independent Inspection: The Role of the Boards of Visitors', in M. Maguire *et al*. (1985).

Wakerley, A. (1984). 'Files', in *NAYPIC News*, issue 9, Bradford National Association of Young People in Care.

Walker, H. (1985). 'Women's Issues in Probation Practice', in H. Walker and B. Beaumont (1985).

Walker, H. and Beaumont, B. (eds) (1985). *Working with Offenders*. London, Macmillan.

Ward, S. (ed.) (1985). *DHSS in Crisis*. London, Child Poverty Action Group.

Webb, D. (1984). 'More on Gender and Justice: Girl Offenders on Supervision', *Sociology* (3), 367–81.

Wilden, A. (1972). *System and Structure*, London, Tavistock.

Willis, P. (1977). *Learning to Labour: How Working-Class Kids Get Working-Class Jobs*. London, Saxon House.

Wilson, E. (1977). *Women and the Welfare State*. London, Tavistock.

(1980). *Only Halfway to Paradise: Women in Postwar Britain, 1945–68*. London, Tavistock.

(1983). *What Is to Be Done About Violence to Women?* Harmondsworth, Penguin.

Wolfenden Committee Report (1957) *Homosexual Offences and Prostitution*, London, HMSO.

Wood, J. (1984). 'Groping Towards Sexism: Boys' Sex Talk', in A. McRobbie and M. Nava (1984).

Worrall, A. (1981). 'Out of Place: Female Offenders in Court', *Probation Journal* 28 (3), 90–93.

(forthcoming). 'Non-Descript Women: A Study of Those Female Lawbreakers Who Defy Description within the Discourses of Femininity,' in progress PhD thesis, University of Keele.

Young, J. (1975). 'Working-Class Criminology', in I. Taylor *et al*. (1975).

(1986). 'The Failure of Criminology: The Need for a Radical Realism', in R. Matthews and J. Young (1986).

Young, M.D. & Willmott, P. (1973). *The Symmetrical Family: A Study of Work and Leisure in the London Region*, London, Routledge and Kegan Paul.

Author Index

Subject Index